D1233985

VIRGIN TRAILS

Virgin Trails

A SECULAR PILGRIMAGE

Robert Ward

KEY PORTER BOOKS

National Library of Canada Cataloguing in Publication Data

Ward, Robert
    Virgin trails

ISBN 1-55263-374-8

1. Mary, Blessed Virgin, Saint-Cult-Europe.   2. Christian pilgrims and pilgrimages-
Europe. 3. Ward, Robert-Journeys-Europe. 4. Europe-Descriptions and travel. I. Title.

BT652.E85W37 2002   232.91'094   C2001-900616-0

The publisher gratefully acknowledges the support of the Canada Council for the Arts
and the Ontario Arts Council for its publishing program.

We acknowledge the financial support of the Government of Canada through the Book
Publishing Industry Development Program (BPIDP) for our publishing activities.

Key Porter Books Limited
70 The Esplanade
Toronto, Ontario
Canada M5E 1R2

www.keyporter.com

Text design: Peter Maher
Electronic formatting: Heidy Lawrance Associates

The publisher has made every effort to contact the copyright holders of material
produced in this book. We would be pleased to have any additional information
regarding this material.

Printed and bound in Canada

02 03 04 05 06 07 6 5 4 3 2 1

With love to Mom, Dad and Michiko

THANKS TO MY EDITORS, Andrea Bock and Susan Renouf, and my agent, Denise Bukowski, for their immaculate assistance. To Tim Cloutis and Pat Aldighieri for tireless patronage of the arts. To Dennis Bock for never ceasing to inspire. To my friends in Milano and their families for warm hospitality. To Jack Fairey for giving my ms the old once-over. To Professor Janine Langan for first bringing these things to life for me. To the Ontario Arts Council and Toronto Arts Council for financial assistance. And once again to Michiko, just because.

Caminante, son tus huellas
el camino, y nada más;
caminante, no hay camino,
se hace camino al andar.

Traveler, your footprints are the road,
there is no other;
traveler, there is no road,
you make the road by walking it.

ANTONIO MACHADO, *Proverbios y cantares*

"For all my years, the only piece of wisdom I've acquired
is that time doesn't have to move forward.
The noblest achievement of the imagination is to make it run
some other way, and terminate in beauty and forgiveness."

DAVID GELERNTER, *1939: The Lost World of the Fair*

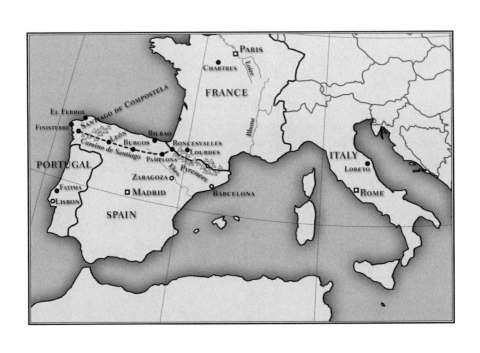

CONTENTS

THE VIRGIN
AT THE END
OF THE WORLD
FINISTERRE

YOU COULD SAY it had been an eventful summer. Lourdes in June. A walk across Spain in July. And now here I was at the end of the world.

They call it Cabo Finisterre, Cape End-of-the-World, and if that appellation isn't dramatic enough for you, the shoreline hereabouts, where so many ships have come to grief, boasts the title of la Costa de la Muerte, the Coast of Death. Three days' walk past the city of Santiago de Compostela, this is the westernmost point of continental Spain, dry land's last mighty heave before it slips beneath the Atlantic waters.

The Roman legions, it is said, built an altar at Finisterre to wish the sun godspeed on its nightly journey to the underworld. This was a holy place, too, for the pagan Celts, worshippers of water and stone. And Christian souls were drawn here from the very beginning of the pilgrimage to Santiago. They came to stand on the cliffs and see, perhaps for the only time in their lives, the crawling vastness of the great, salt Ocean. In the year 1467, twenty-five years before Columbus, a German pilgrim gazed out from the tip of the cape and said: "Here, there is nothing but sky and water. They say no one can cross it and no one knows what lies beyond."

The enduring symbol of the pilgrimage to Santiago de Compostela is the cockle-shell—the *coquille Saint-Jacques*. It's an odd emblem for a road that passes through mountains and semi-deserts, far from any ocean.

Associations suggested for it have ranged from the outstretched fingers of a begging hand to the sex of Venus. But surely what it indicates is the memory of a time when the true end of the road was not Santiago but the Atlantic shore, the end of the world, where the pilgrim would snatch a shell up from the beach to say, "I was here," before turning to start the long walk home.

Of course I would like to say that I made it to the end of the world on foot. On the map it looks like just a hop from Santiago to the ocean shore and I'd already walked 400 miles. But in fact it's sixty miles more, and my feet were in no mood to negotiate. I left my pilgrim's staff at the doors of Saint James' cathedral and grabbed a seat on the morning bus to Finisterre.

The ride passed without event. Two hours of low hills and farmland, the villages few and far between. I was thankful I hadn't walked. After a while, I closed my eyes and when I opened them again we were cresting a ridge and a vast lake of turquoise had opened before us. So this was the end of the world.

It seemed agreeable enough. At the foot of the promontory, the village of Finisterre lay decaying in the slow, picturesque fashion of fishing villages everywhere. Waves sparkled, fishing boats bobbed, and people stood talking loudly to the same people they had talked loudly to every morning of their lives. I stopped for coffee in a bar hung with black and white photos of olden-days sailors and fishermen, then followed the sea road out towards the lighthouse.

The church of Santa María de las Arenas, Saint Mary of the Sands, stands just where the road begins to climb. It's a sturdy little stone church that has toughed it out against the Atlantic gales for eight centuries. The door was ajar as I passed, so I thought I would take a look inside. I had been hiding from the midday heat in places like this for weeks now, scrambling like a lizard in search of the coolness of stone. Here, for the first time, the doors and windows opened onto the cry of gulls and ocean air.

The place was empty save for the pilgrim's usual companions—the Apostle James and Jesus Christ, his mother, the saints. The crucified Savior's body hung limp behind the altar. Life-sized, molded from cow-skin, it was jarringly real with its wild black hair, haggard face, gaping wounds. And this Christ of Finisterre has a fearsome reputation. Once, a Moorish raider raised a sword against him; the infidel's arm froze in mid-stroke, and he and all his companions were converted on the spot. Whether you're Christian or not, it's hard to feel easy in such a presence.

Yet Christ seemed out of place in this crisp maritime light. The legend says that fishermen found him floating on the sea, and truly he had the air of a fragment of Levantine driftwood washed up by chance on the Atlantic shore.

I moved on. The pilgrim's friend, Santiago, was standing by, decked out in his broad-brimmed hat and all-weather cloak, looking just as he had in dozens of churches along the way. Here, he had reached the end of his road. Other saints dozed in chapels or hung from walls, their faces and attributes comforting, familiar; there were no surprises here.

And then, in a rear chapel, I came upon an image different from any I had seen on the Camino. It was the Virgin Mary walking upon a storm-tossed ocean with the infant Jesus in the crook of her arm. The gaudy silver crown on her head identified her as the Queen of Heaven, but she had the curly auburn locks and straight, narrow nose of a Galician beauty. As she gazed towards heaven with eyes full of glory, a pair of sodden mariners in oil-skins hauled themselves from the deep by the hem of her gown.

This was the Mary of the local sailors and fishermen. It was not a particularly attractive statue, nor a famous or even a venerable one. In a snide mood, one might call it kitsch; but three weeks in Lourdes and seven on the Camino had worn some of the snide off me and I could see a beauty based not on the judgment of the eye, but of the heart.

As I admired the statue, it occurred to me what a faithful, though silent, companion Mary had been over the past three months. I had hardly noticed her in Lourdes, so taken had I been with Bernadette, or on the Camino, where all the attention was on Saint James. But she had always been near: in Lourdes as a creature of light and air, presiding over the thousand small miracles that took place there each day; on the Camino as a queen of the earth, enthroned in every church with her child in her lap. Now here she was again, at the end of the world, strolling over the waters of death. Truly, she was Our Lady of the Four Elements, at home on the sea, on the land, in the sky.

And though I had seen her wear many faces, many names, she was always herself, recognizable at once as Mary the Mother of Jesus. Perhaps this was why I had taken her for granted; it was easy to feel that one knew her, when really one knew nothing at all.

I stood in the church, as the shadows of seagulls criss-crossed the floor and waves broke on the shore beyond, humbled by the depth and humility of love that had crafted this simple statue and placed it here. And I thought that if I were the kind of person who believed in signs, I would take this as a sign that I should write something about the Virgin Mary.

Unfortunately, I am not the kind of person who believes in signs.

Good rationalist that I am, I believe in chance, coincidence and the human propensity to seek out patterns and meaning in the world. I don't really believe in a higher consciousness out there, but if there is one, I'm sure that it has more important things to do than plant messages for me in remote seaside chapels. I consider myself an atheist, though I'll settle for "agnostic" just to avoid being dogmatic, for my atheism is not something I arrived at and feel the need to defend. It is simply the habit of mind I inherited from my upbringing. I was not brought up to believe in God, and to begin now would take every bit as great an effort as for a life-long believer to stop.

And yet, and yet . . . Here I was. I had just completed one of the great Catholic pilgrimages. I had spent three weeks in Lourdes. How was an atheist to account for such behavior?

I can only say that for as long as I can remember I have been pressing my nose up against the windows of faith, trying to catch a glimpse of what goes on inside. I am fascinated by religion in the way one is fascinated by the things one doesn't have. I wonder what it is to walk into a church anywhere in the world and feel at home; to pray in the certainty that somewhere your prayer is being heard; to unlock by word or gesture the inner chambers of ritual. I love the sensation, too, of the ego flowing into and merging with some wider sea. This, not loss, but expansion of the sense of self to take in other people, a landscape, the interior of a cathedral, a starry sky is a human gift that can be experienced without the aid of organized faith. But so many of the artifacts and rituals humans have crafted to induce it—music, architecture, dance, poetry, painting—lie in the realm of religion. And so I find myself in places such as Lourdes and Santiago.

In fact, my project this summer had been to take notes for a book about pilgrimages: not only religious ones, but secular as well—to battle-fields, literary shrines, the last resting places of rock stars. Now, in this tiny chapel at the end of the world, by chance or by design, I was being tendered a remarkable proposal: that I set aside the rock stars and poets and dead soldiers and turn my full attention to the Virgin Mary.

Did anything in my background qualify me for such a task?

My previous contacts with the Virgin Mary and the Catholic religion, though not insignificant, had tended towards the idiosyncratic. As a child, I had a prized collection of Christmas stamps featuring paintings of the Madonna. By the age of eight, I already knew a Botticelli Virgin from a Murillo or a Velasquez. (Murillo was my favorite, but that was before I discovered Bellini.) Somewhere along the line my coin collection, too, came to include a noteworthy Virgin. The piece in question was actually not a coin at all, but a small, oval medallion that bore the astounding date of 1830. I remember carrying it in my pocket for a time as a talisman. It seemed an exotic thing to do.

It was around this time that I made my first Catholic friend, Dougie Walker. Dougie lived in the house kitty-corner to mine and attended not Victoria Park Elementary School as I did, but an establishment that went by the outlandish name of "Our Lady Affattama." He wore a jacket to school, had priests and nuns instead of teachers, and attended special classes for something he called "cattakism," though from what I could make out it had nothing to do with cats. My first lesson in religion was Dougie informing me that as I was not a Catholic I must be a Protestant. Apparently that was how things worked.

And then there was Saint Mike's. When I enrolled at Saint Michael's College, the Catholic enclave of the University of Toronto, I believe I did so under the impression that the place would have a medieval air about it; that its library would be staffed with cowled monks, its text-books written on parchment. Instead, I found myself in a beehive that buzzed with the concerns, beliefs, traditions, literature, art, heroes, saints, philosophy and polemics of *contemporary* Catholicism: a whole Catholic parallel universe, in short, that was and always had been going on next to my own without my ever knowing it. Saint Mike's opened the door to this universe. More importantly, it inspired me to go and discover the old Catholic homelands of Italy, France, Spain and

Portugal, where to my eternal gratification I discovered the truth in Hilaire Belloc's ditty:

> Where'er the Catholic sun does shine,
> There's music and laughter and good red wine.

And I may as well mention, if I'm fishing for signs from above, that while at Saint Mike's I nursed a melancholy crush on more than one resident of Loretto College; though I cannot say I ever wondered (as I trolled St. Mary Street, angling for a glimpse of my Beatrice) just what or where the original "Loretto" might be. At least I had figured out by then that "Our Lady Affattama" was, in fact, Our Lady *of Fatima*.

Somehow this didn't look like much of a foundation for a book about the Virgin Mary. And yet there seemed to be a need for such a book, for nearly all of the books I could find about the Virgin, once I had begun to look, were written by and for believers. There is no lack of books on Islam by non-Muslims, or on Napoleon by non-Frenchmen. Why weren't there books about the Virgin by non-Catholics?

Mary, after all, can claim to be the most famous woman in history. (And "history" is the correct word here, for behind the eternal Mary, the myth, the archetype, there stands a real woman.) Who is more widely recognized? Who has been depicted more often or more lovingly in art, or more celebrated in music? In whose name have more wars been fought, empires built, great endeavors launched?

Of even greater interest to me was the twenty centuries' worth of stories that cluster around her, the accounts of her life and her miraculous interventions in human affairs that spring everywhere like wildflowers. Mary has been, if nothing else, a figure to whom and through whom humankind has expressed its deepest longings, dreams and fears. One doesn't need to be Catholic to appreciate such beauty.

This is not to say that I had no reservations about dealing with Mary. The fact is, the Blessed Virgin has not always kept the best company. Her name and divine authority have been invoked by bigots and fanatics. Dictators and authoritarian church leaders have held up her unquestioning submission to the Lord's will as model behavior for citizens and believers. In short, the revolutionary tradition of kindling bonfires with statues of Our Lady exists for a reason. Yet the more I came to know

Mary through my readings and travels, the more I felt that essentially she was on the side of the people, that she was not a goddess of the victors, but a consoler and a healer. So although I was still no believer in signs, I decided that I would try to write about the Virgin Mary.

Of course, this raised the question of where I was to look for her. If it were her Son I was pursuing, the obvious place to start would be the Bible, where almost all that is known or believed about him is recorded. But the Bible tells us little of Mary. In the Gospels of Matthew and Luke, we meet her only in the stories of the miraculous events that surround Jesus' birth and infancy. Her shining moment comes in Luke, where she receives the Annunciation, the news that she is to bear the Messiah, with the words: "Behold I am the handmaid of the Lord; let it be to me according to your word." The Gospel of John passes over these scenes, but finds her in the end at the foot of the Cross. It is John, also, who tells of the Marriage at Cana, where Mary urges Jesus to address the beverage situation (the fact that he agrees, grudgingly, to perform the water-into-wine miracle has long been taken as evidence that he can never refuse his gentle mother's bidding). The Virgin's only other appearance in the Bible comes after the crucifixion, in the Book of Acts. There, she joins the Apostles on the Day of Pentecost, providing support for the tradition that she was active in disseminating her Son's message after his death.

Everything else that is or has been believed of Mary—of her miraculous conception and prodigious childhood, of how she walked with Christ to Calvary, of her later life, death, and Assumption into heaven, and of the million visitations, great and small, that she has made upon the world since then—all of these came later, elaborated (or revealed, as the believer would say) fragment by fragment over the course of two millennia. The Virgin is a composite of legends, traditions, dreams, apparitions, poems, miracles and newspaper reports. Above all, she is image: the silent image of sheltering motherhood cast in light from the windows of Chartres, enthroned in the churches of the Camino, standing fairy-like in the Grotto of Lourdes. Religions have been built upon the words of Moses, the Prophets and Christ; but Mary does not *say*; she *is*.

So there was no obvious place to begin a search for her. I needed to piece her together like a mosaic. It seemed, then, that the way to proceed was to visit some of the places where she had revealed herself, to listen to what these places said to my own "secular" soul, and to walk a mile with the pilgrims where I could, for it was they who had drawn me to this theme in the first place.

This was no spiritual quest I was proposing. I had no thought of discovering the One Great Truth along the way, though I did happily anticipate encountering many small ones. My simple aim was to try my writer's hand at an archaic profession: that of the *madonnaro*, the painter of Madonnas.

The venture was entirely my own, I picked an itinerary that suited me. I would track Mary through the Latin nations of Western Europe, under "the Catholic sun." I would start in Paris with Notre-Dame and the apparitions of the rue du Bac. Next, I would make a long-overdue visit to Chartres and its celebrated cathedral. As I had already spent some weeks in Lourdes, I would pass through swiftly this time; but I would repeat the Camino, to feel again a pilgrimage through my feet and to watch for the Virgins along the way this time. From Santiago I would proceed to Fatima, then Zaragoza, home of the Virgen del Pilar, and Montserrat, near Barcelona, with its famous Black Virgin. I would visit Rome, the city of the Virgin *par excellence*, in the throes of a Jubilee year, and finish my travels in the original Loreto (with a single "t"), on the night when Mary's Holy House was first borne there by the angels.

As things worked out, my itinerary changed on the fly. It was, after all, just the worst time of the year for a journey. Not even the Catholic sun was shining through the windows of Chartres. The Camino was miles of open road with snow, wind and rain to keep me company. The pilgrim tide was low in Fatima. Montserrat had been damaged by an earthquake and no Spanish tourism office would ascertain for me if it was accepting visitors. Rome's Jubilee had almost run its course.

But we cannot always choose our seasons. The accidents of timing, if that's what they are, only mean that one sees something or speaks to someone different than one would otherwise have seen or spoken to. The thing is to get out on the road and start walking. The rest will follow.

BODIES

IN MOTION

PARIS

Tourists and Worshippers

Off the Métro at Cité. Two-at-a-time up the spiral stairs that ring the iron-clad exit shaft. I issue into the perfect morning like vapor from the smokestack of an ocean liner.

Paris again. First stop: Notre-Dame.

On my maiden voyage to Europe in 1983, Paris was the first city I visited on the Continent. Arriving sleepless at seven in the morning, I rolled off the overnight bus from London and went wandering the streets without a map, overwhelmed to find myself acting in a foreign film with no captions. Before long—because that is how gravity operates here—I found myself in front of the cathedral. I gazed bleary-eyed across the *parvis*, hearing Charles Laughton's Quasimodo howling, "Sanctuary! Sanctuary!" Then I made a beeline through the peaked portal of Saint Anne and into the lofty candle-flickering womb of the church. There was a coolness, a faint aroma of incense, the still, constant light of the rose windows. It was early on a weekday morning, and Notre-Dame was all mine.

It was mine though I had never been there before, because I *knew* Notre-Dame. I knew it from postcards, movies, brochures, books, photos. I was a pilgrim, a cultural pilgrim, discovering what every pilgrim discovers: that foreknowledge of a place confers a sense of title. I had left behind my tidy, modern country, my New World suburb of Europe, and crossed an ocean and the abyss of centuries to claim this place as my own. Now, as I paced the length of the cathedral in the still, constant light of the rose windows, I felt that I had come into my inheritance. I took a deep breath of incense and fell asleep slumped in a rear pew.

BUT NOTRE-DAME is not only *my* inheritance. It is a family heirloom of "the patrimony of humanity." And the better part of humanity looks to be here today, lined up waiting to get in. The ample plaza before the cathedral is called the *parvis*, a corruption of *paradis*, but today it is less a Paradise than a Babel of excited tongues. It's a Sunday morning, fifteen minutes before mass, but few of us are here for a religious service. We are here to see the Cathedral of Notre-Dame de Paris, Our Lady of Paris.

The first shrine to the Virgin Mary on this site was consecrated around the year 600. It was not the first Marian church in France, nor was it even the most important church in Paris. That honor went to Saint Stephen's Cathedral, in whose shadow Mary's chapel rose. Indeed, when the marauding Vikings in 856 allowed the Parisians (for a price) to choose three churches to be saved from their plundering, the Virgin's church was not among them. But in the aftermath, as the French surveyed their charred capital and asked themselves just how effective a patron Stephen had been, they decided to rededicate Paris to Mary. A new cathedral was built for her and when the Vikings came looting again in 885, they found themselves up against new fortifications and a new divine protectress. Paris had to withstand four harrowing years of siege, but the Normans withdrew in the end—for the last time, as it turned out—and Mary reigned supreme, the savior of Paris.

As I stand in line, gently putting off the postcard hawkers and the wind-up-birdie sellers, it strikes me as curious how the name "Notre-Dame" has come to signify the building, as though the dowager cathedral herself were "Our Lady of Paris." This is the most famous of all the churches in the world dedicated to the Virgin, a logical place, one would think, to embark on a search for Mary. Yet for some time now, the female figure most closely identified with the cathedral has not been the Virgin Mary, Our Lady of Paris (who stands high on the windy parapets, looking out over her city), but the gypsy Esmeralda. Does Mary still live here?

The young Korean couple in front of me ask if I will take their picture. I don't know if they really want the whole monumental portal of

Saint Anne in the frame, but they're going to get it anyway. Notre-Dame has three portals. Each depicts in its tympanum (the pointed arch above the doorway) a moment of sacred history and Mary figures prominently in two of them. Above the portal on the right, through which we will enter, she is seated, steadying the boy Jesus in her lap with her left hand while in her right she holds something that looks like a giant toilet brush. In this characteristic depiction, the Virgin is referred to as the *sedes sapientiae*, "seat of wisdom," although here she looks very much like a mother and very little like a seat. In the tympanum above the left portal, it is Mary's death and her coronation as Queen of Heaven that are featured. Her Son now is grown, but he inclines his head with reverence towards his mother as angels set the eternal crown upon her brow.

And above the central doors? There sits Christ the King, dividing mankind at the final judgment. The blessed at his right hand ascend to heavenly bliss; the damned on his left sink to eternal damnation. Mary is present too, but she withdraws before the calm majesty of her Child. The Portal of Judgment is the name of this doorway and good Christians once must have shuddered to pass through it. They need shudder no more. It is closed to the public. One enters and exits this house of Mary by the gates of mercy.

A certain number of today's visitors acknowledge that they are guests of Mary by dipping their hands into the ornate finger bowl that stands at the door, bringing the water to forehead, chest and shoulders, then bending a knee in the direction of the altar. Most of us, however, traipse in as though this were a train station or an office building. We regard this place as in some way our own. It's the patrimony of humanity, remember? If we think of ourselves as guests at all, it is as guests of the French government. The thought that we may be guests of the deity doesn't cross our minds.

But now, with mass about to commence, the secular mob is reminded just whose house this is. For while the worshippers pass freely through the barricades and take their place in the warmly lit pews before the altar, we the unhallowed tourists (like the damned souls on the portal of judgment) are steered into the outer darkness by an entry-level Saint Peter. The message is clear: My friends, when there is no mass in progress, you are free to roam and gape and muse. If it suits you, you may even lie down in the pews and dream that Notre-Dame is all your own just because you've seen it in a Disney movie. But when the holy service is in progress, this cathedral becomes what it has always been: the House of the Lord and his Mother and their People. So try not to make a nuisance of yourself.

The organ clears its metally throat, the priest enters the starting blocks, the lips of the choir part, and the crowd around me strains to see, some raising their arms to peer through the eye of a handi-cam. In the calm pool of light at the center of the cathedral, the worshippers sit rapt as the priest explains (not for the first time) what it is that drives men to sin. Meanwhile, the secular hordes keep swelling through the big brass doors, surging up the aisle till they meet the barriers, pausing an instant to take in the service, then retreating to form little eddies around the souvenir stall. Along the way, they slow to peer with scant interest into the chapels of Sainte Geneviève, Saint Landry, Sainte Clothilde, Saint Vincent de Paul. Everyone admires the regal fourteenth-century crowned statue of Mary ("the best known among the thirty-seven representations of her in Notre-Dame") and the radiant rose windows. A few even light a candle in front of the bronze crucifix presented to the cathedral by Napoleon III, or the statue of Our Lady of Guadelupe, or the Virgin atop the pillar near the exit.

But do they do so as worshippers or as tourists? It's not easy to tell, as they half-turn, candle in hand, to pose for a photo.

IN THE HEAT OF THE FRENCH REVOLUTION, pent-up rage against the Church found an outlet in the vandalization of the great medieval cathedrals. The unfettered mobs of Paris hauled the statues of kings down from the facade of Notre-Dame (it didn't matter that they were kings of Israel so long as they were kings) for the sheer fun of knocking off their heads and pitching them into the Seine. The scene must have resembled the public vendettas enacted against statues of Marx and Lenin after the collapse of the Communist regimes. Then as now, there were some who wept for the fall of the old idols, others who deplored the breakdown of public order, and a few who kept an eye on the main chance. It was one of the latter who spoke before the revolutionary committee of the city of Chartres in 1793. He foresaw the day when the Christian faith would be only a distant memory and the people of the world would flock to admire the beauty of France's Gothic churches—and pay good money for the privilege. This, he maintained, was reason enough to preserve them.

Could that sage pass through the portals of Notre-Dame today and see the crowds snapping up, not bones of saints or icons of the Virgin, but slides, coffee-table books, videos, postcards and bookmarks, he would consider his predictions fulfilled. For although it is true that the Christians haven't yet forsaken the house of their Mother, they are far outnumbered by those who have come solely to take in the architecture; visitors who see, when they look around them, not the House of Mary, but Mary's museum.

Let's call it "The Notre-Dame-de-Paris Museum of the Catholic Religion." Its "permanent displays" consist of paintings, stained glass, sculpture, ecclesiastical objects and the structure itself. All of these features originally served as vehicles of religious instruction or devotion; they pointed beyond themselves to the Kingdom of Heaven, were alive with its reflected holiness. Today they are appreciated as art, valued for their aesthetic qualities or the workmanship they display. They point not at the beyond, but at the historical moment and artistic milieu that produced them. They are objects and, as such, are as lifeless as the glass cases of amphorae in a museum.

In the eyes of the secularist, the "museum-goer," Notre-Dame has lost its sacred sheen. Or at least, the specifically Catholic nature of its sacredness has worn away, leaving a residual sense of generic holiness a little different from what one might feel in a Japanese temple or a Turkish mosque. And yet our "Notre-Dame Museum" remains a place of worship—place of *secular* worship. Just look at us, the tourists, our arms crossed, voices hushed, setting step before measured step as we make our way around the ambulatory. What pilgrim could be more reverent?

The question is, to whom have we come to pay homage? To Our Lady? Not at all. We, the secular pilgrims have come to honor "Man." Man the builder. Man the artist. Man the deviser of complex belief systems. If we feel awe in this place, it is for the ingenuity of the architects, the skill of the craftsmen, the deep and audacious faith of the medieval Parisians. We have come to admire the human capacity for creating beauty, and perhaps also to wonder what has become of it. We move through Notre-Dame, in John Ralston Saul's memorable phrase, "in a vague, unfocused manner as if [we] expected to come across the trace of some lost promise."

And all the while, in our vague, unfocused midst, the believers, the museum's "living exhibits," are going about their spiritual business. The believers of Nortre-Dame are not pilgrims for the most part, but local worshippers (though one might argue that a worshipper's every trip to church is a little pilgrimage.) It's easy to pick them out, for like different species of birds, worshippers and tourists have their own, distinct ways of relating to the cathedral. Thus, while the tourist's visit to Notre-Dame takes the form of a slow, circular grazing ritual, the worshipper alternates profound, centered stillness with bursts of purposeful action.

Observe the tourist-cum-museum-goer, one such as myself, how he strolls from chapel to chapel in Notre-Dame, just as he would stroll from painting to painting in the Louvre or cage to cage at the zoo, hoping always for a surprise, a diversion to fill his eye or engage his mind for a moment. He keeps moving because there is no natural place or reason for him to stop, nothing really for him to do here except look. Hence, his typical trajectory is once around, his feet padding a slow rhythm while his eyes flit from point to point, snatching up impressions to toss into the sieve-like shopping basket of the memory. If there is time and the crowd isn't too great, he might sit in one of the pews for a few minutes to "take it all in." After that, he can in good conscience send a postcard home to say that he has "done" Notre-Dame.

The worshipper, by contrast, assumes a seat near the center of the church and focuses her being on the altar, whether there is a service in progress or not. When her prayers are said, she goes to make confession or to visit a chapel. She does not trifle along the way with other chapels and their artistic treasures and, when she kneels to pray, it is with scandalous disregard for whether the object of her devotion is a work of the thirteenth century or the eighteenth, of the Flemish school or the Provençal. Nor is she ever "done" with Notre-Dame, because sometime in the next few days she will be back again to take Holy Communion, renew her prayers, make a confession. The worshipper, in short, comes not—or not only—to *experience* the church, but to *make use of* it.

And this is where the tourist and the worshipper part ways. For the tourist, ultimately, is alienated from much of what he encounters here. His experience is that of a living object observing a dead one. At best, if the fire of his imagination is strong enough, he can blow some life into what he sees, making it glow a little. Sooner or later, however, he will probably run out of wind. The believer, on the other hand, encounters something living in Notre-Dame. Her church has a pulse; a sense of touch, and hearing; it responds to her.

It must take real concentration to find that pulse in today's scrum, however. Today even the candle-lighters look suspiciously like they are enjoying "an interactive experience." It is one of those patrimony-of-humanity moments that deliver much less than they promise because, in the end, something that belongs to everyone has ceased to belong to anyone.

Enough, then. The sun is shining and Paris awaits.

Looking back from the middle of the parvis, up the soaring facade, I see the Virgin where she rises like an exclamation point before her great rose window, asserting her Ladyship over all she surveys. But there are higher parapets still, and there the tourists lord it, striding back and forth, posing for photos by the gargoyles, pointing out to each other the sights of the shimmering city.

Do these barbarians on the ramparts mark the end of Mary's reign? Is her devotion destined to wither in the dry heat of secularism?

Or have I just been looking in the wrong place?

140, rue du Bac

"On a midsummer's night—July 18, 1830—Our Lady came to Paris. She came, not to the shadowy vastness of her Cathedral of Notre-Dame, but to the narrow back street called the rue du Bac …"
Saint Catherine Labouré, Joseph I. Dirvin, C.M.

Over the bridge to the Left Bank, then west along the Seine. It's a glorious day, the sky the blue of the tricolore, and those smoke-puff clouds straight out of a painting by the Douanier Rousseau. There are the bookstalls by the Seine selling Toulouse-Lautrec posters, the lovers lost in each other's arms, the dog shit. Across the river stand the long walls of the Louvre, high temple of art. On this side, a little further on, is the Musée d'Orsay, Impressionist showroom, where the cultural pilgrims who spent the morning at Notre-Dame admiring the creations of medieval Parisians can spend the afternoon admiring the taste and ingenuity of their nineteenth-century descendants.

But turn away instead into the narrow and sinuous rue du Bac. It is a ten-minute walk to number 140, a walk that feels not like a pilgrimage to a shrine of the Holy Mother, but like a shopping expedition. A leisurely Parisian shopping expedition in search of beautiful, useless things—an  eighteenth-century atlas, a Chinese umbrella stand, a sack of nougatines or candied chestnuts. My guidebook proclaims, "You can fill your grocery basket as fast as you empty your pocketbook on the rue du Bac."

Like every street in Paris, the rue du Bac is flagged with historical footnotes. Number One was once the address of the real-life d'Artagnan, while the barracks of the Grey Musketeers were close by at numbers 13 to 17. And in the block north of the suggestively named rue de Babylone stands a true Paris landmark, featured in *Fodor*, *Frommer* and *Fielding*: the Au Bon Marché department store.

Au Bon Marché was the child of Aristide Boucicault, the emblematic self-made man of the Third Empire. Boucicault started out with thirty-six square yards of floor space and ended up master of a 31,000-square-yard, Eiffel-designed "modern bazaar." His little empire was established upon the recognition and exploitation of the great new consumer constituency of the mid-nineteenth century: the young woman with disposable income. Au Bon Marché's success was such that Zola himself felt called upon to take a kick at it. His journalistic novel *Aux bonheur des dames* revealed how Boucicault drove small competitors into bankruptcy, exploited floor workers, and used manipulative advertising to separate young women from their earnings. While the book did nothing to slow Boucicault's momentum, it may well have served as a handbook for his emulators. To this day, Au Bon Marché remains *au courant*. An elevated walkway passes over the rue du Bac to the new Store Two, home of "La Grande Épicerie," where shoppers can select from 150 varieties of tea and 240 cheeses.

Across the street, the rue du Bac offers one more point of interest: a five-storey non-entity, with bars on the ground-floor windows and a statue of the Virgin in the niche above the gate. The address is 140, and it is a building you could pass a thousand times without a glance if it weren't for the mendicants hovering at the entrance and the crowds with name-tags and matching travel totes who periodically erupt from its courtyard into the street. A modest plaque by the gate (far less conspicuous than the red "Garage Exit: No Parking" signs) reads, *La Chapelle de la Médaille Miraculeuse*.

If a passing visitor were sufficiently intrigued to look for 140, rue du Bac in her *Frommer* or *Fodor* or *Fielding*, her *Lonely Planet* or *Let's Go*, she would find nothing. And that is strange, considering that each year something in the neighborhood of two million people pass through these unprepossessing gates. In fact, after Notre-Dame and the basilica of Sacre-Coeur (with its magnificent views over the city), this is the most frequented church in Paris. Granted, the majority of the visitors are French—indeed, Parisian. But not a day goes by without travelers from every corner of the world converging here by the busful.

Why, then, is it not in the tourist guidebooks?

For the simple reason that *tourists* don't come here. *Pilgrims* come here. And not those cultural or aesthetic or spiritual pilgrims who flock to Notre-Dame, but real, old-fashioned Catholic pilgrims who come all this way just to say a prayer in a holy place, as pilgrims for a thousand years and more have come to Jerusalem or Santiago or Rome.

Thanks to 140 rue du Bac, Paris can claim to be one of those points on the map where the contemporary Catholic pilgrimage trail intersects the route of the tourist. But even here, tourists and pilgrims pass in the night. A Marian pilgrim may only see the Louvre, the Eiffel Tower, the Arc de Triomphe, even the cathedral of Notre-Dame, fleetingly from the window of a tour bus. By the same token, a tourist on her way to Au Bon Marché would probably take a glance into this nondescript little religious compound on the rue du Bac and keep walking.

Still, considering that the first travelers' guides to Europe were written for pilgrims to Rome and the Holy Land, it's a little ironic that such an important pilgrim center doesn't make Mr. Fodor's cut. If we could press him on it, doubtless he would rationalize the omission on the grounds that the Chapel of the Miraculous Medallion is simply of no artistic or historical interest. While pilgrims wouldn't take much issue with the first point, they would hardly agree with the second. From their point of view, this chapel is of terrific historical significance, except that they are thinking not of secular history but of "salvation history": the gradual unfolding of God's plan for humankind. In the eyes of many Catholics the apparitions of the Virgin at the rue du Bac in 1830 represent Mary's first important intervention in modern history, the forerunner in a series that would continue through Lourdes and Fatima (to name only the most famous) and on to the present day. From the rue du Bac, through the device of a simple medallion, Mary spoke her message of hope to all the world.

WHERE TO BEGIN THE STORY of the Miraculous Medallion? Try here: It is the 1870s, and this is the house of the Daughters of Charity in Reuilly, a suburb of Paris. The nuns, a couple of dozen all told, are gathered in the common room for an hour of recreation. One is reading. One writes in her journal. Yet another stands looking out the window, mutely fingering her rosary. There are nuns in pairs or small groups, chatting quietly. Several younger sisters are talking in louder voices, now and then bursting into giggles.

One stolid, oldish nun sits by the Sister Superior, sewing up a worn garment. She is a woman in her late sixties: plain, thin-lipped. A bit of a cold fish. And clearly not as genteel as the others; the fingers that ply the needle are thick and tough, hardened by years of work. Absorbed in her needlework, she shows no interest in the conversations that buzz around her.

The younger sisters have slipped into a topic that is evidently a frequent source of idle speculation: Who can she be, the nun to whom Mary appeared more than forty years before? Everyone knows that she was a novice at the rue du Bac, but there were so many, and now they are scattered about different religious houses. Many, indeed, have died. Will the world ever know the seer's name? One of the girls, aiming to shock her companions, announces with a sniff: "Well, I think it's all a lot of nonsense. Whoever she was, I don't believe she even saw the Virgin. She probably just saw a picture of her."

This is going a little far. The other girls are hastening to protest when a slow, clear voice from across the room cuts them short.

"My dear. The Sister who saw the Holy Virgin saw her in flesh and bone. The same as we see each other now."

Everyone in the room catches her breath. They are as surprised, perhaps, at who has spoken as at what she has said. It is the old nun. She holds the girl's eye for a moment. Then, without another word, she goes back to her needlework.

CATHÉRINE LABOURÉ, Zoé to her family, was precocious in her devotion to the Blessed Virgin. When her mother left the world, worn out by the production and maintenance of seventeen children, the nine-year-old girl climbed up on a chair and took the statue of Mary down from the shelf: "From now on," she said, "you will be my mother." A rather theatrical-sounding act of devotion, yet performed in private; the family servant witnessed it only by chance. This fact gives us our first clue to Cathérine Labouré's character and subsequent career. For all her life, she would keep her dramatic spiritual life close to her chest.

Older sister Marie-Louise taught Cathérine the work of the stable, the garden, the dovecote and the house, then left her to manage on her own when she went to pursue a religious vocation with the Sisters of Charity. The twelve-year-old handled the huge task with skill, while never neglecting her daily appointment with the Lord: six o'clock mass at the church of Moutiers-Saint-Jean, four kilometers away. She also began to practice private mortification, fasting and kneeling for hours in the village chapel before the painting of the Annunciation to the Virgin.

During these years, Cathérine had a portentous dream. She was in her parish church. The priest was a man she had never seen before; a man with knowing eyes, a full beard and a most impressive nose. After the mass, he beckoned her to follow him, but she turned away in fear. "You run now," the old priest said, "but someday you will come to me. God has plans for you. Don't forget it!" Several years later, on visiting the house of the Sisters of Charity in Châtillon-sur-Seine, Cathérine would see a painting of Saint Vincent de Paul and recognize the priest of her dream. She accepted this as a sign of her calling.

Saint Vincent de Paul, "the father of the poor," had founded the Sisters of Charity together with Sainte Louise de Marillac in the early 1600s. The Sisters, in their distinctive blue uniforms and "flying nun" hats, had represented a social revolution in their day and a revival of Christianity from the roots. They were the first female religious order to escape the cloister and enter the life of the world to care for the urban poor. Later, they would assume the role of the "angels of the battlefield." They were the *de facto* nursing corps of France, and in April 1830, at the age of twenty-three, Cathérine Labouré entered their seminary at 140, rue du Bac.

There, as foretold, she found Saint Vincent de Paul waiting for her.

Mere days after Cathérine's arrival, the remains of the beloved saint were restored to their mother church for the first time in forty years. They had been forty years of turmoil for the Church, as the after-shocks of the Revolution continued to rock its foundations, and during all this time the body of Saint Vincent de Paul had been shunted from safe house to safe house around Paris to prevent its desecration. Now at last the Archbishop of Paris judged the time ripe for an old-style public display of devotion.

For three days, the sacred body in the silver coffin made its slow progress through the streets of Paris. Hundreds of thousands turned out to watch it pass. But this glimpse of holiness granted to the public was nothing compared to the private vision enjoyed by Cathérine Labouré. For in those same three days, in the little chapel on the rue du Bac, hovering above a case that contained a bone from his right arm, Cathérine saw the heart of Saint Vincent de Paul. No other part of him; only his heart.

On the first day, the saint's heart was white, and to Cathérine that whiteness signified peace, calm, innocence and union. On the second day, it glowed red as fire; to Cathérine, this signified the fire of charity that should burn in the hearts of the sisters. On the third day, the heart was a gloomy brick red, and this color imported great sadness to the seer's heart, a sadness that she felt somehow presaged political strife.

The commemoration of Saint Vincent de Paul passed, but Cathérine's visions had only begun. On the day of the Holy Trinity, she saw Jesus in the wafer during mass. He looked like a king, carrying his cross upon his breast. But suddenly his royal vestments and cross fell from him, and Cathérine understood that the King of France, too, would soon lose his crown.

As these dreams and visions came to her, Cathérine obediently imparted them to her confessor, Father Aladel. He did his best to pacify the young woman. Doubtless, he had seen such cases before: ingenues with imaginations over-heated by the novelty of this environment of prayer and sanctity. Still, nothing could have prepared him for July 19, the feast of Saint Vincent de Paul, when Cathérine confessed that she had passed the better part of the previous evening in the company of the Blessed Virgin Mary.

On the evening of the eighteenth, after speaking to the novices of Saint Vincent's great love for the Virgin, the director of the seminary of the rue du Bac had given each a special treat: a morsel of cloth from one of the saint's own garments. On an impulse, Cathérine tore hers in half before she went to bed and swallowed a piece. Then she prayed to Saint Vincent and went to sleep sure that she would see the Virgin.

At 11:30, even as the elements of the holy relic were passing into the fabric of her body, Cathérine Labouré heard a voice call her name. She drew back her bed-curtain, and saw a child dressed in white.

"Get up at once and come to the chapel. The Virgin is waiting for you."

After an instant of doubt, Cathérine rose and dressed herself while the child waited at the head of her bed. Then she followed—him? her?—down the hall, their way lit by mysterious beams of light. The doors to the chapel should have been locked, but they opened at a touch of the child's finger. Within, all the candles and torches flamed as for midnight mass. Cathérine's guide led her to the sanctuary, instructing her to pray and wait. The minutes passed slowly and Cathérine was starting to worry that someone would discover her when again she heard the child's voice:

"Here is the Virgin! Here she is!"

She heard a sound, "like the *frou-frou* of a silk dress." A moment later, she was kneeling at the feet of Mary. The Virgin sat in a chair and Cathérine rested her hands in the Holy Mother's lap. She called this "the sweetest moment of her life." Then the Virgin began to speak.

"My child, the Good Lord wishes to charge you with a mission. You will suffer great hardship, but you will overcome all by recalling that what you do, you do for the glory of God.

"The times are ill. Great evils will fall upon France. The Cross will be scorned; the Archbishop will be stripped of his vestments; blood will flow in the streets; the entire world will fall into misery. But come to the foot of this altar. Here, the gifts of God will be bestowed on all who ask for them with faith and fervor, on the great and the small."

Cathérine stayed at the foot of the altar, her hands resting in the lap of the Virgin, for she knew not how long, until she felt "as though something had been extinguished."

"She is gone," said the child.

As Cathérine returned to bed, the two o'clock bell chimed. This homely, unlettered French village girl had just spent two hours in the company of the Mother of God. What saint or mystic could claim more?

Father Aladel was naturally taken aback by these new extravagances. And all the more so when, over the course of the following week, everything that Cathérine had predicted came to pass. Three days after the colloquy with the Virgin, King Charles of France, in a surprise bid to seize back his divine right, dissolved the national assembly. The public rose, driving the King into exile, then turned against the Church, his ally. Blood flowed in the streets of Paris; the Archbishop, "stripped of his vestments," went into temporary hiding with the Sisters of Charity. And Father Aladel began to take notice of Cathérine Labouré.

In the months that followed, as order was restored to the capital, Cathérine experienced no further visions.

Then, on November 27, at five-thirty in the evening, as she sat in the chapel during the silent meditation following the day's reading, she heard again the fateful *frou-frou* of silk. There was the Virgin, dressed in dawn-white, hovering beside the painting of Saint Joseph. Her veil was drawn back to reveal her face. Her eyes were raised towards heaven. She was standing on a sort of ball and in her hands Cathérine saw a globe. Suddenly, the Virgin spread out her fingers, showing them resplendent with rings. The rings were studded with jewels, great and small, that cast rays of light so bright that the Virgin's feet were lost in the dazzle.

Cathérine heard a voice: "This ball which you see represents the entire world, and particularly France, and each person in particular. It is the symbol of the graces bestowed on those who pray for them."

As the voice spoke, a nimbus began to form around the Blessed Mother. In the upper part, Cathérine—who had only recently learned to read—could make out words written in letters of gold: *O Mary, conceived without sin, pray for us who have recourse to you*.

"Have a medal stamped on this model," said the voice. "All who wear it around their neck will receive great graces. Graces will abound for those who wear it with faith."

Slowly, the entire tableau turned on its axis. Now, where the Virgin had stood, Cathérine perceived only an "M" with a cross above it and below the holy hearts of Jesus and Mary, his bound with the crown of thorns, hers pierced with a sword. Cathérine understood that this was the flip side of the medal. With that, the vision evaporated.

The next day, Cathérine came to Father Aladel with new instructions. One can imagine his delight. Despite the girl's run of prophecies in the spring, the priest wasn't prepared to commit himself to the stamping of a medallion. Cathérine, however, was not easily put off, especially as the Virgin continued to appear to her in holograph-style apparitions. Years later, other sisters would remember that they often heard raised voices from behind the closed door when Cathérine Labouré met with her confessor.

Early in the following year, Cathérine finished her novitiate at the rue du Bac. She was sent out to the veterans' hospice in Reuilly, at that time a suburb of Paris, and near enough to the mother-house that Aladel could continue to act as her confessor. Her time was now devoted to the quotidian worries of cooking for sixty mouths. Her apparitions had come to an end forever.

But the history of the medallion was just getting underway. Father Aladel had had some months to reflect. He suspected that Cathérine's apparitions were fantasies. But what if they were not? What if Mary had chosen him for her singular attentions, and he had not paid heed? He decided the safest approach was to inform the Archbishop of the matter and leave it with him. To Aladel's surprise, the Archbishop declared that he saw no harm in stamping a few medals; in fact, he asked that the first few be set aside for himself. So it was that in July of 1831, Father Aladel placed in the hands of the sisters the exemplars of what would soon be known as the Miraculous Medallion. Cathérine Labouré displayed no surprise, receiving hers with the simple words, "Now it must be propagated."

Paris was passing through a cholera epidemic that summer. The Sisters of Charity, in their ministrations to the sick, ran through the original batch of 20,000 medals in no time. Another stamping was authorized, and another. Tales of miraculous cures and conversions multiplied. Within three years, the Medallion was circulating throughout France, Italy, Belgium and Switzerland, and there was no end to the list of prayers answered through its agency.

By the 1850s, distribution of the Medallion had exceeded the hundred million mark. The effect on Catholicism was electric. For a century the Church had been under siege—from *philosophes*, Freemasons, the

Hapsburg Emperor Joseph II, the French Revolution, anti-clerical governments in Spain and Portugal, and Napoleon. Now at last this radiant sign had come from above, urging Catholics to fight on. The Virgin had worked a great revival in faith and devotion, and the way was paved for Pope Pius IX's momentous declaration of 1854: that she had been conceived "immaculately," without sin, just as the message on the Medallion proclaimed. The pronouncement was to receive its divine seal of approval in 1858 in Lourdes, when a shepherd girl named Bernadette, who wore around her neck a copy of the Miraculous Medallion, saw a woman who called herself "the Immaculate Conception."

Through all these tumultuous events, no answer was forthcoming to the question on everyone's lips: Who was the seer of the rue du Bac? Cathérine Labouré had made Father Aladel promise back at the beginning, before he had any reason to trust in her visions, that he would never reveal her identity. She held him to his promise for life.

Thus freed of the celebrity and torment that would be visited on Bernadette, Sister Cathérine toiled in contented obscurity, tending to the old codgers of the veteran's hospital and trying to shepherd them to God. (One folk remedy she employed against the most hardened sinners was to steep a copy of a prayer to the Virgin in their wine before serving it to them.) She took the hospice's farm in hand, tending the rabbits, chickens and cows, the garden and the orchard, as in her youth. She kept up contact with her brothers and sisters who lived in Paris, discreetly funding the education of a nephew who ended up as a missionary in China. And as the years passed and the number of sisters surviving from the year of her novitiate declined, she found herself the object of speculation. One nun remembered: "When I was at the seminary in the rue du Bac in 1855, many sisters told me, 'Today, the sister who saw the Holy Virgin is tending the cows at a house in Paris.' But when I was sent to the hospice of Enghien and went to work with Sister Cathérine, I said, 'No, it can't be her. She is not mystical enough.'"

Indeed, in the investigations conducted after Cathérine's death to establish her candidacy for sainthood, few sisters confessed to having noticed anything remarkable about her, beyond an exemplary raptness during prayer. Their descriptions portray her variously as capable, stiff, sharp-tongued, devout and a little dotty—but hardly mystical. Fearlessness was another of her attributes, as she demonstrated during the Commune of

1871, when she defied a band of armed vigilantes who had come looking for gendarmes who were hiding in the house. She even availed herself of the opportunity to hand out some Miraculous Medallions to the *communards*.

And though Cathérine never saw the Virgin again, she continued to hear from her. Mary spoke to her in prayers, relaying instructions for the reform of the Sisters of Charity (she was particularly troubled about laxity among the sisters, including frivolous reading and lack of fervor in praying the rosary), and reminding Cathérine that she expected a statue of herself holding the globe to be placed in the chapel of the apparitions. Father Aladel, ever dilatory, died in 1865 without having commissioned the statue, meaning that Cathérine was compelled to reveal her secret to her superior, Sister Dufès, so that this last item of business could be tied up.

Nor did Sister Cathérine ever lose her knack for predictions. From time to time throughout her life, the future came to her in flashes. Then she would make remarks that, though they had no bearing on the present conversation (and confirmed some in their view that she was not quite all there), proved prophetic in retrospect. It is not surprising, then, that no one paid her any mind as she placidly told them, from the outset of 1876, that she wouldn't live out the year. In fact, she died at seven in the evening, December 31. When Sister Dufès was sure that Sister Cathérine was no longer listening, she gathered the nuns together and said, "Yes, it was she who saw the Virgin."

Cathérine Labouré was canonized in 1947. She is known as "the Saint of Silence."

ENTERING THE COURTYARD of the chapel, I feel like I'm back at St. Mike's College. The architecture is of the neo-Institutional school. A brick-and-concrete alley with high walls on either side. Glassed-in reception office at the gate. Display cases, pastoral posters and offices on the right; on the left, a row of terracotta plaques depicting the virtues of the Miraculous Medallion. It cures. (Little Jean Ribet, seven, of Toulouse, suffering from a dreadful sickness identified as *mal de pott* sits up in bed and smiles.) It converts. (Jewish financier Adolphe Ratisbonne, on receiving a Miraculous Medallion from a friend, has a vision of the Virgin and finds the true faith.) It protects. (In 1915, as Au Bon Marché goes up in flames, the Virgin casts her fire-resistant mantle over the chapel.) The door to the chapel of the Medallion is at the far end of the courtyard opposite a kiosk that sells books and postcards of Stainte Cathérine and Saint Vincent de Paul.

Right now, there is only a handful of people poking around the courtyard. A peek into the chapel, however, reveals a mass in progress. That's where everybody is.

So I stroll about the courtyard, reading the notices on the walls. There is a table of the Announced Pilgrimages for October. Neat little cards slipped into notches indicate anywhere from two to ten groups scheduled each day for the next few weeks, including arrivals from Poland, Indonesia, Guyana, the Congo, Québec, Scotland, Australia, Korea, Thailand, and various parts of France.

It occurs to me that this would be a good moment to check out the Miraculous Medallion shop, before mass lets out. I find three cheery Sisters of Charity in blue minding the till. Their wares, laid out on the counter before them, consist of medallions. Some are a little bigger, some a little smaller, others a little shinier or a little cheaper, but they all have an image of the Virgin on the face and, on the obverse, a big "M" for Mary, a cross and two hearts.

The flyleaf to Joseph Dirvin's biography of Cathérine Labouré, published in 1949, claims that "Catholics are, from their earliest childhood, so familiar with the Miraculous Medal that they are inclined to take it completely for granted. . . . That is indeed our attitude to elemental things generally, like light and air; and this attitude in regard to the Miraculous Medal shows how elemental it has become in Catholic piety."

These words were written near the crest of a wave of Marian fervor that had started with the appearance of the Miraculous Medallion. That wave would roll on through the 1950s with the pronouncement of the dogma of the Virgin's Assumption—the doctrine that Mary ascended directly to heaven on passing from this life—and a crescendo of calls for her recognition as co-redemptor of humanity alongside Christ. The Second Vatican Council of the early 1960s, however, took a step back from these extremes of devotion to Mary and since then the Medallion has become less pervasive than light and air; so much less that most of my North American Catholic friends have never heard of it.

Ah, but I know the Miraculous Medallion!

For now, as I lean over the counter of the shop, I recognize this little metal oval as the talisman of my childhood, the one I used to carry in my pocket. I wonder now how such a thing ever fell into my hands. I vaguely remember hearing that my grandmother was once Catholic. Perhaps the Medallion was hers. Later, when I put the question to my mother, she looks up from her crossword and says:

"Oh yes, Mom was a Catholic all right. But after your Uncle Roger was born she was sick for a long time, too sick to go to church. Well, the priest began to come around to the house telling her that she'd better show up for mass or she'd be excommunicated, if you can imagine. I don't know how long this went on, but Pop finally got fed up with it and he tossed the priest right out of the house. Threw him down the stairs was the way he always told the story, though I don't know if he really did anything of the sort. In any case, the priest went right ahead and excommunicated her that Sunday. And that was it for her. She didn't just stop being Catholic, she stopped believing altogether."

Now when I look at my Miraculous Medallion, I can think about how close my mother came to being raised a Catholic, and say, if it is not inappropriate, "There but for the grace of God …"

At last, mass begins to let out. It's letting out reluctantly, however. A few people in a hurry to get somewhere squirt through the courtyard to the rue du Bac. And the rest of them? I make my way gingerly into the chapel and there they all are, still sitting. Several have gone to the front of the chapel to kneel and pray before the altar (placed on the spot where the Virgin sat) or the statue of Our Lady with the globe (in the place where the Miraculous Medal was revealed to Cathérine Labouré) or the glass casket that holds the earthly remains of the saint herself. A few whisper, read, write. The rest just sit, in utter silence, eyes cast forward in contemplation or prayer.

My mind goes back to the "thou-shalt-not" sign at the entrance to Notre-Dame: ideograms of a cell phone, a dog, an ice-cream cone, a skateboard, all struck through with red lines and below, the plaintive reminder, "This is a place of silence and prayer." There's no need for a sign like that here.

I scan the faces, trying to get a sense of who these people are. They look like locals, not pilgrims. The usual lunch-hour crowd? Most are women, but there is no shortage of men. Generally, they're middle-aged or older, but there are university students and young parents as well. The majority aren't terribly well-heeled, but there are business jackets and designer bags to be seen. Africans and Asians are well represented, but they are still in the minority. In other words, it's not much different from what you'd see in the Paris streets.

The chapel where the Virgin elected to appear is an undistinguished place indeed. And this probably suits the congregation just fine. If Chagall had done the stained-glass windows or Rodin the statues, then there *would* be need for a thou-shalt-not sign at the door. A guidebook would call the art saccharine (the prim angels are actually playing harps) but people don't come here to look at the art anymore than they go to a bank to admire the architecture. They come here to talk to Mary.

And there she is—looming over the altar, front and center, angel-supported on a roil of clouds. Metallic beams of light shoot from her outspread fingers. A halo of light bulbs illuminates her golden crown. There may be, as they say, thirty-seven Marys in the cathedral of Notre-Dame, but there is none like this one. The Mary of the rue du Bac is not a Virgin and Child but Our Lady serenely alone, as she appeared to Cathérine Labouré. This is not the first time the Virgin has been depicted without her son. But in prior paintings and images, where she appears alone as "the Immaculate Conception," she is a young girl, not a mother. In the rue du Bac, Mary appears in the role of the mother not so much of Jesus, as of the congregation and the seer herself. She is the good mother who was longed for by Cathérine Labouré, and later by Bernadette of Lourdes and Lúcia of Fatima.

And what of the crucified Christ? Well, he is here too, in a most tiny and delicate rendition, placed somewhat below the level of his mother's feet. A Catholic, toeing the party line, would most likely explain that Mary's outspread hands direct the worshipper's attention to her Son. What the untrained eye perceives, however, is a divine and powerful woman reaching down to raise her child to heaven.

The statues that flank the altar only serve to elevate Mary further. On the right, she stands with the globe in her hands, as she appeared in Cathérine Labouré's vision. In her virgin whiteness, she is every bit the peasant maiden, as home-spun as Cathérine herself. Normally it is Jesus who holds the world-ball in his hands, but in the Chapel of the Miraculous Medallion, it is Mary. And of course our world is such a handful that she has had to place her child in the care of his father. Yes, there to the left of the altar stands Joseph with the infant Jesus in his arms.

Hail Mary, Holy Working Mother!

Fifteen minutes after mass has ended, a hundred-odd people remain scattered about the chapel in as near perfect silence as a hundred-odd people can achieve. I wonder how they can focus their inner voices for so long. Don't their thoughts slip away like street urchins into the unswept alleys of the mind? What do they take away with them from this place? Peace? Clearer thoughts? New resolutions?

Prayer was not something we did at home, except once a year when the "Selkirk Grace" was admitted as a Burns Night tradition. A few times, I remember, I did try the prayer-before-bedtime routine. It was something I had seen so often on television that I took it to be a normal way of behavior to which, through some oversight, I had never been initiated. I would get on my knees, as one did, and pray for Mommy and Daddy, then toss in some special wish for myself. It was never quite clear to me, though, to whom I was addressing my prayers or why anyone would be interested in them. Even as a child I never had the sense that anything out there was listening.

A few years ago, while living in Japan, I discovered a different way of prayer, one not based on dialogue. Its chief appeal, in fact, was that it quieted for a time the nattering "I"; that insistent and—in my case, at least—mostly querulous inner voice that has maintained its running monologue these thirty-odd years. I would like to claim that meditation *silenced*, rather than *quieted*, the inner voice, but I never achieved that level of stillness. At most, an instant might pass when the only sound in my mind was something from without: a bird singing, a woman laughing, a truck coming to a slow stop in the street outside my window. And there it would be again. That voice! All full of itself now, because it had managed to shut up for a minute.

The silence of Zen prayer, like a breeze that disperses the mist of the self, seems quite different from the silence of Christian prayer, where the reality of the self and the selves of those for whom one prays is never in question. Yet both types of prayer begin with receptivity—as Cathérine Labouré, not a saint known for her eloquence, explains in a few well-chosen words:

"When I go to the chapel," she says, "I put myself there, before the Good Lord, and I say to him: 'God, here I am. Give me what you will.' If he gives me something, I am well pleased, and I thank him. If he gives me nothing, I thank him all the same, because it's no more than I deserve. And then I tell him everything that comes to my spirit. I tell him about my sorrows and my joys, and then I listen. If you listen, he will speak to you, for with the Good Lord one must both speak and listen. He always speaks when one comes to him humbly and simply."

I wonder again, as I did in childhood, what is it like to pray? Perhaps if I focus on the Virgin, and try to think of each member of my family and wish some good on them . . . Is that how it's done? I cast up the faces on the screen of my mind's eye one at a time, like a slide show. My, but I have a big family. Within seconds it's already becoming clear that this is something that requires practice and discipline. My mind chafes at even this small effort to concentrate. Should I kneel? Maybe the physical discomfort would help me to focus. …

I have barely set my knees to wood, however, when a clamor of voices pierces the chapel. Something is astir outside. My apologies to any family members I haven't prayed for yet, but they'll just have to fend for themselves.

For outside, the courtyard overflows with pilgrims! All decked out in matching blue nylon jackets embroidered with the image of the Virgin and just as noisy, pushy, cheerful and cranky as any group of people who have been cooped up in a bus for too long. So much for any notion that a pilgrimage has to be plodding, sober and holier-than-thou. They're all speaking English, though about half, including the tour guide-cum-priest, look to be ethnic Filipinos. Where are they from? My question is answered as a blue nun breaks the surface of the crowd: "More brochures for the Americans!" she hollers.

Two men wheeling a bundle part the masses.

"Clear the way now! Careful!"

They pull up outside the chapel and set about loosening straps and unzipping zippers as an expectant crowd gathers around them. The blue-canvas-enshrouded object that is strapped to their trolley is too big to be a Stradivarius, though they're handling it like one. The butterfly that eventually emerges from the cocoon is a three-foot-tall wooden statue of the Virgin draped in blue, hands joined in prayer, head tilted slightly to one side. She's the one I once knew as Our Lady Affattama.

The men rig her out with care, draping her in a silver gown, setting a veil on her head, a rosary in her slender hands. From a sports-bag emerge planks and poles, and in an instant the men's practiced hands have assembled a pre-fabricated portable shrine and established Our Lady thereon.

"Now, we'd like to have her somewhere near the front," explains one of them to a nun. "If we can just take her once around first, so everyone can have a look, then set her near the altar. This lady's traveled all around the world. People are going to want to see her."

A French woman leans in to caress the statue: *"Ah, c'est belle!"* she coos.

"Please don't touch," says the man, brushing the woman's hand away and directing her attention to the sign at Our Lady's feet that reads, in English and Spanish:

Don't touch her. She will touch you.

Then the shrine is hoisted and borne into the chapel like the Tabernacle, the joyful pilgrims following in its train. They keep streaming in from the rue du Bac as the chapel expands loaf-and-fish-like to contain them. Almost overwhelmed by the Americans is a small Japanese party, who have arrived in the same moment and now find themselves pinned to the walls of the courtyard like movie cowboys trapped in a canyon as a stampede passes.

There is no longer silence in the chapel, but the uproar of hundreds of voices. The worshippers who had lingered after mass give way to the pilgrim hordes. Their clamor, though jarring at first, is not meant as a sign of disrespect. On the contrary, it's a sign that everyone feels at home in this House of Mary. In a few minutes, every peregrinating bum has found a seat and a warm cheer goes up as the priest calls for a round of applause for Our Lady.

Forty years ago, the Second Vatican Council ("Vatican Two," as it is commonly known) decreed procedural changes that were meant to increase the people's sense of participation in the mass: turn the priest towards his auditors, cut the Latin, let communicants accept the Host with their hands. This priest is one of the unanticipated fruits of the reform. He's a showman and a cheerleader. He twangles the heartstrings, jerks the tears, plays for laughs. He speaks the people's language only too well ("We're going for broke because we love God!") and the rise and fall of his voice picks up the congregation and swings it around like a censer.

He kicks off today's performance with an anecdote. He has just been to Italy, he says. The people he met there have "everything." But are they happy? Not at all.

"'Look,' I told them, 'you have Ferraris. You have cellular phones. You have jewelry. My goodness, some of you have private helicopters. So why are you not happy? What is it you don't have? I'll tell you. It is the most important thing. You don't have the love of the family!'"

Italians without love of the family? What is the world coming to? But a murmur of assent goes up from the crowd. Of course, the love of the family.

"But this is not only in Italy," the priest continues. "Look around you! Look around the world today and what do you see? Wealth. Incredible wealth. The sort of wealth our parents could never have dreamed of. And at the same time, unhappiness. Marriages breaking up. Families breaking down. Suicide. Divorce. Child abuse. Abortion. Am I right?"

He's right. So right. Wealth and misery.

"Despite all our wealth, despite all our wonderful possessions, our cars, our homes, our trips, our jewelry, our toys, we . . . are . . . unhappy. Unhappy. And why? Why are we unhappy?"

The crowd knows why, but they want to hear it from him. He lets their anticipation build, then blows it away with a whisper.

"Because we lack love.

"Yes, we have forgotten how to love. Our love, the thing we *call* love, is only pleasure. Someone pleases us and we say, 'I love you, I love you.' But when they stop pleasing us. Aha! Then we say, 'I don't love you anymore. I've found someone new to love.' So love today has become something *pro-visional*.

"But love, real love, is not provisional. It is *un-con-ditional*. And what do I mean by unconditional love? Well, listen to the words of John: 'For God so loved the world that he gave his only Son, that whoever believes in him should not perish but have eternal life.'

"*That* is love. That is real love. Not provisional. Unconditional. Love."

There is silence again in the Chapel of the Miraculous Medallion, but a different silence now. A rapt silence. Not the silence of prayer, but of waiting. And when the priest feels the silence is enough, he leans in to the microphone, leans in, till we can hear his breathing. Then he begins to croon, soft and low, the first verse of "What the World Needs Now is Love."

Saint Burt Bacharach, pray for us.

42

TOWARDS THE END OF THE SERMON, the basket goes around. It comes back full of greenbacks. The congregation exchange the Peace of Christ, that lovely ritual of sharing a handshake and a smile with everyone around you, including the ones you don't know. They all look like awfully nice people, happy to be here. The ladies in front ask where I'm from. They're from Canada, too. Small world. Then everyone launches into "Amazing Grace." Everyone except the ones who've just received communion and have the pursed, thoughtful lips of those who hold God in their mouths.

The priest is running through the afternoon schedule:

"Now please go straight to the buses. Our next stop will be Our Lady of Victories church. We have about fifteen minutes there. After that—please, if I could have your attention!—after Our Lady of Victories church, due to traffic congestion, we will *not* be going to the Basilica of Sacre-Coeur. Instead, we'll be sight-seeing until five o'clock, at which time we will check into our hotel. At six-thirty, we're having a Chinese supper. Any questions? No? Then can I remind you once more of our spirit of silence. For every grace we receive, let us remember to give silent thanks."

And then, having laid out his flock's busy temporal and spiritual agenda for the day, he remembers where he is and relents a little.

"Ah yes," he says, "and maybe while we're here you'd like to pray to the body of Saint Cathérine Labouré."

How often, in the churches of Europe, does one see the statues of the dead lying atop their tombs, sleeping their little mortal sleep, sometimes with their faithful hounds warming their feet, and think, "How lifelike." Now, as I stand above the glass case that contains the body of Cathérine Labouré, I'm thinking the opposite: "How statuesque."

Yet that's Cathérine Labouré. Or most of her anyway. Her heart is elsewhere, and the hands joined in prayer at her chest are made of wax. But the rest is all her. She was exhumed in 1933, during the process that led to her beatification. Despite fifty-six years in the tomb, the medical examination revealed her body to be "in a perfect state of conservation, having retained all its suppleness." Her advocates were thrilled; a well-preserved corpse, especially one that gives off a sweet odor (the original "odor of sanctity") has always been considered a sign of holiness. Sister Cathérine was given a light coat of wax and placed in the chapel of the rue du Bac for all to see.

And the woman in the glass case opposite? That would be Sainte Louise de Marillac, co-founder of the Daughters of Charity and a most holy woman.

And that thing on the wall? Why, the heart of Saint Vincent de Paul. The very heart Cathérine Labouré saw in July of 1830. Like the rest of the saint's body, it went into hiding during the Revolution. For fifty years, all trace of it vanished. Then it turned up in Lyon, concealed in a cavity hollowed out from the pages of a book.

The cult of relics has faltered badly in recent years. Just look at our use of the word itself to denote something outdated and a little fusty. Yet for most of the Christian era, a relic was a thing of great potency, a living thing to be worshipped, treasured, feared and even—if the opportunity presented itself—stolen.

Once, the hunger for relics was so ravenous that Hugh, Bishop of Lincoln, bit a finger off an arm of Mary Magdalene so that he could have a piece of her for his own diocese. The monk Arinisdus of Conques joined the religious community at Agen and spent ten years winning the community's confidence until at last the opportunity arose for him to steal the body of Sainte Foi and spirit her back to his own town. The desiccated corpse of Saint Mark was smuggled out of Alexandria under a load of pork so that the Muslim customs officers wouldn't delve too deeply.

We laugh or wince at such stories today, for we are not at ease with death and the dead. In this respect, we resemble the Romans and the Jews of Christ's day, who regarded corpses as a pollution and removed them as far from the living as possible. But where it was death's power that the ancients feared, it is its apparent powerlessness that frightens us today. We do not readily conceive of matter as being infused with life. Like Lear, we know when one is dead and when one lives—or we think we do—and a dead body, for us, is matter.

But for the early Christians, those scandalous Christians, the sting of death had been pulled. Their God had valorized human flesh by entering it and dying in it. Their holy books preached a day when the dead would rise and be whole again as in life. Thus, they accepted death with courage, in hope of the resurrection, and in imitation of their Lord. And the bodies of the martyrs, who died with the adrenaline of faith coursing through them, came to be prized and worshipped.

The first Christian shrines were built literally "on the bones of the martyrs": the Vatican, for instance, was originally no more than the cemetery across the Tiber (and therefore, remote from human habitation) where the Apostle Peter had been interred. To this day, an altar is defined by Roman Catholic canon law as "a tomb containing the relics of saints," and an office of the Vatican exists to supply the required relics to new churches. In the early days of the Church the doctrine developed that a saint, though dead, remained physically and spiritually present in her relics. Thus, to possess a bone, a fingernail paring, a lock of hair, even a piece of cloth that had touched a saint's body, in life or in death, was tantamount to having the saint herself on hand with all her powers of intercession at the throne of God.

Before measuring the distance between the minds of a modern tourist and a medieval pilgrim (or even, for that matter, between a modern pilgrim and a medieval pilgrim), one must understand that a medieval pilgrim traveled primarily to see and pray to relics; in the Michelin guides of the Middle Ages, a city's star-rating was based on the relics it boasted. A head of John the Baptist (and he had several) was the pilgrim's Eiffel Tower; a spine from the crown of thorns, his Arc de Triomphe.

Today's pilgrims, however, show no more than a passing interest in the body of Saint Cathérine Labouré or Saint Vincent de Paul's shrunken heart. They are mere objects, dead and unavailing. The focus today is on Mary. The undying Mary. *Mary was here* and, for the pilgrim, this chapel still glows like radium with her presence.

OUTSIDE THE CHAPEL, one of the custodians of the pilgrim Virgin awaits her egress. He's a self-effacing man in a nylon sports jacket who looks like he'd be more at home running a hardware store or coaching a junior hockey team than traveling the world with Our Lady of Fatima. But then, as the example of Cathérine Labouré shows, the Virgin often calls the least likely candidates.

"Who are we?" He is a man who picks his words with care. "We are a group that organizes and participates in pilgrimages involving the statue that you have seen. There's only two of those statues in the world that the Holy Father has authorized to travel. This one's based in the United States, but as you can see, she's traveling."

"She's on tour?"

"She's traveling. People want to see her. This way, they don't have to go to Portugal. She comes to them. And we've had many stories of miracles.

45

Women have told us, 'My husband had cancer and after I prayed to that Virgin he was cured.' And she has cried. More than thirty times, from what  I have been told. You've seen her, she's wood. But actual tears have come out of her eyes. I'd suggest you speak to her custodian. He could tell you in more detail."

I promise that I will, though I'd much rather hear it from him. Somehow the miraculous sounds even more so when heard from the mouth of a hockey coach.

"So where have you been so far?"

"Well, we started off in Fatima. Then we went on to Garabandal in Spain. Have you been there? It's a very exciting place. A lot going on there. We spent two nights in Garabandal. Now just this one day in Paris. We go overnight from here to Rome to take part in the Jubilee. After that, we'll go to Medjugorje in Yugoslavia and then to the Holy Land. Seven countries in three weeks. Only Marian shrines."

"That's quite a trip."

"Quite a pilgrimage, yes."

The Lady arrives along with her custodian. The man in the sports jacket excuses himself; he's got a job to do. The pilgrims make their boisterous way back to the buses.

Seven countries in three weeks; only Marian shrines. Not everyone's idea of fun. But then I think of the poor tourists at Notre-Dame, pacing around the perimeters, peering into the chapels, scarcely knowing what they're looking at. At least the pilgrims feel welcome where they go.

Sainte Thérèse de Lisieux, Pèlerine

The day is waning as I wind my way back down the rue du Bac. I cross the Pont Royal, where satiated culture vultures clutching Musée d'Orsay and Louvre shopping bags stand admiring the Seine and the sky. The Tuileries is milling with people. A festive pro-Israel demonstration is getting underway and the Champs-Élysées has been converted into a promenade. This must be the "traffic congestion" the priest at the rue du Bac was referring to. Leaving the crowd behind, I head up towards the Madeleine.

A few blocks to the east, fronting a dull little square, is the Church of Notre-Dame des Victoires. It's a stern-faced, unwelcoming sort of place, but the pilgrim group chose it as their only stop in Paris besides the rue du Bac. What did they hope to see here? The answer soon becomes apparent: This is the seat of the Universal Association of Marian Prayer.

Notre-Dame des Victoires is dedicated to Mary, "Refuge of Sinners," a Mary who promises "to accept all, whoever they may be, without regard to race, culture, religion, atheism, indifference. For Mary is the refuge of all men; that is to say, of sinners." Now that sounds like unconditional love.

Father Defriche-Desgenette, the founder of the association, was appointed pastor of Notre-Dame des Victoires in 1832. In those days, according to Desgenette, the clergy were so despised by the working men of the quarter that "they dared not go to the bedside of a dying man until he had lost consciousness." Yet his divinely inspired decision to dedicate Notre-Dame des Victoires to Mary's Immaculate Heart brought the locals back to the Church. From this modest beginning, the Archconfraternity of Notre-Dame-des-Victoires went on a tear that paralleled the spread of the Miraculous Medallion. By the time of the founder's death, it boasted twenty million associates worldwide.

But this is not the only attraction Notre-Dame des Victoires offers to pilgrims. There is also its association with Sainte Thérèse de Lisieux.

On the whole, the Virgin Mary's rise in prominence over the past century has coincided with a decline in the adoration of saints. The anthropologist Victor Turner speculates that this is partly due to the saints' ties to the places where their relics rest. Of the Virgin, however, there are no bodily relics; she was "assumed" into heaven upon her death. She slipped the surly bonds of earth, leaving not a hair behind (or not much more than a hair, as various churches have claimed to possess her fingernail clippings, articles of her clothing, her wedding ring and vials of her milk). Mary abides now in a timeless placelessness, free to light down among us when and where she will.

In this era of the Virgin, few new saints have achieved a truly international following: Sainte Thérèse de Lisieux, who often prayed here at Notre-Dame des Victoires, is one of them. In recent years, she has even acquired something approaching Mary's "freedom of movement."

Though she died an obscure death in a convent at the tender age of twenty-four, Thérèse Martin achieved posthumous renown through the publication of her diaries. The little saint won hearts with her lucid prose, her fine attention to the movements of the spirit, her bravery in the face of a drawn-out death from tuberculosis, and—not least—with the rash of miracles that were subsequently attributed to her intercession. "I will spend my heaven doing good on earth," she had declared and apparently she meant it.

Thérèse led a circumscribed life, even by the standards of her era. Her devout parents, Louis and Zélie Martin (themselves currently candidates for sainthood), had first aspired to a celibate, or "Josephite," marriage. Their union remained unconsummated for nine months, until their parish priest convinced them they owed God children. Evidently well-persuaded, they set about their Christian duty with a vengeance, in the end producing nine offspring. All of the five who survived childhood became nuns.

The lone journey of Thérèse's brief life was to Rome, where she went in the company of her father to beg the Pope's permission to enter a convent although under age. Given such limited travel experience, she would seem an unlikely patron saint for the far-flung missions of the Catholic Church. Yet so she was declared in 1927. And while this may seem only another example of the often eccentric logic of patron sainthood (Saint Stephen, who was stoned to death, is the patron of bricklayers), Thérèse has responded to the call in her usual manner. Her journeying, like her publishing career, her celebrity and her miracles, has been posthumous.

In life, Thérèse Martin maintained a correspondence with two missionary brothers who were laboring in the fields of the Lord. In one of her letters, the saint-to-be announced: "Despite my smallness, I would like to enlighten souls. I have the vocation of an Apostle. I would like to travel the earth, to proclaim the Good News in all five parts of the world and even in the remotest isles." A century after her death, Thérèse's wish is coming true as her body, encased in its jewel-box of a coffin, circles the earth.

It was in October of 1994 that the saint first took up her pilgrim's staff for a tour of the parish churches of France. The response of the faithful and the word of conversions and cures was so strong that 1995 and 1996 saw her touring Belgium, Luxembourg, Germany and Italy. On International Youth Day, 1997, she was in Paris with the Pope (her body rested here, at Notre-Dame des Victoires); then on to Switzerland,

Austria, Slovenia and Rome, where she received the diploma of "Doctor of the Church."

By 1998, she was ready for something more ambitious: a year in Brazil. She recrossed the Atlantic to Holland in 1999, then ventured east to Russia and Kazakhstan. Later that year she appeared in Argentina for the Sixth Latin-American Missionary Congress before conquering the USA with a whistle-stop, four-month tour of the nation's 112 parishes. The Jubilee Year 2000 saw her wintering in the Philippines, Taiwan and Hong Kong, then returning to Italy in time to meet the pilgrim masses. Nor are her travels anywhere near an end: Mexico, Lebanon and Canada are on the schedule for 2001. (As I write, the little saint is in Québec, where, according to newspaper reports, she is giving Harry Potter a run for his money.) 2002 will take her to Australia and "the remotest isles" of Oceania. Africa awaits in 2003.

As she winds her jet-trail ribbons round the globe, the body of Sainte Thérèse reverses the normal flow of pilgrimage: rather than the people coming to the sacred, the sacred is going to the people. Like the little Lady of Fatima whom I saw this morning at the rue du Bac, or the peregrinating Pope John Paul himself, Sainte Thérèse in her tiny gilt coffin exploits the miracles of modern transportation to be in all places at all times.

She proves in the process that the age of relics isn't over yet; that life can still inhere in that which seems dead.

Saint Jacques

And one more stop before I leave Paris. On that first, long-ago visit, I fell in love with a certain medieval tower that stood on its own, not far from Notre-Dame. It looked like a castle, but it was just a huge, solitary, jutting tower with a park around it full of scruffy characters. It wasn't open to the public as far as I could tell, and I couldn't imagine what point such a structure could serve. Nor did I much care; it was just so European.

I had no idea, either, who that man was standing up there on the parapet with an angel by his side. With his cloak, his staff and his broad pilgrim's hat, he had the air of a watchman on guard over the city or a sailor on the lookout for land.

But now, as I see him again for the first time in years, I recognize this solitary watcher as my friend and companion, the pilgrim saint and saint of pilgrims: Saint Jacques, Saint James, Santiago. And I understand that he is up there not only to look out, but to welcome.

"¡Hola peregrino! Welcome to Paris!"

What is he doing here so far from Spain? And why is he facing northwest when his body lies in Santiago, far, far to the south? The plaque on the fence outside the tower tells me that this, the Tour Saint-Jacques, is all that remains of the Church of Saint-Jacques-des-Boucheries, demolished by the Revolution in 1797.

Well, it was good of the vandals to spare the old saint at least. Just seeing him up there makes me feel like I have a friend on the road. Since, as I remind myself, I don't believe in signs, I do not take this as an omen that he is watching over me in my travels. But that doesn't stop me from saluting with a discreet wave.

OUR LADY OF THE BEAUTIFUL WINDOWS CHARTRES

THE SKY HAS THREATENED rain since early morning. From the window of the train, I watch the stony spires of Chartres Cathedral prick into sight against a dreary October sky. I deposit my bags at an anonymous hotel, climb the road to the cheerless, unpeopled cathedral plaza, and take some pictures that will all turn out gray. I try my hardest to admire the acid-rain-corroded sculptures of the cathedral's facade, but an ashen patina is starting to form on my pupils. I have to get inside.

I blink away the change in the light as I cross the threshold. Then, for the first time today, I smile. It is just as I had hoped. Even on a day like this, the windows are full of color. It is not the vivid color of a summer day—that must be blinding!—but it is a bold, warm color nonetheless. Today the windows speak in hushed tones, but they speak. For the rest of the afternoon, I wander the cathedral, eyes upward, watching and listening. This time of year, with so few distractions, one can almost hear the voices of a thousand years ago. There is a temptation to amplify these voices into trumpets of faith, joy and certainty; the challenge is rather to tone them down until they sound like the voices of people one might know.

For many, Chartres is *the* great Gothic cathedral, and it is celebrated above all for these walls of color and light, its windows that make up a Bible-in-glass. Almost all of the windows date back to the early thirteenth century, after 1194, when the old cathedral burnt to the ground. Chartres at the time was one of the great pilgrim centers of Europe, and a new house for the holy relics and the pilgrim masses was needed as quickly as possible. The windows were the contribution of the town's guilds. The armorers, water-bearers, shoemakers, butchers, fishmongers, tanners, masons, furriers, weavers, carpenters, coopers, blacksmiths, apothecaries, drapers, sculptors, wheelwrights and wine merchants all pitched in to sponsor their own sets of windows. You can make a game of identifying the donors by the "signature" panes that depict them hard at work, skinning, tanning, weaving, draping, mongering. It's a shame none of the modern professions are represented: the waiters' guild serving disgruntled tourists; the concierges snoozing at their reception desks.

The colors of the windows warm the eyes and that warmth is communicated to the mind and the body. You need a coat in here but you don't feel the cold. I pick up a guidebook to know what I'm looking at, but most of the time it hangs loosely from my hand. The colors speak for themselves. I spend two days in Chartres, nearly all of that time in the cathedral. Outside there is only the drab modern town. I'd eat in here if they'd let me.

Recently, I saw a movie by the Chinese director Zhang Yimou called *The Road Home*. Strangely, it reminded me of these days in Chartres, how gray they were on the outside, how colorful within. In the film, the hero returns from the big city to the village of his childhood to bury his father. A long flashback retells the idyllic story of how his parents first met and fell in love. To contrast the romantic, elemental past with a present that is older and wearier, the director uses a simple but effective trick: the past he presents in color, the present in black and white. The device reverses our expectations, but captures the very essence of nostalgia.

For of course the past was lived in color. Passions were stronger then. People spoke and acted with a directness and sincerity that eludes them today. They lived closer to the earth. Their work had meaning. Yes, their lives were harder, but their joys were greater. Or, at least in movies and books they were.

Mind you, there have been times in modern history when it was not the past but the future that appeared in color; when people believed that with the help of science, technology, the brotherhood of man or the exercise of reason we were creating a better world. But the present of 2001 is, on the whole, not one of those moments. Science and technology are carrying us along at such a rate that we feel we have lost control of the vehicle. The surrounding landscape is unfamiliar, the way ahead forbidding. More and more, as we look into the rear-view mirror at ways of life that are receding behind us, it seems that the lives of our grandparents had an authenticity, a forcefulness, a closeness to fundamentals, as well as a whole spectrum of emotional colors that have been bled from the present.

Looking back further in time, we tend to view the Middle Ages, too, in color: in *The Name of the Rose* Technicolor, to be precise. It seems to us an era of lively and forceful contrasts, of humor and tragedy, great violence and great romance. This is ironic, for the people of the Middle Ages were, like us, inclined to see their times in black and white. They too were nostalgic, though not for a time within living memory. The long-lost Eden and the heroic early days of the Church were the days they pined for. Yet, at the same time, they were optimistic; not for a world that would be brought about through human efforts, but for the renewed heaven and earth promised by Christ. Those two epochs, the distant past and the awaited future, were the ones the Middle Ages brought alive through the brilliant colors of their cathedrals. What an effect the windows of Chartres must have made upon them as they passed from their monochrome world of plague, poverty, ignorance and injustice—their middle time, suspended between glories past and future—and into this sanctuary of dreaming colors that signified both nostalgia and promise.

The strength of medieval faith stood in inverse proportion to the desperate conditions of medieval life. It would be foolish either to discount the horrors of that world or to romanticize its beauties. That said, I can only conclude that I am a romaniticizing fool. Why else would I be here?

The Virgin's Tunic

Only a handful of worshippers have assembled tonight for six o'clock mass. They sit in the bright Baroque choir, before the four-ton marble statue of the Assumption of the Virgin (which the Revolutionaries, if they'd really wanted to do posterity a favor, would have busted up and carted away). In Chartres Cathedral, unlike Notre-Dame de Paris, the faithful huddle together in the least attractive part of the church, leaving the art and history buffs to roam at will through the candle-lit gloom.

Most visitors come to Chartres today to admire the windows, the architecture and the statuary, as they have since the nineteenth century, when the Romantics rediscovered the beauty and spirituality of medieval art and transformed "Gothic"—a disparaging term coined by the Renaissance— into one of the highest praise. But long before the beginnings of the cultural pilgrimage, Christian pilgrims were coming from all over Europe to pray for a safe childbirth or a cure for their ailments. They were drawn here by the Roman Catholic world's most precious relic of the Virgin Mary.

Mass ends and the congregation heads for the doors. Several women hurry, before the cathedral closes, to offer their prayers at the feet of Our Lady of the Pillar. They kneel briefly in silence, then approach one by one to caress the pillar and kiss it. A tall young woman reaches up to touch the hem of Our Lady's gown. Meanwhile, the departing tourists cast a last glance at the darkened windows, hoping that tomorrow will see them flaming in sunlight.

No one, tourist or worshipper, seeks out the shadowy chapel in the apse of the cathedral where, in an elegant reliquary case guarded by

angels, a simple strip of white silk the size of a winter scarf hangs like a Gaultier creation. Even by day, most tourists and worshippers pass it by without a glance, their eyes locked on those glorious windows. Yet this is the cloth that pilgrims once came here by the millions to see and touch, the cloth that is responsible for all this art and beauty.

IN 1793, WHEN THE REVOLUTIONARIES hauled the *saint-chemise* from its golden cask, they were surprised by what they found. Surprised, because tradition had called this cloth a "tunic" —the very tunic, in fact, that the Virgin had worn when she gave birth to Jesus—and here they had a five-yard length of silk on their hands. It was enough to tunic several Virgins! They proceeded to carve Chartres' most prized possession into ribbons, sharing the portions among themselves as grim souvenirs. The strip of cloth one sees today found its way back to the cathedral after the Revolution (a second is on display down below, in the crypt). It has been rechristened *Le Voile de Notre-Dame*, Our Lady's Veil, though it doesn't look any more like a veil than it does a tunic. Perhaps the answer would be to feminize *"Le Voile"* to *"La Voile."* Then it would be Our Lady's Sail, which would make more sense.

It was in the year 800 that the *saint-chemise* first came west. Charlemagne was about to be crowned Emperor, and the Empress Irene in Byzantium had to send *something* for the occasion. She thought Mary's tunic might do. Only two generations later, on the death of Charlemagne's grandson, Charles the Bald, it passed to the cathedral of Chartres. How did such a precious item not end up in Paris?

For one reason, in France the Virgin was not yet what she would become. Mary had been worshipped in the Eastern Empire since at least 431 (when the Council of Ephesus voted her the title of *Theotokos*, Bearer of God, causing the city to erupt in celebrations and torch-lit processions). Her cult had long since reached Rome, but it was not until the tenth and eleventh centuries brought Western Europe into closer contact with the East that Mary really took off in these parts.

The other reason why Mary's tunic ended up where it did is that Chartres was reputed to have worshipped Mary longer than any city in France, going back to the day in the century before Christ when some local Druids received a premonition of the Virgin Birth. Today, one might suspect this proto-Virgin of being a Celtic mother goddess, but Charles the Bald was no cultural anthropologist. He willed the Holy Tunic to Chartres, where its value quietly set about multiplying.

In 1194, the old Chartres cathedral burned to the ground. What looked at first like a disaster turned out to be a blessing in disguise when, after four days of scrabbling through the rubble, the Holy Tunic was found undamaged. Evidently, the fire had just been Our Lady's way of saying she wanted a bigger, brighter house and, this being 1194, plans were launched at once to cater to her desire.

This was the century, from 1170 to 1270, when some eighty cathedrals, five hundred large churches and thousands of smaller parish churches were raised in France, most of them dedicated to the Virgin. And, while in recent times people have mostly turned to Mary in eras of social upheaval and insecurity, her medieval Queenship coincided with a widespread restoration of public order and a flowering of the arts of peace. The Virgin softened hard northern manners and added grace and beauty to human life.

The building of the Gothic cathedrals was the greatest collective enterprise the West had undertaken since the fall of the Roman Empire. The investment of finances, material, time and labor rivaled the building of the pyramids, while producing something of far more value to its community. In the end, however, the effort beggared the nation. The tremendous wave of focused energy that had carried the project ahead began to wane. Even in Chartres, ambitious early plans for a multi-spired cathedral were shelved forever. But in the year 1200, the passion for building was still young. Pilgrims by the thousands pitched in, hauling carts piled high with construction materials and food for the builders. They sang as they toiled and some flogged themselves lustily. With the help of these penitential *corvées*, the magnificent new cathedral of Chartres was up and running in a lickety-split twenty-six years.

It was built beyond human scale, built vast enough to accommodate the hundreds of thousands of pilgrims who flooded in, year in and year out. Many of these were expectant mothers who brought with them the clothes they would wear during childbirth or bought miniature souvenir shirts made of embroidery or metal. They would reach up to touch the reliquary of the Holy Tunic with their garments as they passed beneath the altar, praying that their delivery would be as safe and easy as Mary's had been. On the greatest occasions—August 15, the feast of Mary's Assumption, and September 8, her Nativity—the multitudes would spend the night in the cathedral to be present for morning mass. The floors were built with a slight incline towards the front doors to help sluice away the unholy mess they left behind.

The sick also undertook the pilgrimage to Chartres, as they do to Lourdes today. Healing waters were drawn from a subterranean well that had been sacred to the Celts and was probably the original object of worship on the site. The customary treatment, nine days in the crypt, sounds insalubrious, but was of well-attested therapeutic value.

The Cathedral was built upon mystical calculations that were intended to put the structure in harmony with the divine. The number of bays, chapels and doorways is a medley of sevens and nines, these being the numbers holy to the Virgin. The cathedral's dimensions were determined using the ancient mystical science of "gemetria," whereby letters are assigned numerical values, then "added up" to generate significant numbers (it was by this method, for example, that the Book of Revelations computed the number "666" from the name of the Emperor Nero). Some of the key measurements of Chartres Cathedral, upon which the ground-plan of the structure are based, include axes and radii of 354, 241, 112 and 96 Roman feet. In his work on Chartres, John James shows that the number 96 can be derived from the words *Beata Virgo*—Blessed Virgin—while *Maria Mater Dei*—Mary, Mother of God—adds to 112. The sum of *Beata Virgo Maria Assumpta*—the Blessed Virgin Mary of the Assumption—is 241, appropriate in that Chartres is the only cathedral dedicated specifically to the Mary who was "assumed" into heaven upon her death. Finally, 354 can be derived from θεοο—God. This last is the longitudinal axis, so that one can picture the infant God laid across the lap of the Virgin, as in the *Sedes Sapientiae*, or Seat of Wisdom motif.

Of course the pilgrim was not expected to be conscious of these features. They were meant to enhance the holiness of the place on a more subtle plane, by echoing sacred resonances. There was, however, one mystical element the pilgrim could not help being aware of: the labyrinth.

The Labyrinth

The labyrinth of Chartres is circular. Its diameter, at just under thirteen meters, equals the width of the nave from pillar to pillar, but the path to its center wriggles 261.5 meters, a good four-minute walk. The path is of white stone laid within black marble borders. It meanders in and out, left and right, through eleven concentric circles to the center where there once was a copper plaque depicting Theseus and the Minotaur.

One's first impulse on seeing a labyrinth is to walk it. It looks like a bit of whimsy, a challenge, if not a daunting one. It would call for a certain concentration, which, combined with all the righting and lefting, would doubtless still the mind, level out the pulse, and balance the hemi-spheres of the brain—all the benefits claimed by modern advocates of "labyrinth therapy."

Now if only there weren't two solid banks of pews overlaying the thing now …

Labyrinths were once a common feature in French cathedrals. (And not only French: Years ago I took a picture of a small labyrinth traced on a pillar near the doors to the cathedral of Lucca, in Tuscany. It is identical to the one of Chartres.) But by the eighteenth century, their original purpose had been forgotten and they came to appear as nothing more

than a trifling, archaic distraction from the serious business of worship. The labyrinth of Chartres is one of the few that was not pried up at that time.

Seating in churches being a relatively recent innovation, the medieval worshipper was free to follow the labyrinth when and as he pleased, on foot or on his knees. En route, as he absorbed the psychological and therapeutic benefits already mentioned, he also took considerable time to pray and reflect, with the result that the journey to the center traditionally took about one hour.

A name commonly given to these labyrinths was "The Road to Jerusalem," though a labyrinth seems an unlikely symbol for a pilgrimage. A pilgrimage, after all, tends to make a beeline for its destination, while a labyrinth takes the most tortuous route. The goal of a pilgrimage lies at the end of a road, but the end of a labyrinth is its center. And where, at the end of a pilgrimage, the pilgrim turns his footsteps home, the center of a labyrinth spells game over.

To perceive that the straight path of pilgrimage and the winding way of the labyrinth are in fact one, we must first ask what pilgrimage signifies. A time-honored answer is that a pilgrim's journey is a distillation of the journey of life, complete with all its riddles, doubts, hardships and temptations. Thus, even though a pilgrimage looks like a straight line on the map of the world (as life looks like a straight line on the map of time), spiritually it is a winding and uncertain way, liable to backtrack and turn from its goal even when that goal seems nearest.

Pilgrimage, moreover, although a journey *out* on the physical plane, is an inward journey on the spiritual, with the pilgrim's true home in God as its destination. The Latin word *peregrinus*—which has come down to us as *peregrino, pèlerin*, pilgrim—originally meant an alien, a man without kin, friends or patrons: an outsider. For Saint Augustine, the Christian was a *peregrinus*, one who wanders the earth, feeling nowhere at home, because his true home is in heaven. "Our heart is restless till it rests in Thee," he wrote (a thought parsed by Sainte Teresa of Avila as "Life is a night in a bad hotel"). From this point of view, ultimate homecoming and reconciliation with God must wait till death. But if pilgrimage is imagined as the journey of our life, then its end *is* death and the new life to come. When the Christian reaches the destination of her pilgrimage, however far she may be from her home of birth, she is only a step away from her home in heaven.

So the labyrinth turns out to be a fitting metaphor for the Christian vision of pilgrimage and life: a winding road of the spirit that ends in the center where the soul rests eternally. And note, too, that it is a journey with a certain outcome. Unlike a maze, the labyrinth of Chartres has no forking paths or misdirections. There is one true way. Only follow and you will reach your goal.

Four Virgins

Though the foremost attraction of Chartres was the Holy Tunic, certain of the 175 images of the Virgin inside and outside the cathedral had their personal followings. Three of the most famous can still be seen: Notre-Dame de Pilier—Our Lady of the Pillar; Notre-Dame de Sous-Terre—Our Lady of the Underground; and Notre-Dame de la Belle Verrière—Our Lady of the Beautiful Window. A fourth met her end in the events leading up to the Revolution.

Two of the remaining Virgins are of wood; the third, of glass. Our Lady of the Beautiful Window is a breath-taking figure, robed in sky-blue against a background of ruby. At three yards in height, she is vastly larger than any of the images that surround her. Her gown forms a protective nimbus around the child, while the set of her mouth declares that, as Regent, she intends to hold the Throne of Heaven till her son is ready to take over—and probably after, as well. The century of Chartres' building was the era of France's most formidable royal women: Eleanor of Aquitaine, "Queen by the wrath of God"; Mary of Champagne, founder of the first Court of Love; and Blanche of Castille, the mother of Saint Louis. It was the era when the French added a piece to the chessboard whose power and scope for action made the King and the Knight seem pitiful creatures indeed. That piece, naturally, they called the Queen.

In Our Lady of the Beautiful Window, we see the Queen of Heaven in the likeness of the Queen of France. French miracle tales of the time endow her with a host of queenly attributes. She is hot-tempered, imperious, jealous, sharp-tongued, arbitrary, but also utterly forgiving. Those who pledged themselves to her did so trusting that she would protect them as a queen protects her vassal. And this meant, above all, shielding them from the hard justice of the King. Christ, in the early Middle Ages, was imagined as Lord and Judge. Since the fourth century, when the Emperor Constantine adopted Christianity, the imperial image of the Son of God as Pantocrator, the Ruler of All, had gradually eclipsed that of the gentle Jesus, mediator between God and man. No longer daring to hope for mercy from the Son, Christians turned instead to the Mother. It was believed that the most heinous sinner needed only trust in her to be saved, as countless tales and poems show.

A robber calls her name from the gallows. At once she flies to his rescue, sustaining him for three days until the miracle is acknowledged and he is cut down. A nun abandons her convent for a life of sin, but never ceases to pray to Mary. When, years later, she repents and goes back to her convent, she finds that no one has noticed her absence: the Virgin has been standing in for her. When a clerk, despised by all but devoted to Mary, meets his end, his body is tossed in a ditch and forgotten. That night, the Queen of Heaven comes in person to the Bishop of Chartres: "Do you suppose it doesn't annoy me to see my friend buried in a common ditch? Take him out at once! Tell the clergy it is my order, and that I will never forgive them unless tomorrow morning without delay, they bury my friend in the best place in the cemetery!"

And then there is the illiterate tumbler who enters a monastery. Unable to keep up with the other monks at prayer, he resolves to please the Virgin the only way he knows how, by tumbling for her. Each day he steals away from mass to her altar in the crypt, where he performs till he passes out from exhaustion. The Abbot, having noticed the monk's daily absence, follows him one day and watches him in secret as he tumbles his way to oblivion. The Abbot's lips set in a frown. "We shall have to see about this fellow," he says. But as he is about to step out of the shadows to give the monk a good shaking, the Holy Mother descends in a glory of angels and archangels with a towel to wipe her tumbler's brow.

This self-willed, spirited creature bears little likeness to the low-key Mother of Cathérine Labouré's visions. Indeed, the profile that emerges from the legends is a curious one: the Virgin Mary as subversive. At first blush, the notion seems absurd. Mary is the Queen of Heaven and Mother of God—surely an establishment figure. Yet in medieval France she used her exalted status to do as she pleased, even when that meant overturning the laws of heaven and earth to save one miserable soul. Mary was the Good Queen, her mercy falling equally on all her loyal subjects, without respect to rank, wealth or influence. Those who showed devotion to her—though weak, imperfect, wicked or penniless—were rewarded, in this life or the next. Those who did not worship her paid dearly for it.

That the heavenly Queen's principle of radical mercy subverted the Christian principle of radical judgment was not lost on my righteous Scots Calvinist forebears. They inveighed against this woman, banishing her from their churches and their homes. Mercy? They would have none of it! A sinner was a sinner and if he burned in hell for it, then God's will be done. It was no less than he deserved.

There was a time when candles were lit to Our Lady of the Beautiful Window, but today she rules only the postcard racks. Instead, it is the gentle Notre-Dame de Pilier, a life-size Virgin atop a stone pillar, who attracts the greatest devotion of worshippers and pilgrims. This Lady has her own little arbor within the stone church, a grove of flickering candles set before an ornate carved chapel. A crown rests on her high French forehead and she is draped in a gorgeous brocade. She was carved in the Renaissance, so care has been taken to make her beautiful. Our Lady of the Pillar is youthful, serene, and very, very dark of hue.

Once, she was painted, but the pigment wore away long ago to reveal the wood tones beneath, and since then she has been known as *la Vierge Noire*, the Black Virgin. Standing before her, my impulse is to fall to my knees and bump my forehead against the floor. If Our Lady of the  Beautiful Window is a Virgin of light, who draws her life from the sun, Our Lady of the Pillar is a Virgin of darkness, deriving her being from the earth and the places beneath.

France, Spain and Italy teem with dark Virgins. An inordinate number of the most famous statues and images of Mary, including those of Montserrat and Guadelupe in Spain, Loreto in Italy, Le Puy and Rocamadour in France, and Einsiedeln in Switzerland, are dark-complexioned. Lately, the question of the origin and meaning of "Black Madonnas" has attracted growing attention. Jungians, artists, feminist scholars, New Agers and historical conspiracy theorists have all been entranced by her archetypal, pagan mystery. At the same time, voices from the other side of the schoolyard have objected that really there is no such thing as a Black Madonna; that most were originally lighter and have simply been blackened by candle smoke, corrosion, aging or the wearing away of paint.

This argument is well-grounded, and one must be cautious in talking of a "cult of the Black Madonna" (though it would make a fine name for a Tintin adventure). Still, the fact remains that by whatever means these Virgins first came by their "blackness," it has become part of their identity. Many Black Madonnas bear nicknames that identify them by their hue, like *la Moreneta*, the little dark one, of Montserrat; and wherever attempts have been made to restore such images to their original paleness, popular outcry has ensued.

How do we account for this attachment? Catholic apologists have often quoted the Song of Solomon—"My love is black, but she is beautiful"— to explain the dark Virgins. But this is, rather, to explain them away. For if the Black Madonna has roots, they lie not in any Old Testament quotation, but in the various cults of the Great Goddess that Christianity and the worship of Mary replaced and overlaid. Isis, Cybele and other of the goddesses were often black, a color that did not carry negative connotations for the pagan world, but rather formed part of a psychological and mythical nexus of the earth, fertility and femininity. What all this has to do with Christianity is a question best answered by the individual worshipper.

The Black Virgin stands in her flickering grove, distant yet near, powerful yet accessible, her sexual allure neutralized by her condition of motherhood. Her devotees kneel to pray before her in the twilight. Then one by one they go to kiss her pillar.

BENEATH THE FLOORS OF CHARTRES, in the ninth-century crypt, rules another black Virgin, Our Lady of the Underground. Legend casts the worship of the first Underground Virgin (for the one we see today is the third) back to a time some twenty-one centuries ago when Druids were inspired by prophecy to make a statue of a virgin with a child. Historians, caring nothing for legend, have proposed the eleventh century as a more plausible date. In either case, the Virgin one sees today, enthroned before a snazzy abstract tapestry, dates back only to 1976.

The crypt of Chartres is as extensive as the cathedral above. It is a somber place today, opened only for special occasions and paying tourists, but once it was a brilliant hive of devotion. The sick in their legions brushed shoulders with pilgrims, saints and the monarchs who enriched the treasury—and the wardrobe—of Notre-Dame de Sous-Terre. She was the Virgin of the mighty, the one they turned to for special favors, well understanding that her services did not come cheaply. In the sixteenth century, the heirless Henry III and his Queen walked year after year the fifty miles from Paris to Chartres in dead of winter bearing gifts to win the favor of Our Lady. Evidently their gifts were never rich enough, for their prayers went unanswered. Royal houses of France rose and fell and Our Lady of the Underground lived and thrived. Robed in the richest fabrics, niched in a profusion of marble and gold, set off by a swirl of angels and censers, she seemed, in her eighth century on earth, immune to political fashion.

But all the while, Our Lady was living beyond her means. Up above ground, the spendthrift canons of Chartres were exhausting her treasure faster than they could rake it in. A Gothic cathedral, they had decided, was too austere for modern tastes; a pristine new choir in Carrara marble was just the thing, with a few gaudy tons of Baroque statuary to tart it up. In order to cover the expenses, from the mid-eighteenth century the canons began to sell off the cathedral's lands and belongings piece-meal. When the proceeds still didn't meet the cost of the marble, bread taxes were introduced, a measure poorly calculated to endear the Church, or Notre-Dame de Sous-Terre, to a restive citizenry.

With the Revolution came the moment of reckoning; Our Lady was made to pay along with the rest of the French aristocracy. One of the first moves of the revolutionary authorities was to close off her crypt to worshippers. The response of the bishop of Chartres was resolute: if the worshippers could not descend to the Virgin, the Virgin would rise to her worshippers. For the first time since the legendary days when the Druids worshipped her in the forest, Our Lady of the Underground moved into the world of air and light, changing places with Our Lady of the Pillar.

If the bishop hoped that her presence would galvanize the anti-Revolutionary forces, however, he was to be disappointed. Our Lady had arrived far too late. She could do nothing to prevent the mob from divvying up the Holy Tunic in September of 1793. She had no say when Catholic worship was prohibited outright soon afterwards. And she did not even survive to witness the final outrage as, on November 29, the cathedral of Notre-Dame de Chartres was re-designated a Temple of Reason, and the Deists and Republicans rattled the stained-glass windows with a chorus of the *Marseillaise*.

The minutes of the revolutionary council of November 9, 1793, contain the following order: "... that the Virgin of the parish church be slaughtered (*abattue*), because it is ridiculous always to see the superstitious devoutly kissing the wooden pillar that sustains her. The council charges the ecclesiastical commission to take down this statue at once." The decision was executed with gusto, the "ecclesiastical commissioners" depillaring Notre-Dame de Sous-Terre with such force that she shattered, her head (or was this only a guillotine-born fantasy?) rolling before the feet of the onlookers.

One councillor subsequently proposed, in the name of good house-keeping, to send "the debris of the Virgin" to the Convention in Paris. But the good citizens of Chartres had other plans for her. A few days before Christmas, they warmed their hands at a bonfire of missals, archives, church furnishings—and the fragments of Our Lady.

That the vandalism of 1793 went no further, posterity—and the hoteliers of Chartres—is forever indebted to a councillor by the name of Sergent-Marceau. The radicals of Chartres, having found that cremating the statue of Our Lady had only whetted their appetite for havoc, were now chomping at the bit to knock down her house. They had started to pick around the edges of the job, bashing heads off statues, but now they were ready to set to work in earnest. Morin, the town architect, argued against the demolition of the cathedral on logistical grounds: it was a huge job and what would they do with the rubble? "A quibble," replied the fanatics, animated by a fever to destroy that was as powerful as their ancestors' urge to build.

It was at this point that Sergent-Marceau rose to speak the words that saved the cathedral:

"Friends, the glory of Chartres offers beauties which have cease-lessly fixed the attention of travelers and attracted lovers of Gothic architecture. . . . The devotion inspired by the priests towards this ugly little Virgin we burned last week animated all the artists of that day to construct this edifice. . . . Let us then preserve it with care, that it may be for Chartres an enduring treasure. . . . And when Liberty has been assured by the affirmation of the Republic, we shall see men scurrying here from every part of the world, enriching us with their gold as they are enriched by the example of our virtues."

Vive la révolution. Bring on the tourists.

After the end of the Terror in 1794, the cult of the Supreme Being quickly withered away. The Revolutionaries wearied of pretending that the ghastly statue of the Virgin of the Assumption (which had arrived from Carrara just in time for the Revolution) was the Goddess of Reason. Freedom of religion was decreed in 1795, and the cathedral of Notre-Dame de Chartres was returned to the Catholics. The devout retrieved Notre-Dame de Pilier from the crypt and went back to kissing her pillar. But the crypt remained sealed and our Lady of the Underground forgotten until the Marian revival of the 1850s, when a new statue was commis-sioned. No one was ever really enamored of this one, and she was super-seded in the 1970s by the present Virgin, who presides today, as she has for ten centuries, over the crypt of Chartres.

THERE WAS ONCE A FOURTH FAMOUS Virgin of Chartres: a silver image crafted in the thirteenth century. She no longer exists, though a depiction of her may still be seen in one of the windows, where a pilgrim is shown praying to her. Her story proves that vandalism is not exclusively the province of revolutionaries.

This Virgin was greatly venerated in the Middle Ages; indeed, she held the place of honor above the altar. Yet at some point her popularity went into decline. Had she ceased to answer the prayers of her suppli-cants? Displeased some powerful lord? Was it that some evil had been spoken of her? Or had she simply fallen from favor, overtaken in popu-larity by new images? Whatever the case, she was shunted in the sixteenth century from the main altar to a rear chapel, perhaps the same chapel that today houses the *saint-chemise*.

For the next two centuries she forged on, doing her best despite her reduced conditions. But then came the debt crunch of the 1760s. The canons of the cathedral went casting about for any little scrap of gold or silver. In a note signed April 6, 1769, Germain Blonnié, a goldsmith of Chartres, acknowledged receipt of twenty-four *livres* for "melting down the Christ and the Virgin of the old altar." The little silver Virgin had been turned into ingots to pay for Carrara marble. (Ironists will be gratified to know that the same goldsmith, now styled Citoyen Blonnié, resurfaces in the 1790s, this time melting down gold and silver that have been stripped from the cathedral by the Revolution. There's a Brecht play in there somewhere.)

It is horrifying to think that an image that had received so many prayers over the centuries could be so blithely destroyed. Then again, the Church could reply that works of religious art are intended to be not receptacles for prayer, but windows to a higher reality; that one prays *through*, not *to*, an image. A statue of Mary is not Mary, and maybe it's better to melt down the images from time to time before they turn into idols.

I FEEL LIKE I'VE SPENT MORE than two days in Chartres, pacing, reading, joining the tour groups at the appointed hours, waiting to be kicked out of the cathedral at night. But two days it is. No adventures have befallen me, no encounters. I have spoken to no one, save waiters and tour guides and the nice ladies at the information desk. It seems as though all of the stories of Chartres are in the past.

Yet the nice ladies tell me that it's different in summer. And not because there are more tourists, but because the pilgrimage to Chartres lives again. It has been growing year by year since the end of the war. The pilgrims arrive now, not by the hundreds of thousands, but by the hundreds and sometimes the thousands. They are students, seniors, diocesan groups, scouts. Many walk at least the last few miles of the way to enjoy the sight of the cathedral spires pricking up from the plain.

No one believes anymore in the tunic of the Virgin. No one expects to be cured by a rest stay in the crypt. There are no more kings hoping to bribe a favor out of Notre-Dame de Sous-Terre. So why do they do it? They do it in homage to and in imitation of those who came before. The pilgrims of old who, looking back from where we are now, seem to have held a purer faith, less clouded hearts; to have lived their lives in color.

PILGRIM, WHERE IS YOUR HAPPINESS? LOURDES

Kristem, waar is uw geluk?
Pellegrino, dov'è la tua felicità?
Cristiano, cual es tu dicha?
Pilger, wo ist dein wahres gluck?
Chrétien, où est ton bonheur?
Pilgrim, where is your happiness?
    —From the pixel board outside the Grotto in Lourdes.

SO THERE I WAS, standing in the esplanade in front of the Basilica of the Rosary in Lourdes, one of a line of human fence posts guiding the pilgrims to their places. They were coming in their thousands, coming "in procession," as the  Virgin had told Bernadette they should. It was the evening procession, so they were carrying those candles with the little paper cups around the top to shelter the flame: *flambeaux*, the French grandly call them, though to me they always looked like flaming tulips.

The sick, as always, came first, pushed in their wheelchairs or drawn in one of the big blue Lourdes rickshaws. It was a mild night, so the hoods of the rickshaws were down, and the passengers sat attentive, listening to the choir sing the Lourdes Ave Maria. They passed on my right, bound for the places of honor at the steps of the basilica. After them came the standard-bearers of parishes in Italy, Ireland, Bavaria, Poland, Normandy. . . . Then, on my left, the rest began to pass: the ambulatory, strolling, not marching, raising their candles and singing *"Aa-ve, Aa-ve, Aaaa-ve Ma-riii-a."*

One stooped, candle-bearing priest detached himself from the body of the procession. He wore a green, white and orange badge that read simply, "Ireland." He began to make his own way down the line, like an ancient general inspecting the troops of salvation. He paused when he came to me, and I had to lean well down to hear him over the glorious din of the choir.

"Where are you from?" he asked.

"Canada."

"Ah, yes. What place?"

"Toronto."

"Ah yes. And how long are you here?"

"About twelve days so far."

"I see. And how many have come to Lourdes?"

"I'm sorry?"

"How many have come?"

I couldn't imagine what he meant. How many had come? You only had to look.

"Thousands," I replied. "There's thousands every day. They never stop."

"I mean from Toronto. How many have come?"

"Oh, from Toronto? Just myself, Father."

"I see. God bless you."

And he continued on his way.

YES, I WAS ALONE and I wasn't Catholic. And those were two very odd things to be in Lourdes. And one other thing: I was happy. But that was not so unusual.

I had been scared about Lourdes. I really didn't have a clue what I was going to do here. I imagined myself watching the pilgrims as from a great distance while they went about their religious business. What common ground could I hope to find with them? Would I even be welcome among them? In the end, the answer to my doubts turned out to be disarmingly simple. Our common ground was work—the care of the sick—and as long as I was willing to work, I was more than welcome in Lourdes, for Lourdes is a very practical place.

I cannot say that faith was never an issue; of course, people were curious about my beliefs and puzzled at what I was doing there. But their puzzlement was of the pleasantly surprised variety. They looked upon me not as an interloper, but an unexpected guest. The pilgrims I met were happy to entertain my questions, eager to talk about their faith, and sometimes, though not always, solicitous of why a nice young fellow like myself was not Catholic. Older men especially, those of an age to be my father, knitted their brows when I said I was a non-believer, as if I had told them that I didn't have a job and they were trying to think who could set me up with one. Lourdes, as I have mentioned, is a practical place.

Still, it took a while for me to meet the pilgrims. For more than a week I stayed to myself, as I had feared, watching everything happen from a safe distance. Yet I didn't feel lonely, for the unexpected had happened: I had fallen in with the rhythms of Lourdes—the ebb and flow of pilgrims, candle-lit processions, late masses at the Grotto, the slow roll of wheelchairs by the river. Then the clash between the ritual cadences of the Sanctuary and the secular beat of a tourist-trap town with its scruffy characters and chirpy shopkeepers—*"Bonjour Monsieur! Merci beaucoup Monsieur!"* And the older rhythms: morning mist and drizzle giving way to brilliant sun, the restless gush of the River Gave, the echoless Grotto.

It helped that I was sick when I arrived. Nothing mortal. Just a nasty cough. Sinus infection. The sort of thing that responds best to a few days of rest. And Lourdes, as millions will attest, is a supremely restful place. Seven days passed like seven weeks and it was a good slowness. Looking now at the notebook I filled during that week, parts read like a dream journal, written in the instant of waking before the soft light of the mind has been erased by the glare of day. I seemed to be seeing two Lourdes: one bustling with pilgrims who occupied hotel rooms and wheelchairs, bought souvenirs, laughed, prayed for miracles and posed tactical challenges to the local administration; the other, a world of ritual and mystery, where humans interacted with the eternal elements of fire, water and stone beneath the disquieting gaze of a girl named Bernadette.

After that first week of wonder was over and my sinuses had cleared, I did what seemed only natural in Lourdes. I tried to make myself useful.

The Place

As you approach Lourdes by train from Toulouse, all is just as it ought to be. There are still cows and sheep in the tranquil fields; there are hay bales and country churches that Bernadette would have known. Then there appears the town itself, not menaced but cradled by the hills that rise on all sides. The conductor calls out, *"Lourdes! Prochaine arrêt! Lourdes!"* and the passengers look at each other and smile. If the Holy Mother was going to appear to a little shepherd girl anywhere, then yes, it would be here.

Step out of the station and you may, if you are very lucky, see the snow-capped Pyrenees off to the left. I saw a mountain the day I arrived, stark and immediate in the highland air. I didn't see it again for two weeks. Only a valley clogged with clouds, so that if I hadn't seen that mountain once, I would never have dreamed it was there. Walking into town, there was a fine view of the castle, handsome upon its rock, the tricolor flying proudly from its ramparts.

And already you're wondering, Where is it? For though the train station stands well above the town, you've yet to catch a glimpse of the celebrated Sanctuary of Notre-Dame de Lourdes.

Bear right and walk down the boulevard de la Grotte, the great trough that drains tourists into the Sanctuary. Lined solid on either side with restaurants, hotels and souvenir shops named for every saint in the calendar, the boulevard at least reassures you that you're on the right path. It's a fifteen-minute walk, more if you have a cane or a walker as so many travelers to Lourdes do, or if you surrender to the distractions along the way—postcards and *menus du jour*, posters of Jesus that wink as you pass, ice-cream stands, busy bar patios, and the hundred thousand Madonnas that fill the shelves of the shops (the Madonna, being tall and slender with a small base, is a highly stockable item).

You leave the last shop behind and you've reached the River Gave. You sense that you're near your goal and you cross the bridge almost without noticing the shallow and swift-running water beneath. You hasten to the gates and there it is, waiting for you.

Disneyland.

Well, it's hard to avoid the comparison. The long, long avenue, and at the end that great, pointy basilica shooting off the rock of Massabielle like an enchanted castle …

The Sanctuary of Notre-Dame de Lourdes is an enormous piece of real estate. It's a healthy stroll—and a hell of a long trip in a wheelchair in the rain—down the avenue that runs from the Porte Saint Michel to the basilica. The avenue is divided by a grassy median, and here at the top there is a little circle with a stone crucifix at the center. The division of the avenue is important, because the two daily processions begin way down there by the basilica, proceed up the right side of the avenue, make a circle here around the cross, then run back along the left side.

Heading towards the basilica, one passes a long, low building on the right. This is the old Accueil de Notre-Dame, where for many years sick pilgrims to Lourdes were housed in no great comfort. On the left is a wide, grassy field that looks innocent enough but in fact conceals an underground basilica that can hold 20,000. Off to the left are the information center, the bookstore, the pastoral center. At the end of the avenue, pilgrims pose for photos in front of the statue of *la Vierge Couronné*, the Crowned Virgin. And we've reached the esplanade, a short-order Saint Peter's Square embraced by two curving ramps said to represent the arms of the Father.

If you are as unobservant as I am, you may realize only now that "the basilica" is in reality two basilicas. That low, rounded one crouching at ground level is the Rosary Basilica. To reach the pointy upper basilica, which is built on top of the rock of Massabielle, one must climb the ramps. It's tempting to head up there to get the lay of the land, but there will be time for that later. This is not Notre-Dame or Chartres or Saint Peter's. No one comes here for the architecture. So one passes instead through the arch below the right-side ramp, and out onto a long, narrow strip of land, with the River Gave on the right and the rock of Massabielle on the left.

First, there is the place where the pilgrims buy their candles. Then a long wall of taps where they fill their plastic Madonnas with water. And then, at last, the thing they have come so far—from Calais, from Singapore, from Bari, from Wicklow, from Zagreb, from Bern, from Chicago, from Cadiz—to see: the Grotto, the scar in the rock face, where the Virgin Mary appeared eighteen times to Bernadette Soubirous from February to July of 1858.

The Story

Such marvelous and extraordinary facts have been related regarding a promenade made each morning for the past fifteen days about a mile and a quarter from Lourdes by a little girl named Bernadette Savi [sic], daughter of a simple working man who lives from day to day by the sweat of his brow, that we cannot pass over them in silence. On leaving the town in the direction of St. Pé, this girl goes to a grotto, situated at the center of a great rock where there flows a stream, not far from the banks of the Gave, and having reached this place, she makes each day at six in the morning an adoration during which she claims to enter into divine rapport with the Virgin, mother of God. From the moment when the child indicates that the holy apparition has appeared, spectators remark that her face grows pale and her hands begin to tremble. This state soon gives way to a gracious smile and emotions most sweet and ravishing.

Short of attaching to these events the significance bestowed on them by public rumor, we pass them on here because we are certain that they have already attracted the interest of the authorities. We assure you that this very day, at eight in the morning, more than five thousand people gathered around the young girl as she prayed in her accustomed place …

From the *Journal de Tarbes*, March 4, 1858

Lourdes is a medieval miracle tale that unfolds in the age of newspaper articles, medical reports, police records and the camera (though Bernadette died in 1879, we have more than seventy photos of her). One can follow frame-by-frame the wholly unforeseeable series of events that would turn a local incident into an international phenomenon. In its day, Lourdes ignited a national polemic and two enormous best-sellers: Henri Lasserre's *Notre-Dame de Lourdes*, which established the legend, and Zola's *Lourdes*, which tried to explode it. It also introduced a new element of drama into the history of Marian apparitions. Traditionally, an apparition had been (as at the rue du Bac) a private encounter between one or several visionaries and the Holy Mother. Lourdes inaugurates the vision as public spectacle.

Yet behind all the sound and fury lies a strangely moving tale from a never-never time before photojournalists and mass-circulation dailies. "Once there was a girl named Bernadette Soubirous" seems the way for it to begin, because the story of the apparitions has so many elements of fairy tale: the brave and pure-hearted heroine, the poor-but-honest parents, the blustering villains who try to thwart her, the secret cavern, the beautiful fairy godmother, the ogre who hears the magic words and turns into a prince. And so …

Once there was a girl named Bernadette Soubirous, a child of fourteen years, the daughter of a good-natured but spendthrift miller with a weakness for the bottle. His latest business had failed and his family was reduced to living six to a room, the room in question being the vermin-ridden former prison cell of Lourdes. Bernadette was a tiny thing, asthmatic, unlettered, but she was the eldest child and her family's tragedies stung her fierce pride. In order that there would be one less mouth for her parents to feed, she spent several months in 1857 tending sheep for her former wet-nurse in the hills above Lourdes.

One day in February, shortly after returning from the pastures, Bernadette went with her sister and a friend to gather wood. Their destination was a lonely spot a mile outside town called Massabielle, the Old Rock. There was a grotto at Massabielle where the pigs of the town grazed, a filthy place, possessed of an ill reputation. Some said it was haunted.

Before the grotto ran a stream, and that day as Bernadette sat to take off her shoes before crossing it, a gust of wind touched her cheek. When she looked up, she could see a young woman standing in a niche above the grotto. Bernadette reached for her rosary in fear. The woman produced a rosary herself and made the sign of the cross. Then she disappeared.

When Bernadette's companions asked what she was looking at, she was amazed that they had seen nothing. She told them about the woman. Of course, the girls couldn't keep such a secret and the rumor of Bernadette's vision blazed through the town. Her mother, fearing scandal, beat her and forbade her to return to the grotto, but Bernadette was too strongly drawn and outside forces were already weighing in. An inquisitive society woman who employed Bernadette's mother as a washerwoman procured a private visit to the grotto with the girl. She came armed with paper and pen, hoping the silent specter would write its name. When Bernadette offered the writing implements, however, the woman of the grotto laughed. Then she spoke for the first time, more graciously, said Bernadette, than anyone had ever spoken to her:

"Will you have the kindness to return here for fifteen days?" she asked.

Bernadette could only answer yes.

And then, before she disappeared, the woman said one more thing: "I do not promise to make you happy in this world, but in the other."

So Bernadette went to the grotto each morning, knelt with her candle and told her rosary till the apparition returned. And each morning more people followed to observe her ecstasy. They saw Bernadette's face change. They saw her smile and cry. They saw her lips form words. But only Bernadette saw and heard the woman. The messages she passed on were terse. For the first few days, "Penance! Penance! Penance! Kiss the ground for the conversion of sinners," was all the woman had to say. Some days, she said nothing at all.

The authorities, meanwhile, were growing uneasy. After the sixth of the fifteen days, Police Inspector Jacomet locked Bernadette in his home, where he taunted the girl, trying in vain to catch her in a lie. He even threatened to arrest her if she went back to the grotto. But Bernadette was not to be intimidated; she returned the next day with the biggest crowd yet and under the protection of gendarmes. Fearful of popular anger, the mayor had revoked Jacomet's ban.

It was on the ninth day that the woman spoke the fateful words, "Drink the water, eat the grass for the sinners." At first, Bernadette started towards the water of the river, but then she turned back to the cave. She fell to her knees, crawled into the grotto and started to dig there with her fingers. A bit of filthy liquid bubbled up through the muck. She raised it to her lips and—with reluctance—drank. Then she yanked out a handful of grass and stuffed it in her mouth. The skeptics in the crowd had seen all they needed to see; they laughed and headed back to town. The little visionary's aunt slapped her for shaming the family. But the faithful knew a sign when they saw one. Two days later, a pregnant woman with paralyzed fingers came to the grotto at first light. She thrust her hand into the water that Bernadette had brought forth and immediately felt warmth coursing through her flesh.

Word of this prodigy spread fast. Fifteen hundred were gathered by the river on the twelfth day, when the woman instructed Bernadette to "Go and tell the priests to build a chapel here so that the people can come in procession." With a resolution that recalls young Cathérine Labouré facing Father Aladel, Bernadette hastened to deliver the message to Father Peyramale, the crusty old parish priest of Lourdes. So far, Peyramale had been content to observe the events at the grotto through proxies, but now this girl had had the audacity to bring her pranks to his doorstep. "You're a little liar!" he exploded. "Tell your lady that if she wants a chapel she'll have to pay for it. And while you're at it, ask her who she is."

Ten thousand, it is said, turned out for the last of the fifteen days. They came expecting a revelation and left disappointed. After forty-five minutes of silent prayer, Bernadette calmly extinguished her candle and went home. On that anti-climactic note the fortnight of apparitions came to an end.

People continued to pray at the grotto, however, and more wonders were reported. Still, Bernadette stayed home, waiting. Three weeks passed. Then on March 25, the Feast of the Annunciation, she felt the call. She went down to the grotto with her candle and knelt in her usual spot. When the woman appeared, she asked her, "Mademoiselle, would you be so kind as to tell me who you are, if you please?"

The woman only smiled.

Twice more Bernadette asked, and still the woman said nothing. But after the fourth time, she opened her hands towards the ground, then joined them again at her chest, looked towards heaven, and said in Bernadette's own dialect:

"Que soy era Immaculada Councepciou."

Bernadette ran all the way from the grotto to Father Peyramale's house in Lourdes, repeating the strange words over and over so that she wouldn't forget them. She burst in upon the priest and exclaimed:

"I am the Immaculate Conception."

Father Peyramale was speechless. When at last he found his tongue, he could only blurt out: "It's impossible! A woman cannot have that name. Do you know what it means?"

Bernadette shook her head.

"Well then, go home. I'll see you another day."

The girl left in confusion, thinking that Peyramale was angry. The truth was, he needed time to compose himself. Bernadette had spoken the magic words that convinced him she was not lying. It was only four years since Pope Pius IX had proclaimed as dogma the doctrine of the Immaculate Conception: that the Holy Mother had been freed from mortal stain at the instant of her creation. How could this sacred formula have come from the mouth of an unlettered shepherd girl, if not through Our Lady's grace?

Stone

Outside the Grotto the rock face is tawny, streaked white and gray like an elephant's flank. Inside, the walls are black, stained by a century of candle soot. In the innermost depth, water drips from the ceiling, and moss and tiny plants sprout from the rock. Where the water drips, the  rock is smooth, cool, glassy. People touch here to feel the wetness.

Pilgrims enter the Grotto one by one in a steady flow, running their left hand along the stone wall. The Virgin never said there was any power or virtue in the stone, so there is no special reason to touch it. But everyone does. Some, eyes clenched, press it with both hands, fiercely trying to draw something from its bareness.

The literature of the Sanctuary assures us that "by pressing their hand on the rock or by kissing it, the pilgrims show their faith in God, who is the rock," but the Sanctuary is whistling in the dark. The reason why the pilgrims touch the rock is old, old and swims far too deep in the oceans of the mind to be hauled up on a fishhook of symbolism.

The Grotto and the area around it have been "improved." Electrical lighting has been installed; the course of the Gave has been diverted to make room for benches and a promenade; the stream where Bernadette knelt lies buried beneath the plaza. A plaque marks the spot, however, and if you kneel there today, pilgrim, and look up as she did, you will still see a strange natural niche above the Grotto, a niche just big enough for a human to stand in, if a human cared to scale the rock to get there. Occupying the niche is a statue of Our Lady of Lourdes—a poor likeness in every way, by Bernadette's estimation.

The first time I visited the Grotto, a woman had prostrated herself in prayer, forehead to the ground, just at the entrance. The Spanish couple behind me started up the Ave Maria in a whispered call and answer. Coolness embraced me. The earth inside, where Bernadette's sister gathered firewood, had been leveled and paved over, and the rubber tires of a wheelchair made a sucking noise on the stone surface. Step by step, the line of pilgrims approached the mystery, the muddy place where Bernadette had clawed with her fingers to release the healing spring. When my turn came, I grasped the metal railing and leaned forward to look. For the first instant, my eyes were dazzled by the spotlight shining from below. Then I made out the flash and leap of water beneath a thick sheet of plexiglas.

The effect was that of a miniature waterfall in a hotel lobby.

Roped in, paved over, floodlit, benches set in front of it, a church plunked on top: so much effort has been made to render the Grotto comfortable, safe and accessible, to contain it and claim it, that it's a wonder it can still capture the mind. But look at the benches, filled with people day and night. There's no need for them to be here. If they want to pray, there are plenty of churches in Lourdes. Yet they linger, thinking, praying or just floating in a pool of stillness.

Of course pilgrims come to the Grotto because they know something mysterious happened here. But they stay because they can *believe* that this was the place where such a thing could happen. The Grotto is a natural theater for the imagination despite all that has been done to denature it.

How must it have been when Bernadette first came here, before the benches and retaining walls and electric wiring went in? A sinister place, one imagines. It's sinister still, eating like an abscess into the base of the rock. Sinister in spite of the towering basilica set over it to say, "This is a Christian place. There is nothing to be afraid of here."

Mind you, an oversight was made with the basilica. It was built to face the castle and the town. So what happens here below, especially late at night when the basilica rides the sky like a gray sleeping ship and the Grotto blazes with candlelight, seems to happen behind the Church's back. The strange hushed services take place out of sight, in a magic cave, at a place that was before the Church, before time.

Not in this world, but in the other

One would like to end the story of Bernadette with "And she lived happily ever after." But sadly, words like "thwarted" and "blighted" are the ones that most often crop up in accounts of her later life. If we can call Bernadette happy, it is not by any secular measure of the word. But then, the woman of the apparitions had promised no more.

I accept Lourdes' invitation to "walk in the footsteps of Bernadette." To the Boly Mill where she grew up; to Le Cachot, the former lock-up where her family lived at the time of the apparitions (the guide asks us to reflect on Bernadette's words, "God chose me because I was the poorest and the most ignorant"). To the font where Bernadette was baptized. And the door she pounded on when she came to tell Father Peyramale that the Lady wanted a chapel. And the place she knelt ...

I walk in her footsteps, but I never catch up with her. She's always around the next corner.

In the months that followed the apparitions, controversy swirled around the grotto. When the civil authorities fenced off the site, its devotees tore the barriers down. The offerings and coins that were left at the grotto were confiscated by the police. Gendarmes were posted to keep people away from the "unauthorized place of worship," meaning that Bernadette's final vision, on July 16, came from the far side of the Gave. There was even a rash of apparitions that persisted for a few weeks until the local prefect threatened to have anyone reporting visions hospitalized. Meanwhile, progressive citizens expressed dismay that the credulous were exposing themselves to disease by drinking the water of the spring.

The turning point came in July, when the Emperor Napoleon III enlisted in the ranks of the credulous. His infant son and heir had recovered from sunstroke after a sprinkling of water that the child's governess had fetched from Bernadette's spring. That October, the barricades came down once and for all.

From then on, it was Bernadette, with Father Peyramale ever looming at her side, who was the calm eye at the center of the storm. One after another, skeptics and ecclesiastical inquiries went at her, trying to find a hole in her story, a sign that she was deluded or lying. All surrendered in the face of the girl's candor. Whether they believed in the apparitions or not, it was clear that Bernadette did. Under subtle questioning, she displayed "charisma" in the oldest sense of the word: a precision, persuasiveness and wisdom beyond her years or education that her interlocutors could only understand as a gift of the Spirit. Meanwhile, the facts on the ground—the cures, the favors granted, the religious fire that burned in Lourdes—spoke ever louder for the validity of her vision. In the end,

Bernadette's story won through. The cult of the Virgin of Lourdes was recognized by the Church in 1862.

After this triumph, what remained for Bernadette? She was a messenger and she had delivered her message faithfully. "Now I am a person like any other," she told an ecclesiastical hearing. But that was only wishful thinking; whatever she hoped, Bernadette would never again be "a person like any other." She was a celebrity, and as long as she remained in the world, she would never enjoy another moment of peace. The growing crowds in Lourdes pressed to touch her, to beg for her blessing, to force money and gifts on her (in the beginning, she would simply let the money fall to the ground; later, she handed it over to the charity box of the church). But Bernadette resisted all attempts to venerate her person. She understood perfectly that she was only a messenger.

She was gently pried from her family and directed towards the religious life. The Church thought it better to get the girl into a convent where she would be sheltered from the crowds and where, perhaps more importantly, she couldn't say or do anything that might be detrimental to the reputation of Lourdes. For the Virgin, moving in her mysterious way, had given the ecclesiastical hierarchy a handful with her choice of messenger. Bernadette was a peasant girl. She lacked religious education. She spoke a French incomprehensible to anyone from outside her little valley. Her parents were an embarrassment to good society. And anxious though she was not to offend, she never developed an instinct for saying what people wanted to hear, but persisted in thinking for herself and saying what she thought. Her Mother Superior was not alone in complaining, "I don't understand why the holy Virgin revealed herself to Bernadette. There are so many other souls more lofty and delicate."

Nevertheless, religious houses eager to have a visionary on staff wooed her with alacrity. In the end, Bernadette chose the Saint-Gildard convent in distant Nevers. She left her village and her grotto forever in 1866, taking the train whose tracks had just reached Lourdes that year, the train that seven years later would be carrying the 20,000 pilgrims of the first National Pilgrimage. Bernadette would not be there to see them. While all the other novices, after taking the veil, were sent to houses throughout France, Bernadette remained in Nevers. She would spend the rest of her days there, separated from her family and her people, frustrated by a sense of uselessness, forever incapable of satisfying her superiors, battling demons as her health deteriorated.

Even in the cloister she remained on show for every nosy cleric who happened by. They would "carelessly" drop objects near her, then ask her to pick them up so that they could have something she had touched. She despised them for it.

Bernadette endured. Like that other girl messenger, Joan of Arc, she was destined for martyrdom. But where Saint Joan's death was fiery and swift, Bernadette's was long and obscure. If ever a body needed the miraculous waters of Lourdes, it was Bernadette. Through the last years of her life, she was racked with asthma, tuberculosis, an aneurysm, a knee tumor, bone decay, abscesses in her ears, bedsores. "I would never have thought that one must suffer so much to die," she once said, as she gazed at her crucifix.

Today, instead of illuminating her city, as Saint Francis does Assisi, or Saint James Santiago, Bernadette haunts Lourdes. Though her "miraculously uncorrupted" body reposes, past caring, on display in a glass coffin in Nevers, her unquiet spirit lingers here. Her great, dark eyes follow the pilgrims from postcard racks, bookstalls, shop windows. They do not seem the eyes of one who has seen something beautiful and holy; they reflect, rather, an unfathomable suffering. It is the suffering of Lourdes. The eyes of Bernadette offer fellowship in the terrible solitude of pain.

One can only hope that her Lady kept her word; that Bernadette is happy in the other world.

Que Soy Era Immaculada Concepciou

Bernadette's Lady sent tremors through the Catholic world when she called herself "the Immaculate Conception." What do these words mean, and what did they imply in the political and religious milieu of the mid-nineteenth century?

Only the Roman Catholic Church teaches that Mary was conceived without sin. The belief is not derived from scripture (though Catholics argue that when Mary is called "full of Grace," it implies her sinlessness), but from traditions that date back to the apocryphal gospels of the Eastern Church. Western theologians of the Mary-smitten twelfth century supported the doctrine with arguments based upon "aptness"; that as

God had the power to give the grace of sinlessness to his mother he must have done so, rather than let himself be born of a mere fallen woman.

Other Christian denominations object to the belief on the grounds that it seems to set Mary on a par with her son. If the Virgin is free from sin at her conception and free from corruption at her death (as the dogma of the Assumption asserts), does that not elevate her so far above humanity as to make her a sort of goddess? Does it not, moreover, render Jesus himself redundant? Naturally, Protestant reformers rejected the doctrine when they broke with Rome, but even within the Catholic Church it always aroused controversy. Aquinas, the supreme philosopher of the Christian Middle Ages, rejected it, as did even Mary's greatest eulogizer, Saint Bernard of Clairvaux. After the Reformation, the Jesuits warned their flock that anyone who denied the Immaculate Conception was well on his way to hell, even as the Dominicans in the church next door preached the opposite. Gangs of hooligans debated Mary's stainlessness in the streets and more than one pope attempted to ban the subject from churches altogether. Through all this controversy, the Church officially steered the middle course: Catholics could believe in the doctrine or not as their conscience dictated.

Then in 1854 Rome changed tack. The doctrine of the Immaculate Conception was declared dogma, a teaching all Catholics were obliged to accept. The force behind this turnabout was Giovanni Maria Mastai-Ferretti, Pope Pius IX.

Pius IX lived in, and made his mark on, "interesting times." It is well-nigh impossible to locate the man beneath all the scorn and praise that have been heaped upon him. To his detractors, he is an egotistical, bullying, anti-Semitic reactionary who tried to drag the Church back into the Middle Ages. To his admirers he is a generous man of deep principles, a hero in a time of disorder, a beacon to believers and "the founder of the Modern Papacy."

To the Romans, at least, *Pio Nono* was "the Last Pope." The last, that is, to rule Rome as both Pope and King. At the time of his election in 1846, Italy was still a checkerboard of kingdoms and duchies and Pius was a temporal ruler whose realm cut a swath across the Italian peninsula. Liberal thinkers of the day, when they projected a unified Italy, often envisioned the Pope as president of a future federation of Italian states, and the flurry of liberal reforms that opened Pius's rule seemed to set such visions within reach: he granted amnesty to exiled revolutionaries, launched railways, established freedom of the press, admitted laymen into the government of the Papal States, and freed the Jews from the ghetto (as well as from their weekly obligation to attend a scolding Christian sermon).

Europe gasped. In Vienna, Prince Metternich declared that the only contingency he had *never* allowed for was a liberal Pope. In Rome, the citizens launched torchlit parades to celebrate each new reform. Throughout Italy, nationalist hopes were sparked. The handsome young patriot-Pope (Pius was fifty-four in 1846) was the man of the hour, the messiah who would rally the people. When the northern Italian states rose against Austrian rule in 1848, all eyes turned his way, assuming that he would lend his arms to the struggle or perhaps even assume a leading role. But Pius did nothing of the sort. As Pope, he could not justify waging an offensive war, particularly against Austrian "children of the Church." He had, besides, no wish to assist in the establishment of any Italian republic that might compromise the temporal powers of the papacy.

Overnight, Pius became as scorned and detested as he had previously been admired. His prime minister was assassinated and he was forced to flee into exile. When the French armies restored him to the papal throne a year later, he was a shrewder and more determined man, the critic and opponent for life of all the "erroneous" teachings of the modern world.

Pius's first salvo in his war against modernity was the proclamation of the dogma of the Immaculate Conception. Not that it was an issue he had to force: Catholics had been united and galvanized by the Miraculous Medallion, and calls for the definition had sounded from everywhere. Still, it provided him with a golden opportunity to show the world the Roman Church militant. Henceforth, this most divisive of Catholic doctrines was to be dogma, and let those who didn't like it be damned.

Pius also seized the moment to consolidate papal power over the Church. By championing the Immaculate Conception, he placed himself at the vanguard of Marian fervor. Now, to be with the Pope was to be with Mary and who dared oppose Mary? The bishops were constrained to lay aside any misgivings and array themselves behind their Pontiff. In the event, their assent went unacknowledged as, for the first time in Church history, a dogma was defined solely by papal authority. Pius's unilateralism anticipated the defining act of his reign, the 1870 proclamation of Papal Infallibility.

Between these two historical pronouncements, Pius found time to compile the infamous *Syllabus of Errors*. This document chastised modernity and all its "isms" one by one, with the ultimate error being the assertion that "the Pope can and should reconcile himself with progress, liberalism and modern civilization."

Pius IX would wear the tiara for thirty-two years—longer than any other Pope. He was on hand from beginning to end as the emerging Italian republic wolfed down the Papal States, taking Rome itself for their final morsel. In September 1870, the armies of King Victor Emmanuel forced their way into the Eternal City and Pius locked himself up in the Vatican, a self-proclaimed prisoner. Not until 1929 would a Pope again set foot in the streets of Rome. But Pius continued to launch missiles from inside the walls of Saint Peter's, forbidding Catholics to participate in the new democracy "either as electors or elected." No quarter was to be given to the modern world, its ideas and its institutions. The Church at its highest levels settled into a bellicose conservatism that would, in the twentieth century, draw it into tragic complicity with the regimes of fascism.

But all of that was far in the future in 1858. In 1858, there was only relief that Catholicism had weathered the tempests of the French Revolution and the Napoleonic era; that, thanks to the Miraculous Medallion, a great revival of faith had taken place; that a cherished belief of many Catholics had been solemnized; and that now, somewhere up in the Pyrenees, the Blessed Mother herself had appeared with the words, "I am the Immaculate Conception" on her lips.

THE LADY WHO CAUSED THIS GREAT stir is curiously innocuous. Especially to a traveler coming fresh from Chartres, the Virgin of Lourdes—the one whose image we see at the Grotto, and multiplied endlessly on the shelves of the souvenir shops—is a bit of a letdown. She has neither the dark, chthonic power of Our Lady of the Pillar, nor the imperial bearing of Our Lady of the Beautiful Window. Her eyes soft-focused heavenward, the Immaculate Conception seems to hover above the earthly passions she has aroused. Yet she remains close enough for pilgrims' prayers to reach her. If Bernadette mirrors Lourdes' pain, the Immaculate Conception absorbs it without ever being stained.

Bernadette didn't like the way her Lady was depicted. She didn't even bother to attend the inauguration of the statue. The sculptor of the Immaculate Conception that stands in the Grotto was Joseph Fabisch, a fashionable artist from Lyon, who knew what a Virgin ought to look like and made her just so. It's intriguing to imagine how different the cult of Lourdes might be had Fabisch portrayed Bernadette's Lady as she appeared, rather than as she should have appeared.

First of all, she would not look like a "Lady" at all. The convention of calling her "the beautiful Lady" goes back to the first newspaper reports, but Bernadette never described her in that way. In fact, Bernadette attributed no sex initially to the creature of her apparitions, calling it only *Aquéro*, "that thing." Later, she would describe Aquéro as a *damizéla*. In

her book on Lourdes, Ruth Harris points out that while this word can be rendered in French as *demoiselle*, or unmarried girl, in Bernadette's dialect it held a further connotation: fairy. And how fairy-like, in fact, the creature was! To the end of her life (and to the annoyance of interlocutors with fixed ideas of their own), the four-foot-eight Bernadette, with her face of an eleven-year-old, continued to insist that Aquéro had been no bigger or older than herself.

This Aquéro, however, was too far from the accepted and acceptable image of the Holy Mother. She seemed an offspring of the grotto and the forest, a throwback to the sylvan nymphs who used to emerge magically from springs and tree trunks. If one reads between the lines of Bernadette's accounts, Aquéro's spritely qualities only stand out the more: she can't be counted on to show up when she promises, she speaks little (unlike the long-winded Marys of the rue du Bac or Fatima), and she replies with an enigmatic smile when asked a question she isn't inclined to answer. Aquéro, whatever she may have been, was not a good, bourgeois Virgin.

So, consciously and unconsciously, artists, the Church and the popular imagination reimagined her; they made her a lady instead of a girl: tall, gracious and trustworthy rather than petite and mercurial. They created a Lady of Lourdes in a form they could understand, and in doing so they fixed especially on one detail of Bernadette's account: the moment before the Immaculate Conception names herself; the moment when she lowers her hands and spreads her fingers.

"Look," they said, pulling out their Miraculous Medallions, "it's the same gesture! She's the same one."

Perhaps time has proven them right.

Waar is uw Geluk?

My first days in Lourdes I spent watching, reading, listening, racing to get a handle, any handle, on it all. Everything I saw was Important. I was seized by a fever to marshal evidence, to catalogue.

I recorded the place-names on the banners in the afternoon and evening processions: Leisure Time Travel Pilgrims, Liverpool; Bayerisches Pilgerburo; Our Lady and Saint Wilfrid, Blyth; Limburg, Nederlands; Notre Dame d'Europe, Gibraltar; Associazione Sant'Agnese, Torino; Orden Franciscana Reglar, Almagro; Our Lady Queen of Heaven, Dublin Airport; Immaculate Conception, Stockholm; Le Petit Train de l'Amitié, Dunkerque; Parish of the Most Holy Rosary, Tullow.

Rheinmaas was there with their glow-in-the-dark standard that looked like a pub sign, and the Legion of Mary with theirs of the Lady of Fatima. There were groups who walked behind the flags of Switzerland and Poland, Portugal, Croatia and the United States of America. And, of course, there were Les Pèlerins de l'Eau Vive, "The Pilgrims of the Living Water," each carrying a small sign with the legend "Lord Jesus, cure us of alcohol."

I pored over the testimonials chiselled into the walls of the basilicas:
"Thank you Good Mother for giving us a child."
"I prayed to Mary. She miraculously protected me through the war. 8 May 1919."
"CV—YD. Two hearts united by Our Lady of Lourdes."
"Thanks to Our Lady of Lourdes for protecting the pilgrims of the 6th gray train in 1908 from the accident that took place in Pau Station."
"She cured me. She converted him. Thank you."
"Thanks to Our Lady of Lourdes for success in my exams."
"A mother thankful for the Christian end of her son, providentially succored by a missionary in Annam where he was devoured by a tiger."
"On Christmas Day, at midnight, my son was cured. Thank you Good Mother."
"Merci Merci Merci Merci Merci."
I observed the pilgrims' observances:
Eucharistic procession in the afternoon. Rosary procession at night. Lighting candles. Drawing water. Touching the stone. Praying at the spring. International mass in the underground basilica. Kneeling where Bernadette

knelt. Going for a bath. Walking the stations of the cross. Leaving flowers at the statue of the crowned Virgin. Buying souvenirs.

I kept a running tab on the languages in which the Hail Mary was recited at the nightly procession: Maltese, Hungarian, Polish, Croat, Portuguese, Slovak, Irish Gaelic (which manages to be both guttural and lilting), Tagalog, Arabic, Swedish, Slovene, Indonesian.

One cataloguing night, I fell under the spell of the pixel board by the Grotto. All day and all night, this pixel board broadcasts the words of Mary to Bernadette in the six "official" languages of Lourdes (french-english-dutch-italian-spanish-and-german running top-to-bottom neck-and-neck). Fortunately Mary's messages were few, concise and easily translated. They blink in an endless spool, so that in five minutes you can read the story of Lourdes in telegraphs, like this:

> Mary said:
> "I do not promise
> to make you happy
> in this world,
> but in the other."

Under some strange compulsion, I jotted lines at random from all six languages to make a kind of pixel-board-of-Babel poem.

Afterwards, one question lingered with me. Curiously, it lingered in Dutch.

Kristem. Waar is uw geluk?

Christian, where is your happiness?

Pilgrims

I'm outside the pilgrim center looking over the schedule that's been posted for a Franco-Portuguese group. They've got quite a weekend lined up.

Off the train Saturday afternoon and straight to the stations of the cross. Mass at 5:30 in the upper basilica, then candlelight procession at 8:45. Sunday's religious marathon starts off with spiritual ablutions—confession from 7:30 to 8:30—followed by mass at 9. One more hike around the stations of the cross at 11. Then lunch break, followed by an "Encounter for Reflection" at 3. The gang will be marching under the team standard, "*Portugais de France*," at the 4:30 Eucharistic procession, then attending evening mass at 6. One more rosary procession at 8:45. The train leaves early Monday morning, but there'll still be time for a 6:45 mass at the Grotto. Somewhere in there, too, they'll be shopping for souvenirs, walking in the footsteps of Bernadette, taking a dip in the baths, lining up at the taps and, oh yes, eating.

It strikes me that one reason I like Lourdes so much is that I'm not on an organized pilgrimage.

But while Lourdes may not sound like most vacationers' idea of a good time, it pulls in five million people a year. That's the population of a large city (or a small country) running the taps, fondling the stone, squinting at Bernadette's spring through the plexiglas. Enough to make Lourdes the most visited spot in France after Paris.

Who on earth are these people?

The number-crunchers at the Sanctuary of Our Lady are assiduous in amassing and sifting information about the pilgrims. Their findings tend both to confirm and shed light on our experience of Lourdes (as only statistics can). First of all, the Sanctuary distinguishes between *excursionistes*—visitors who do not stay the night—and *séjournants*—those who do. The fact that the average séjournant spends not just one or two, but three-and-a-half nights in Lourdes points to the importance of this distinction: you're either in-and-out or you're here for the long haul. As it turns out, fully 60 percent of Lourdes' annual visitors are in-and-outers.

Their numbers would include a certain number of tourists—travelers who have dropped in to see what the hubbub is about (or, like two otherworldly Japanese girls I met, to see if the miracle-baths really work)—but one can assume that the majority come for religious motives; they are pilgrims.

Nonetheless, the pilgrim experience of séjournants and excursionistes will differ vastly. In the time he has allotted for Lourdes, the excursioniste can only hope to visit the Sanctuary, make a prayer and pick up some water. If this was his goal he will be satisfied—in much the same way as he is satisfied coming home from the market with his shopping done. But generally, one hopes for something more from a pilgrimage. Some kind of insight, growth, personal transfiguration. Short of a miracle (an event that can never be ruled out in Lourdes), one day is not enough time to be transfigured.

Formerly, of course, the time a human soul needed for real growth and transformation was built into the experience of pilgrimage. A pilgrim in the days of foot travel might devote weeks, months or years to his journey. It was not that he had any choice in the matter, travel was a slow business. But virtue was born of necessity. This was the time he needed in which to grow. Today's pilgrim seldom enjoys the benefits of slowness. Planes, trains and automobiles are at his disposal. He has no excuse not to be back in the office on Monday.

Lourdes has reached a compromise with this modern reality by taking a water-over-stone approach: pilgrims are asked to make a modest commitment of time—a few days, a week if possible—on a yearly basis. It still doesn't sound like much, but over the course of years this periodic spiritual refreshment has an effect, for Lourdes is an extremely concentrated experience. It is so because the Sanctuary of Notre-Dame is a world unto itself, adjacent to but separate from Lourdes proper. Whereas in Rome or Paris, pilgrims find themselves at sea in a teeming city, the pilgrims in the Sanctuary of Lourdes *are* the city, the ever-changing citizenry and workforce who animate this miniature society. The Sanctuary's year-round paid staff numbers less than four hundred. All the rest are pilgrims.

It is pilgrims, of course, who make up the massive daily processions—singing, parading their banners, hoisting their candles. But it is also pilgrims who lead the processions, who take the sick from the trains and care for them during their stay and staff the baths and hostels. The priests, readers and other celebrants of the holy ceremonies always include pilgrims as well. One might think of the Sanctuary of Lourdes as a vast stage where pilgrims act out a Christian drama. The amazing thing is that the cast changes by the week!

In this light, the excursioniste, who comes and goes in a day, must inevitably stand at the periphery, more spectator than participant, more tourist than pilgrim. But then, Lourdes is a spectacle and a spectacle needs spectators: they also serve who only stand and watch.

As for the two million séjournants, the pilgrims who stick around, the Sanctuary divides them into three categories: private pilgrims, small groups and official pilgrimages. "Private pilgrims" comprise everyone imaginable: the postman from Poitiers with the withered hand who liked to drive down for a couple of days when he got the chance (but when I told him I'd been here for two weeks, he shook his head and whistled:

"Two weeks in Lourdes? I'd throw myself in the river"); Satoshi, from Japan, who converted to Catholicism last year for reasons he preferred to keep to himself; Jan, who popped in from Amsterdam to ask the Holy Mother for advice about her next step in life; the Filipino family at my hotel who were traveling with their own priest. They step out of Lourdes Station into the crisp air, saying, "Well, here we are." In the days that follow, they will join a procession, light a candle, and fill their blue Madonnas with Lourdes water. Many, like my friends from Milan, volunteer in advance to staff the baths, do station duty, organize the crowds at the processions. Individually, the private pilgrims may not make a big splash, but their million little splashes add up.

"Small groups" include people like the busload of Finns who occupied my hotel for four nights. (I know it was four because the man in the next room snored like a beast in pain.) They may have a mass spoken in their language at the Grotto (typically at 6:45, before liturgical rush hour). They walk behind the standard of their parish or their national flag at the processions. Some even come to the microphone during the evening mass to say the Ave Maria in their own tongue. One night, I met a group from Lebanon that consisted of four boys and a Lebanese flag. They carried the flag in the rosary procession, got "a special welcome tonight to our friends from Lebanon," went to the microphone in front of all those thousands of people to recite ten times "Salaam aleichem Miriam" [sic], and made quite a hit afterwards with some American girls.

In 1998, nearly four thousand groups from seventy-five countries registered their visit with the Sanctuary. There was a group of fifty from Iraq and another of forty-eight from Russia. There were eight groups from Taiwan, ten from Singapore and fifty-three from Japan. English Canada beat out French Canada twenty-one groups to six. Even little Gibraltar launched four groups with a total of 215 pilgrims and five priests.

But while the "small groups" add color and spice to the mix, it is the "official pilgrimages" that are Lourdes' bread and butter. These pilgrimages can involve hundreds or thousands of pilgrims. They commission their own trains, or charter planes if they're coming from Ireland and England. They occupy whole floors in the *accueils* (pilgrims' hostels with full medical facilities). They stay for longer than anyone else—up to six days—and most of them return annually.

The majority of the sick and mentally or physically handicapped pilgrims in Lourdes come with official pilgrimages. They arrive accompanied by full teams of doctors and nurses and at least one companion for each person requiring care. Official pilgrimages are epic ventures: planning and fund-raising, largely through church sales, lotteries and parties, go on throughout the year.

Big David from England spends a dinner outlining the logistical challenges of getting the annual Easter pilgrimage over from his diocese: transferring hundreds of individuals who cannot transfer themselves from buses to ferries to hotels to trains, making sure that luggage and fold-up wheelchairs end up in the right hands, booking rooms at several hotels in Calais because there isn't one hotel big enough for the whole group, ensuring that each pilgrim's individual medical needs are attended to. And all these arrangements are complicated to the *n*th degree by the policy of shuffling the sick and the caregivers so that everyone, every day, gets a new companion. One can see why official pilgrimages stay so long in Lourdes: it wouldn't be worth the trouble, or the stress on the sick, to come for less.

Not surprisingly, many parishes hand over the running of their pilgrimages to "chains," big-scale operations that make pilgrimages their business. The largest of these, the Italian Unitalsi, operates its own accueil in Lourdes, a twelve-storey complex called Salus built exclusively to house Unitalsi groups. (When I ask my friend Maurizio if Unitalsi is a non-profit organization, he replies, "Very much so; they operate on an enormous deficit.")

Because of their numbers and their identifying clothing, because you see them day in and day out, the faces of the official pilgrimages are the ones you remember as the faces of Lourdes: the high school students from Lyon in their red pea caps, toiling behind wheelchairs on the hill to Marie St.-Frai; the Unitalsi groups in their navy-blue t-shirts, waving their arms over their heads and singing on the platform as a train departs; the ranks of elderly Dutch sitting stolidly through the international mass; the squadrons of Spanish nurses laughing and smoking like coal furnaces in their pre-war headscarves that make them look like nuns.

Official pilgrimages know the place, they know the people, and they know their part in the show. Many of the pilgrims have been coming for as long as they can remember, and Lourdes for them is an album of memories, a reference point in their lives, a second home. They rediscover here a sense of community and the deeper meanings of their religion that are so easily lost in the quotidian world. They are pilgrims in a full, rich sense of the word.

According to the Sanctuary, two-thirds of those who come to Lourdes for the first time come out of curiosity or hoping for a cure. But three-quarters of those who return do so "in the name of devotion, the desire to do service, and for the encounter with the Virgin."

In other words, they may come the first time as tourists, but they return as pilgrims.

Arrivals

On the morning of June 10, a train arrives from Arras bearing 240 sick pilgrims—*les malades*. The train is scheduled to arrive at 7:16, and by 6:45 teams of *brancardiers*—the French and foreign volunteers who will assist in moving the sick—are already hanging around the platform having a smoke in the cold morning. As the hour approaches, they begin to roll wheelchairs out of the waiting hall. Soon the platform is lined with them: ancient cushionless blue steel industrial-strength monsters that work on the dolly principle: tip her back and push like hell. Most are dedicated to someone: "In memoria Francesco Giannino, Milano," "Clara II." Built to last and with no concession to comfort, the Lourdes station wheelchairs have been shuttling invalids and the elderly from the train platform to the bus loading area since the war (the Crimean War, that is).  Remarkably, though Lourdes Station handles something in the neighborhood of 50,000 handicapped passengers per year, low-tech and high manpower remain the order of the day.

The train pulls in at 7:30. Of course the handicapped on board aren't equipped with their wheelchairs; a standard wheelchair is simply too wide to maneuver in a train passage and there's no place to park it anyway. So station wheelchairs (not the Lourdes classic, but a lighter, narrower model) are rolled into the trains by the brancardiers and, one by one, the malades are fetched out. Fortunately, the floor of this morning's train is level with the platform, so ramps can be laid down and the sick wheeled out without too much effort. In many trains the floor is three steps up from the platform, meaning that those in wheelchairs must be hoisted down, which requires five sets of hands.

The goal of the operation is to get all the invalids off the train and onto the bus that will take them to their hotels or accueils. To this end, a more-or-less spontaneous division of labor takes place. Some brancardiers help invalids from the cars to the platform; others run a shuttle between the platform and the buses; a third crew loads the buses as they arrive, then accompany them to their destinations.

It sounds like a military operation, but it looks like a bomb scare, with people scurrying in every direction. Lourdes functions not by precision, but by numbers and goodwill. Each volunteer helps according to his or her means, which means that some don't help very much at all. But no one who wants to lend a hand is turned away and that policy is hard to fault in an age when millions of workers are declared "redundant." In Lourdes, everyone pitches in and, somehow or other, sooner or later, God willing, everything gets done and no one gets killed in the process.

The platform is full of greetings and kisses between the waiting bran-cardiers and their colleagues from Arras who have arrived with the train. Lourdes is always a homecoming. Nurses trot up and down the platform laden with quilts to keep the sick from freezing. Seven people fuss over the job of getting one woman on a stretcher properly tucked in. It takes several minutes, but no one gets flustered and the woman looks happy. Many of the sick are quite capable of walking from the train to the waiting area, but few are given the chance. They are snapped up instead by the wheelchair brigade who circle like hungry cabbies. In Lourdes, hospitality for the sick and elderly begins the moment they arrive at the station.

A little toothless man with a young nurse in tow declines to enter the Hall des Malades till he's had a cigarette. He begins to talk to me, but whether its his toothlessness or his accent, I can't make out a word. His nurse smiles and translates.

"He says it's cloudy. He wants to know when the sun will come out."

He takes another drag and turns to me again. This time he starts me out with something easy.

"Lourdes," he says with spirit. "*Loooourdes.*"

By 8:40, the platform is almost clear, but the unheated Hall des Malades is still full of invalids who wait, uncomplaining, for their buses. Joelle, the French Railways welcome officer, looks at them and shakes her head.

"The poor things. But you know, I see them arrive and I see them leave. They look younger when they leave."

City of Miracles, City of the Sick

The association of Lourdes with miracles has become a cliché. This holds all the more here in Lourdes itself. Mention that the weather cleared up just in time for the procession (as it always does) and someone will laugh and say, "It's a miracle." Spot a wheelchair without an occupant, somebody's bound to point and gasp: *"Un miracle!"* As I write, I must constantly suppress the urge to say, "But the real miracle of Lourdes is …"

The Sanctuary bookstore carries a number of titles on miracles. My favorite is *Les miracles . . . tout simplement*: the Idiot's Guide. If you already have a grasp of the basics, you can take a look at *Lourdes: Miraculous Cures (Who, When and Where)* by Dr. Theodore Mangiapan, former president of the Medical Bureau of Lourdes. To comfort the faithful and confound skeptics, monographs complete with x-rays and medical charts are available dealing with each of Lourdes' three most recent miraculous cures. But one title goes for the throat: *Are There Still Miracles at Lourdes?*

The miracles have grown scarce recently. In the early days they ran thick and fast—in 1858, there were over a hundred declarations of cures, seven of them recognized as miracles by the Church. By the First World War, nearly 4,500 more claims had come in, thirty-three of them deemed miraculous. The fifties was a boom decade, producing ten miracles, four in the *annus mirabilis* 1950 alone. And then came the sixties—only one miracle. Two in the seventies. One more in the eighties.

Has the water of Lourdes lost its kick?

By the reckoning of no less an authority than Dr. Patrick Theillier, president of the Medical Bureau of Lourdes, an average of fifty-seven pilgrims per year claimed to have undergone a cure during the years 1858 to 1914, an era when the annual run of pilgrims was 5,600. That's a one-in-a-hundred shot, pretty decent odds. But the number of cures during the period 1914 to 1928 fell to one in seven hundred pilgrims; for

1928 to 1947, it was one in sixteen hundred. Today, the odds are infinitesimal. You'd think that even the most hardened gambler would pass on such a long shot.

And yet they keep coming, more and more every season, filling up their jugs, splashing in the baths. Don't they know the age of miracles is over?

Two reasons immediately suggest themselves for Lourdes' enduring allure. The first, as we shall see, is that Lourdes today is more than just a city of miracles: it is the city of the sick. The second is that pilgrims to Lourdes have maintained a healthy skepticism. Skepticism? Wouldn't "credulity" better describe the attitude of people who come here hoping that somehow a bit of water is going to cure their diabetes or make them see again? But no, skepticism is the word. The pilgrims are skeptical of the Church's reluctance to recognize miracles.

Of the thousands of cures the waters of Lourdes are popularly claimed to have effected, the Church has deigned to recognize only sixty-six as miraculous. The fortunate sixty-six and the details of their cases are on display in a little photo gallery tucked away in the arcades on the right side of the esplanade: from Catherine Latapie (diagnosis: ulnar paralysis due to traumatic elongation of the brachial plexus) who in March 1858 put her paralyzed hand into the spring and immediately felt the life returning; to Jean-Pierre Bély, crippled for years by disseminated sclerosis, who arrived in Lourdes on a stretcher in October 1987 and left three days later on his feet. (He didn't report the miracle to the Medical Bureau for nearly a year, partly because he was ashamed that he had been cured when others had not.)

But you only need to chat with the pilgrims to know that the sixty-six officially recognized *miraculés* are only the tip of an iceberg. Other accounts abound. Naturally, a good many are apocryphal, of dubious verity, or colored by an optimism born of desperation (there is no shortage of testimonials in the basilica for "expected" cures). On the other hand, there are plenty of soundly documented cases for which the only adequate word seems to be "miraculous."

Consider the testimony of Jean-Pierre Bély, a man who had been unable even to sit up for eighteen months prior to visiting Lourdes and receiving the sacrament of the sick:

"There I am on my bed, happy, a little euphoric. . . . That is when a sensation of cold came over me. . . . My jacket was put on my shoulders, but I became more and more cold. A penetrating cold envelopes me. Someone gives me a blanket, but nothing can stop this sensation of cold. A hot water bottle is slid under my covers. …Then, slowly, the cold diminishes in intensity, and it is replaced by a warmth that is at first gentle. I close my eyes while thinking that I am going to be able to go to sleep. This sensation of heat goes through all my body, starting at my feet and climbing up the spinal column. The heat increases a degree at a time, and quickly becomes difficult to bear. Instinctively, I push the covers to the foot of the bed and with a hand I put the hot water bottle aside. I then discover that I am seated on the edge of my bed, astonished and surprised to have made these gestures with such ease, while that same morning, it had been difficult to hold in my hands a small missal. I stay there seated, trying to understand what is happening to me. …"

What was happening to Monsieur Bély was a miracle. It was not promptly hailed as one, however. Lourdes does not operate that way. Instead, his case was monitored by his own doctor, his neurologist, the head of the University Hospital of Poitiers and the International Medical Committee of Lourdes for a period of nearly twelve years. The Committee didn't hand down its cautious decision until 1998: "It is possible to conclude with a good margin of probability that M. Bély suffered an organic infection of the type multiple sclerosis in a severe and advanced stage of which sudden cure during pilgrimage to Lourdes corresponds with a fact unusual and inexplicable to all the knowledge of science."

One may ascribe this cure to psychosomatic causes, the power of prayer, the intervention of the Blessed Virgin or the agency of pixies. The inescapable fact remains that such events occur at Lourdes with a certain regularity. "And if it can happen to him …" reasons the pilgrim.

The recent decline in the incidence of miracles indicates not a reduced efficacy of Lourdes' particular magic, so much as the fact that Lourdes sets its standards for miracles so high. From the very outset, Lourdes answered the scorn of the secular world by inviting it to come see for itself. Even that godless creature Zola was given the run of the place (though, in the event, he betrayed the trust of his hosts). A Lourdes Medical Bureau was founded as early as 1884, with the mission of providing preliminary diagnoses so that claims of cures would have a medical foundation. Since 1954, the International Medical Committee, a body that includes non-Christian physicians, has acted as a higher court to judge cases sent up by the Medical Bureau. Before a miracle is ever proclaimed, the case must pass before the eyes of dozens of doctors. The conditions a cure must satisfy are precise and stringent. There must be a previous, complete diagnosis of an actual illness. The prognosis should be clear cut and possibly terminal within a short time. The cure should be sudden, without convalescence, complete from the beginning and definitive. Any treatment prescribed must not be considered as the cause of the cure, or even of favoring it. It is—excuse me—a miracle that any cure meets these extraordinary standards.

Yet while Lourdes is to be admired for exposing its claims to the full light of science, the policy is sometimes taken to perverse extremes, as in the case of the quadriplegic woman who recovered after taking a bath, save for one hand that remained paralyzed. The verdict? An incomplete cure. When it plays by the rules of science rather than faith, religion assumes a defensive posture. It even seems at times that the Church is embarrassed by the miracles, inexplicable, pre-modern things that they are.

Happily, the pilgrims still know a miracle when they see one.

There are other sorts of miracles that occur in Lourdes, however, not as flashy as the blind seeing or the lame walking, but no less real. They are the primary reason why pilgrims keep flocking in even as the net miracle rate declines.

In her book, *Lourdes: City of the Sick*, Doctor Catherine Watling tells the story of Con Brannigan, a former shepherd who has been utterly crippled by multiple sclerosis. He is now confined to a hospital where he "stares at the same piece of wall all day, every day." Knowing that Con has no interest in religion, Watling is puzzled when the parish priest suggests she take Con to Lourdes. Then she realizes that he is simply proposing "the only type of holiday possible for Con Brannigan." So she and Con go off to Lourdes, with surprising results. It is not that Con leaps from his wheelchair and starts turning somersaults. He doesn't even find faith in God. But for the first time in years, he smiles and laughs. He is on a trip, after all, meeting new people, participating to the extent that he can in the world of the mobile. In Lourdes he is tended to, taken out and shown around. In the few years that remain to him, Con's trip to Lourdes is the one thing he has to look forward to, and to look fondly back upon in the course of a long, lonely year.

There are tens of thousands of Cons: the sick and the elderly—especially those without families—whose "only possible holiday" is a trip to Lourdes. And Lourdes gives its all for them, from the moment they arrive at the airport or railroad station. The sick are the first to be welcomed, the first to be blessed, and the first to be offered the Sacrament. In processions, it is always the wheelchairs and stretchers that lead the way and take the places closest to the altar while the sound stand in silence behind.

Sickness, in Lourdes, is an honored state, for the sick here are not simply individuals with infirmities, they are The Sick who Christ called and blessed and healed. I have said that Lourdes can be thought of as the stage for a Christian drama. That drama is the enactment on earth of Jesus' word that in the Kingdom of Heaven the last shall be first. There is nothing sanctimonious or condescending in this. All understand their role in the ritual. The volunteers come here prepared to serve; the sick, to be served. The unanticipated consequence is that Lourdes, drizzly, dolorous, Virgin-ridden Lourdes, is a very cheerful place. One of the most cheerful on earth, in my experience.

"Sickness" in Lourdes is as normal as health. Mentally handicapped adults walk in the processions arm-in-arm with their families and caregivers. In the town, where the streets are lined with red wheelchair-paths, groups of malades sit laughing in bistros. The underground basilica, the huge new Church of Saint Bernadette and the hostels of the Sanctuary are all built to accommodate wheelchairs and stretchers. After a few days, I grow so used to the sight of disability that my perceptions become inverted: I take a baby stroller for a wheelchair. I see a woman holding her husband tenderly by the stump of his arm, then realize he is simply holding his arm behind his back.

The parade of sickness through Lourdes today is nothing compared to what it was one hundred years ago, when so many disfiguring and virulent diseases lay beyond the reach of medicine, when public hygiene was still in its infancy and antibiotics were not yet widely available. Yet it seems that as medical knowledge has advanced, our tolerance of disease has diminished. We do not like to admit pain and disability into our sterile, orderly world; they embarrass us. So we close our eyes to them or put them somewhere out of the way. Lourdes breaks down the walls that are built around the sick, creating a world where disease and disability are not sentences of exile.

One afternoon, I go to see the Cité St. Pierre, in the green hills above the town. This is another of Lourdes' new vocations, a residence where the poor and the poor in spirit can stay for a nominal price. The shuttle bus is packed with folk from Waterford and I find myself wedged in among three jolly nurses, Mary, Maureen and Maire.

"We're here with 110 invalids, it's our one day off, and look at this one, still in her uniform," says Maire of Maureen. "Me, I'm traveling incognito."

Mary is concerned whether the mass she has ordered will be said.

"Look, they've given me the card, but they didn't even ask me the name of the person it's for. They just took my money."

"I suppose you have to fill the card in yourself, Mary," reasons Maureen.

"Sure you're right, but I'm just thinking, if I'd done that in Waterford, they'd have writ the person's name down in a book, wouldn't they have?"

"Well, I'm certain they would have, but we're not in Waterford, are we?"

Before Mary can respond to this rhetorical question, Maire interjects with another:

"Will wonders never cease?"

She is pointing out the window of the bus. We look and see camels grazing and languishing on the Pyrenean hillside. They look quite at home. There are trucks scattered about the meadow. The circus has come to Lourdes.

Cité St. Pierre's motto is *Paix Silence Paix*. Peace Silence and, once more, Peace. There are moss-covered rocks, old birch, fields of grass (including tall stuff that's been left to grow). The place is tended, but not overly. The birds are deafening.

I stroll up the hill with Mary, her brother Michael and their two companions, Anne and Jimmy. We're on our way to see a replica of the chapel in the countryside where Bernadette the shepherdess used to take her flocks. Michael's a chatty one. As we go, he keeps stating the obvious to his chum.

"Oh, there's some nice trees over there, Jimmy. You don't see ones like that in Ireland. . . . There's the little chapel up ahead, we'll be there in no time. . . . Lovely flowers these ones are. . . . It's a little steep, this bit, Jimmy. . . ."

Several minutes go by before it dawns on me that Jimmy is blind.

Fire

Lourdes is always on fire. In front of the Grotto stands a tree of candles. Near the baths there are "silos" full of candles dedicated by pilgrims. In the nightly procession, pilgrims carry candles in little paper holders. There are so many candles that they can't all be allowed to burn at once or the basilica might go up in smoke. So pilgrims at the Grotto are "invited" to light their candle, hold it as they make their prayer, then extinguish it and lay it in a basket. The Sanctuary assures us that all these candles "will be relit during the winter months, thus prolonging your prayer during your absence." The fires of Lourdes never stop burning.

Candles are one of the few things you can buy within the Sanctuary. The big yellowy ones range from about four to fifty pounds. The pilgrims who splash out 800 francs on one of them can often be seen doing a victory lap of the esplanade carrying the monster on their shoulders before they take it to the silos. There are smaller candles for sale, too. White, with a tinge of blue at the base. These are tall as well, about three feet high, but slender.

The silos stand between the Grotto and the baths. They are corrugated-iron sheds with rings to hold the candles upright and metal trays beneath to catch the wax. The candles burn in dutiful rows. On a sign near the candles a prayer is written in six languages. The English reads: "Like Bernadette with her candle. / Here I am Mary. / I entrust you with my intentions. / Stir up in me faith hope and love. / Help me to bear your light to the world.

Candles have resonance in Lourdes. Once, when Bernadette was praying at the Grotto in her customary trance, the crowd noticed that the flames of her candle were licking her hands. A doctor who was on the scene rather ostentatiously pushed his way to the front to time the phenomenon. Afterwards, he studied the girl's hands but found no injury. The incident is immortalized among the stained glass windows of the basilica, an allegory of Science confounded by Grace. The doctor looks as stunned by the evidence of his watch as doubting Thomas by the evidence of his fingers in Christ's wound.

Pilgrims like to "personalize" the big candles with their signatures, a photo, a symbol of their group. An Irish group has signed their names in black pen the length of this one. Right now, it's Kathleen Ryan who's melting away. On another candle is taped a photograph of Bernadette. The tape covers her eyes, her stubborn peasant eyes that saw what they saw, whatever anyone said. In a few days the candle will burn down to the level of the photo and Bernadette will turn to carbon.

A Filipina girl cautiously lights her candle from one that is already burning. She lowers it into place with both hands, her lips moving in tentative prayer. She is trying to find the right way to do this. A young man, big and blond, stands close by a stall of candles, steadying his camera. He aims across the top, shooting to catch as many flickering wicks as he can. He has a professional camera and it will take a lovely picture. It will look like hope, harmony and peace. But mostly hope.

Further on, in the very last silo, old candles are burning down to a pool of flaming liquid. They have lost all semblance of order and are

becoming mere fire. The candle man comes with his dark goggles and long iron poker to subdue the unruly flames.

My fourth night in Lourdes it rained. It rained quite heavily in the afternoon, then settled to a persistent drizzle by evening. From the ramparts of the basilica, the old castle looked like the Chateau d'If poking out of an ocean of mist. I had decided to watch the rosary procession that night from above, and I was starting to wonder if it might not be canceled. This was hardly weather to be taking sick people out in. But then I heard it, from half a mile away, that persistent call of "Ave . . . Ave. . . . Aa-ve Ma-rii-aaa," and soon a candlelit river was flowing before me. The rain couldn't keep them away; they had simply equipped themselves with umbrellas. The ones who couldn't be bothered with umbrellas held candles anyway and the rain did not extinguish them. Fire and water had called a truce for the evening.

The rosary procession and the late-night crowds around the Grotto had quickly become my favorite part of Lourdes. The afternoon procession, held under the auspices of the Father and the Son, was a good show with a dash of pomp, but after a couple of times I could take it or leave it. The candlelit evening procession in honor of Mary, however, I never missed. Claire, a sweet young thing from Normandy who thought me rather odd, asked once if it was the spiritual atmosphere that attracted me to the rosary processions. I had to think for a moment before I told her that, no, it was the *secular* atmosphere. The rosary procession was simplicity itself: only a cross borne by one man, an icon of the Virgin, and the people. Holding hands. Pushing wheelchairs or sitting in them. Singing the old songs. Relighting candles on a windy night.

If one image could express the gentle mood of the rosary procession, it is this: a tall young man stands on the road, beneath the trees in the esplanade. He is looking up into the gathering dark, lost, it seems, in reflection. A woman, probably his mother, kneels in front of him. And the entire pro- cession waits patiently behind till she has finished tying his shoelace.

But on this night, no one stopped to look up into the rainy sky. The pilgrims made their way up the esplanade and down the esplanade and into the square before the Basilica of the Rosary, following the voices on the loudspeakers, alternating songs with the muttered recital, easy as breathing, of the Ave Maria in every language under heaven. *Béni soit, benedetto sia*, blessed be the fruit of thy womb, *le fruit de vos entrailles, il frutto di tuo seno, el fruto de tu vientre*. The lovely soprano filled the sanctuary with the bright liquid of her voice. And the rain kept falling.

Gradually, the procession reached the square. The sick, in their wheel-chairs and chariots, were rolled up to the steps of the church. No more than twenty tonight; it really was that cold. Then one more rickshaw careened in, holding a long and elegantly reclining woman who looked, from a distance, like Bette Davis. As the healthy took their ranks behind, the square bloomed with tiny flames and umbrellas in a thousand colors and patterns.

Squinting down over the field of candles through rain-splashed glasses, I saw a tapestry shot through with gold thread, the twinkling embers of a burnt-out forest fire, the torches of an advancing army. Kosovo was in the news those days, tales of villages in flames, but this wasn't the same element. In Kosovo, the fire of fear was burning. The fire in Lourdes was the soft, contained fire of hope. Then I understood that part of the magic of Lourdes was to tame the forces that frighten us, transform them into symbols of God and the Holy Mother's love. Like Bernadette, the pilgrims cup fire in their hands without being burnt.

The service was nearly over when a figure I recognized stepped out of the crowd. He was a young black man with dreadlocks, whom I had noticed in the afternoon procession, pushing a German or Dutch man in a wheelchair. I had seen him again since. He was hard to miss, with his low-crotched jeans and long hair.

Tonight, however, he was decked out in a formal brown jacket and pants. In his left hand he held a large candle; in his right, a round silver object. Evidently he had a part in the program. Slowly, with the assurance of an acolyte, he climbed the stairs of the basilica, his arms extended. He sank to his knees, facing the choir, then turned his face up to the rain.

"What a beautiful gesture," I thought.

The security guards thought otherwise.

One moved in directly from the wings, ready to remove this uninvited presence by the swiftest means. A priest intervened to slow the guard, but by then the young man was rising to his feet and heading for the choir. Now priest and the security guard both made a grab at him. The young man shook them off and began to shout. Just at that moment, as it happened, the guest readers stepped forward to bid their goodnights and the little drama fell into the background. The priest settled things down and the young man was allowed to exchange the gesture of peace with the clergy and choir.

He stayed on after, complaining to the guards and the priest with gentle persistence. I caught only snatches of his labored French. *"Vous avez oubliez,"* he kept repeating, though I couldn't make out what it was he felt they had forgotten. The priest finally threw up his hands and strode into the church. The guards walked the man to the gate, one on either side, as the still-lit candle bobbed in his hand.

I caught up with him at a souvenir shop where he was addressing a few of the pilgrims from Wexford. A couple of them could barely contain their anger as they turned away. I asked him why he had done it.

"The music," he said. "It was the music. Six days now I have been here, and every time, when I heard that music, I've wanted to praise God. Tonight, he made me do it. The Holy Spirit made me do it. He made me a fool in the eyes of the world." He spoke in clear, slightly accented English. He was taller than I had realized, and I found myself looking up into his moist, unblinking eyes.

"I have discovered myself here. I have discovered my calling. I've learned that I have been hiding from myself. But now I know that I am chosen. I am a saint and I must listen to my father and do his bidding. My father talks to me twenty-four hours a day. I hear his voice always. I heard it in the music tonight."

He spoke slowly, not expecting to be believed. There was still that reasoning, almost pleading, note to his voice, like the man who stops you on the street with his hard luck story. And then he showed me his hands, still speckled with wax, and two marks that could have been cigarette burns in the center of his palms. His voice dropped.

"I was crucified on May 5. Two policemen assaulted me. They came to my apartment and asked for my papers. When I couldn't show them, they beat me. Since then, I have had these marks. I am the crucified one."

He was in awe of his own suffering, of the magnitude of his calling. He kept his hands displayed so that I could look, confirm. I felt scared for him then, because I am a child of my time, and saints and prophets make me nervous. My sole, sensible concern was that he not get in trouble with the authorities here in the city of Our Lady.

"I do not care about danger," he sneered. "I must do as the Spirit teaches me. I must speak as the Spirit speaks through me, even if *your* society cannot hear. If you take my life, I will only go to my Father. Jesus said, 'He who saves his life shall lose it. And he who loses his life will be saved.'"

It was another line from the Bible, "Am I my brother's keeper?" that was running through my mind. I felt somehow responsible for this man, yet I had no idea what I could do for him. Should I pretend to believe him? Try to reason with him? Take him to a doctor? I didn't know. In the end I wished him Peace and left him to his visions. He made the sign of the cross on my forehead with his waxy thumb. I hurried across the street in the rain.

The Blue Madonna

"Tutto questo—mi—ripugna," says Claudio, spelling out each syllable.

Claudio is an imposing fellow, with his animated salt-and-pepper eyebrows, and though normally droll and kindly, he is capable of verbal violence.

On this occasion he has chosen the verb *ripugnare*, which translated directly into English comes out rather clumsily as "All of this is repugnant to me," but has in Italian an acerbic directness: "All of this repugns me."

We are standing in front of a typical souvenir shop in the boulevard de la Grotte. Claudio is glowering at the 3-D posters whose images change with your point of view: Jesus on the cross opens then closes his eyes; Bernadette bows to the Virgin; the Pope appears full on, then in profile, as if in a wanted poster; the faces of Jesus and Mary alternate with a scary three-eyed mid-stage. But Claudio's repugnance stretches beyond these manifestations of kitsch to embrace the whole commercial ghetto that lines the streets to the Grotto. The sign outside one souvenir shop sums it up: *"Tourisme et Réligion."*

The Musée de Bernadette has a revealing model of Lourdes-and-vicinity in 1858. There is the old town, huddled close around the castle; the mysterious Grotto, far beyond the river; and in between, several square miles of farmland just waiting to be snapped up and transformed into the Las Vegas of prayer. Most of the land from the Gave to the Grotto was embraced by the Sanctuary, but there was still plenty of room by the river for hotels, shops and restaurants to metastasize. From a developer's point of view, the Immaculate Conception could not have chosen a better place to appear to Bernadette Soubirous.

Claudio is not the only Catholic to be "repugned" by the commercialism of Lourdes; many are turned off by what they see as a proliferation of money changers in the temple. The Sanctuary takes itself off the hook by pointing out that the money changers aren't actually *in* the temple, they're outside the gates, beyond Our Lady's jurisdiction. The Sanctuary itself is pure: the only use you'll find for money there is to buy a mass. And, in any case, as the official guide book reminds us, "The commercial and souvenir shops are necessary, as people do not want to forget the graces of God received and make them known to others."

Of all the items purchased by pilgrims to keep them in mind of the graces of God received and make them known to others, the champion is the water bottle. After all, how can a pilgrim come back from *Lourdes*, for God's sake, without water for everyone he knows? To service this need, the souvenir shops provide a whole range of containers. There is the petite perfume-bottle style in plastic or glass (sometimes bearing the provocative legend, *Eau de Lourdes*), the syrup-bottle type with corks and the canteen style with straps. The most common model is squarish, functional, and made of clear plastic. It comes in five sizes, from a half-liter (personal use) to ten liters (parish size), and generally carries a picture of Bernadette kneeling before the Virgin with the upper basilica poking up anachronistically in the background.

A more elegant container, better suited for gift-giving, is shaped in the form of Our Lady, with a blue twist-off crown. She has a blue sash on her dress, sometimes holds a golden rosary, and comes in four sizes, from about six inches to a foot high. The Blue Madonna, as I think of her, is made of a clear, but slightly cloudy plastic, and though I will be accused of irony, I must say that she is as beautiful as plastic gets. It is touching to see a pilgrim at the taps filling a row of Blue Madonnas, each one as upright and humble as a prayer. The Madonna is also available in white plastic and glass, but these materials are not as suggestive as the cloudy plastic. Another design adds a kneeling Bernadette at the Virgin's feet, but this is an awkward composition, difficult to pack, and evidently not a big seller.

Apart from water containers, other items on sale in this precinct of Moloch include Lourdes letter-openers, fridge magnets, church keys, candles, mints, rosaries, eau de toilette (not to be confused with eau de Lourdes), baseball caps, key rings, wind-ups that play Ave Maria, and the inevitable floating pen (turn it over and the Virgin rises from the Grotto up to heaven). All items are available in just the size, color and language you were looking for at the queen of souvenir shops, the Palais de Rosaire, a grand emporium that, to its everlasting credit, does *not* carry those 3-D posters that morph as you walk by, and is also about the only tourist establishment in Lourdes that closes on Sundays.

With all respect to Claudio, I like the shops. Isn't there something medieval in their hurly-burly of religious commercialism? It's too bad they don't sell relics.

If you wonder how the 17,000 citizens of Lourdes put up with the five million pilgrims who descend on their town each year, the answer is that much of the time they don't need to. Lourdes is, in effect, two cities. The one we think of when we say "Lourdes" is the low city, the city of Our Lady, which lies on an east-west axis and comprises the Sanctuary and the commercial streets that feed into it. This is the city of tourists and pilgrims. Above it reposes the high city, the proud, ancient city of Lourdes, which runs its own way on a north-south axis. This is the city where people live, buy cars, rent dirty videos and get divorced; where men sit in bars watching the tennis from Roland Garros or go out to cheer for the local rugby side (one year, all but one member of the French national rugby team hailed from Lourdes); where you can buy books that do not have a saint on the cover; and where the Regional Association of Firemen holds its annual fair with miniature fire trucks and paintings by school kids. It's also where the Lourdais go to church—those who do. There are a few hotels in this part of town, as well as the train station, but there is nothing really to keep travelers up here, so before long they all roll down to the Grotto.

It's not a bad place, this other Lourdes, and it's a shame that most tourists don't get to see it, though the Lourdais probably prefer it that way. It allows them to maintain the illusion that their prosperous, raffish little town and the tourist hell-hole bearing the same name exist in different universes. I stayed in a pension up by the train station. After I started volunteering, I could have moved to cheaper dorm lodgings near the Sanctuary. But I preferred to maintain some distance, mental and physical, from the city of Our Lady. In the high city I could go to the market and buy a loaf of bread and a wedge of goat cheese, pick up some fruit from the cheerful old trollop with the bad teeth and dirty hands who always gave me more than I asked for (and charged me for it). I could sit in the park with the local derelicts, then take my *Herald Tribune* to a teashop and never know I was in Lourdes, except for the parties of nuns who occasionally stopped to peek in the window at the cakes.

One Sunday afternoon, I watched the local motorcycle club roar down the main street under police escort in a hellacious stream that took as long to pass as any rosary procession and drowned out the bells of the parish church with its thunder. This too was Lourdes.

Eucharistic Procession

Four-thirty. Minutes to go before the Eucharistic procession. The banners of the basilicas of the Eternal City—San Paolo, San Giovanni, San Pietro, Santa Maria Maggiore—glint in the sun that has (miraculously) succeeded a long day's drizzle. The standard-bearers are receiving marching orders from their gravel-voiced captain.

"No no no. *Balance! Balance!* Look, take it like this or you'll end up on your backside."

He stands behind one of the standard-bearers, a slip of a girl. The base of the standard is set in a leather holster just above her crotch, and she's holding it low, like a caber she's preparing to toss. The captain reaches around to adjust her grip.

"Stand straight. Raise your hands. Don't lean back. That's it."

At the far end of the esplanade, the choir is warming up, trying to really grab the high note of the "Ho-saaaa-na" by the throat. At the portable altar in the center of the plaza, three sets of pristine-white priests practice maneuvers with ponderous urns. Each gripping a handle, they run the urns up and down the stairs of the altar, up and down till it looks like they're in training for the next Vatican Games. Four men in black, suited up like pallbearers, heft a life-size cross. A matching set of white nurses, holding banners depicting the four evangelists, wait behind.

The Eucharistic procession is one of Lourdes' long-running daily highlights. It is a crowning moment for the official pilgrimage groups, who turn out in full strength behind the banner of their parish or diocese or organization. It gathers the various national tribes together beneath the single canopy of Catholic worship. It offers a bright and shimmering spectacle, pleasing to God and man. It answers those who criticize Lourdes for being too Mary-centric, since the highlight of the procession is the elevation of the Host, the Body of Christ. And it has been, even more than the baths, the scene of miracles over the years.

There was the legendary John Traynor of Liverpool: riddled with bullets in the Great War, epileptic, incontinent, confined to a wheelchair for three years. The doctors had tried to have him put off the train on the way to Lourdes, convinced he was about to give up the ghost. But Traynor survived the journey and was borne on a stretcher to the Eucharistic procession. As he saw the Host passing before him, he suddenly experienced feeling in his right arm—so much feeling that he broke the fastenings on his stretcher. This was miracle enough, considering that the nerves of his right shoulder had been severed by a bullet eight years before and the arm paralyzed ever since, but more remarkable still was Traynor's sudden conviction that he could walk. He tried then and there to get to his feet, but the brancardiers, assuming he was hysterical, administered a sedative injection. This only served to delay the fulfillment of the miracle. First thing next morning, Traynor leaped out of bed, dodged the hospital staff, and sprinted several hundred yards over gravel to prostrate himself in prayer at the Grotto.

And Alice Couteault: suffering from multiple sclerosis, afflicted for more than a year by a spastic gait, she too had to be carried to the Eucharistic procession. A few minutes after receiving the Sacrament, she found herself able to walk normally again. Her husband, who was waiting on the platform at Poitiers to take her home, passed out cold when she skipped down from the train and ran to meet him.

And the thrice-miracled Marie Bigot: for the two years prior to her pilgrimage in 1953, she had been blind, deaf and paralyzed on her right side, but during the Eucharistic procession, she felt a cramp in her right foot. Within hours, she had recovered full use of her right arm and leg. She returned to Lourdes the following October, primarily so that the Medical Bureau could monitor her condition, though of course she once again attended the procession. This time, she suddenly found that she could hear the singing of Ave Maria. And Our Lady of Lourdes wasn't finished with her yet. A few days later, as she lay on the night train home, enjoying the sounds around her for the first time in years, she opened her eyes and saw the lights of a station flashing by.

It strikes me, as I retell these stories, that I want very deeply for them to be true. That if someone offered to debunk them, I would say, "Thank you, but I'd prefer you didn't." Some part of me clings to the hope that stories can end this way, that tragedy can give way to comedy. Cardinal Newman once remarked, "A miracle is no argument to one who is de-liberately, and on principle, an atheist," but I can't agree. My own atheism lives happily alongside a belief in miracles. I don't necessarily find a miracle to be a convincing argument for the Christian faith, but it still makes a case for the power of the unknown. It suggests that for all we know, we may still know nothing and this thought gives me comfort.

In his novel about Lourdes, Émile Zola fictionalized the cases of three famous miraculous cures. He had them all relapse into sickness on their return home, thus neatly "proving" his thesis that the *miraculées* were only hysterics duped into a temporary recovery by Lourdes' hyper-religious atmosphere. The only problem—as Zola well knew—was that the real people he based his characters on never did relapse. Neither did Marie Bigot, Alice Couteault or John Traynor, who returned to England a healthy man, took a job pitching two-hundred-pound bags of coal, and continued to collect a full veteran's pension for the rest of his days because no mechanism existed to rescind the pension of someone who had been deemed permanently disabled.

Yet the guardians of the Sanctuary, forever sensitive to accusations of superstition and mumbo jumbo, continue to exercise extreme discretion in dealing with Eucharistic procession miracles. Thus, when blind sixteen-year-old René Scher turned to his companion during a procession in 1966 and said, "I can see," he was hustled off to the Medical Bureau as unceremoniously as a fur protester at a fashion show. Scher, who had been "permanently" blind since a childhood operation, first saw a white flash that he took to be the holy wafer, then the dark masses of the trees overhead. By the time he reached the Medical Bureau, enough sight had returned for him to pick out distant objects at the request of the doctors, who, unfortunately for the pilgrims in attendance that day, were the only ones to enjoy this edifying spectacle.

Funny place, Lourdes.

BUT THE BELLS HAVE STARTED TO RING, and a race is on to get wheelchairs in position. The sick who want only to watch the procession need to be parked in the shade before the esplanade can be closed off. Urn-bearers, evangelists and cross-toters have to squeeze their way through the Dutch wheelchair squadrons. A Spanish man suddenly shows up at the barrier pushing a shopping cart piled high with ten-liter jugs of miracle water. Wheelchairs start to back up behind him as the brancardier remonstrates with him in French.

The procession has assembled across from the Grotto. At a word it sets off, hospital beds and wheelchairs leading the way. The infirm come rolling in waves across the bridge, some holding canes in their laps like the instruments of their martyrdom. A gray-bearded Down's syndrome man-child gazes from side to side with unguarded curiosity. An old French woman leans her chin on one hand and waves with the other, like the Queen Mum in her royal car. A nun leans forward, tense and uncomfortable at being served. A fellow in a tartan cap stuck with Lourdes pins counts his rosary. One woman suddenly goes into a panic, takes over the wheel from her caregiver and steers herself out of the cavalcade.

There are patients laid out on their backs beneath many-colored quilts, others zipped up to the neck in cocoons. Two obese women hold hands as they roll along. Often the pushers look older and not much sturdier than the pushed: a man with one arm pulls a rickshaw; a grandfather supports the head of a long-haired young girl as he guides her chair.

After the sick come the bishops and priests, the doctors and nurses and hospitalers. There are standard-bearers not only from Rome, but from Dunkerque and Balsall Heath and the Women's Catholic League and Cloyne (and who would have dreamed there could be so many people in wheelchairs in Cloyne?), then the acolytes with their urns, the nurses with their evangelists, and the black-suits bearing their cross. The

 bishop who will perform the mass paces beneath a silk canopy like an Oriental potentate in an Italian opera. Last come the silent thousands, the ambulatory, the common pilgrims.

Looking down from the ramparts, I think of the stained-glass windows in the Rosary Basilica that depict scenes from the life of Bernadette, and the "common people" who crowd the edges of those scenes. The pilgrims crossing the bridge right now in their drab brown slacks, black skirts, blue jeans, their pumps and sensible moccasins and Reeboks, their matching blue shoulder bags (courtesy of "Leisure Tour Pilgrimages"), their baseball caps and cheap silk scarves, their green and red vinyl windbreakers— these are today's common people. They come from many nations, but they all look much the same. Even pilgrims who have come from the exotic Philippines, Singapore, Japan.

They proceed along the arcades, then turn into the long avenue that runs from the esplanade to Porte St. Michel. Tourists and pilgrims, come to watch or bear witness, line both sides of the avenue observing the simple spectacle of a mass of people walking.

The loudspeakers send out the voice of the choir. The procession continues to the top of the avenue, circles the crucifix and heads back down the other side towards the esplanade. Here come the cross, the urns, the evangelists. Here's the bishop beneath his canopy, the standard-bearers, the priests, the doctors and nurses. Here they all come, led by a single hospitaler who draws them forward like a mime pulling an invisible rope.

All the while, the run-on rhythm of recitation provides the bass line. A verse from the Gospels. A petition to God. A new voice, a new language. French English Italian Spanish German Dutch. Then a Christe Eleison, a Hosanna, an Ave Maria, and on to the next hymn.

The wheelchairs and their occupants are steered to the foot of the altar.

"You are present among us now as you were on the roads of Galilee," sounds a woman's voice over the loudspeakers. "Lord that I may walk."

"Lord that I may walk on your way," a man responds.

The standard-bearers climb the ramps to the upper basilica and drape their flags over the balustrades. The banners of the basilicas of the Eternal City—San Paolo, San Giovanni, San Pietro, Santa Maria Maggiore— hang proudly back-to-front.

"Lord that I may hear."

"Lord that I may hear your Word."

The protagonists of the mass with their urns and banners and cross, the bishop beneath his canopy, take their places around the altar. The acolytes tip their urns and the sound of running water is heard over the loudspeakers. Slowly the rest of the procession fills the square, row on row, thousands deep, expectant.

"Lord that I may see."

"Lord that I may see your light."

The roof of the bishop's canopy is a tapestry sparkling with wheat and grapes, pools of water, urns of flame. The white-clad priests kneel hieratic, like donors in a Renaissance painting. The bishop raises the golden disc of the ciborium and slowly turns. Silence falls over the vast square. The crowd cross themselves or drop to one knee at the sight of the Body of Christ. Priests fan out among the sick to administer the Sacrament.

Directly below me, near the benches, is a child of two. His mother, who holds him on a lead, is engaged in prayer. I can see the bulge on his crown from here, his tonsure of fine blond hair. A bird has caught his attention. He points at it and squawks, attempting language. His voice is the only human sound rising from the vast plaza. He spreads his arms and toddles after the bird, his leash slowly paying out as he moves away from the bench. Then his mother decides he has gone far enough and gently reels him back. The boy leans forward with a breathless squeal, defying gravity.

A bell rings and the service is over. The crowd exhales. They all take off in the direction of the Grotto, racing to line up for the baths, to grab a place at the taps.

Water

The Lady told Bernadette: "Go and drink at the spring and wash yourself there." The taps and baths allow all pilgrims to follow this injunction (though somehow the command to "Eat the grass for the sinners" has never found its way into the ritual practice of the Sanctuary).

Bernadette's spring burbles out 27,000 gallons of water a day. It's an awesome amount of liquid for a little girl to have drawn out of the ground with her fingernails, but that's part of the miracle: twentieth-century demand was anticipated right from the start. The water is retained in two underground reservoirs and to ensure its equitable and convenient distribution there is a long row of taps in the wall alongside the Grotto. Pilgrims are encouraged to drink, wash and fill their containers with water from the taps, though they are enjoined not to take "excessive amounts."

The Sanctuary assures us, "The spring water of Massabielle is not magic water: analysis of the water shows it to be ordinary drinkable water without any special properties." This was a big letdown for the mayor of Lourdes at the time of the apparitions, dashing his visions of a spa and a bottling factory. Lourdes water, far from being "magic," isn't even "holy water"; that is to say, it is not blessed by a priest. Initially, the distinction between the holy and the merely miraculous was lost on me. Anxious not to offend religious sensibilities I used the taps sparingly, sneaking discrete sips. But when I observed the casualness with which the water is treated by believers—other brancardiers would fill up their empty water bottles with it on a hot day, or wash their grimy hands after running out the rope at a procession—I began to enjoy the taps. I can attest that the water, aside from working wonders, is cold, tasty and refreshing.

While the focus of the pilgrim to Lourdes is the spring and its miraculous waters, there is another conspicuous source of water nearby: the River Gave. I'd encountered the Gave already on this trip in a town called

Lescar, once a stopping place on the road to Santiago de Compostela. There, as here, though the river is not wide, it is strong enough to drown a man, and it was the custom once of wily boatmen to capsize boatloads of pilgrims, sparing only their goods from a watery end. Pilgrimage is a more civilized activity today than it has been.

The Gave is a noisy little river. Shallow and swift flowing, it doesn't look like much of a threat to mankind. Surely drinking from it would bring greater harm than falling in it, as the aroma suggests that the Hôtel de la Solitude and the other establishments upstream have found their own uses for it. (One pilgrim legend holds that it is polluted only where it runs through the town; it turns pure when it passes the Grotto.)

A century ago, a stream flowed into the Gave between the Grotto and the place from which Bernadette saw the apparitions. The asthmatic girl had been ordered by her mother to keep out of the water so she stopped on the far side. The stream, which plays such a central role in the story, disappeared long ago beneath the paving stones because it was limiting access to the Grotto. The Gave was also deemed inconveniently close to the spring, but it is too wide and stubborn to be smothered, so it was rechanneled instead, then left to flow noisily, as it has flowed since some distant Ice Age, down from the Pyrenees to the ocean.

I am disappointed that the Gave is not paid more respect. I realized this one night when I saw a group of worshippers sitting by the river across from the Grotto. They had lit candles and set them in a row atop the retaining wall. The effect was striking, and my first thought was, "How beautiful. They're praying to the river." Obviously I'd spent too much time in Japan, where nature can be prayed to because, of course, they were doing nothing of the sort. They were praying to the Virgin of the Grotto from the place where Bernadette had experienced her last apparition. The Gave was only a prop in their ritual. For the first time, Lourdes exasperated me, though the fault really lay with Christianity and the whole Western way of thought, with its tedious exaltation of the human, and its refusal to concede selfhood or soul to other living beings.

If you back away from the Grotto, back, back, until you are leaning against the wall with the river behind you, then the already subdued human sounds—the mumbled prayers, the wheelchairs sticking to the paving stones, the pilgrims talking low, the "Sssshhh!" over the loudspeakers when people forget that this is a place of prayer—are all immersed and drowned in the restless, restful whisper of the river.

The Hospitalité

After a week in Lourdes, I felt I had some idea of the history of the place and how things worked there. My health had been restored by wonder water, sleep and Ave Marias. I was all set to pitch in and help out. I didn't reflect too deeply on the eccentricity of this impulse. Why I, who have never been generous with my time (or Catholic), should suddenly want to throw myself into the service of Mary was a mystery. Or perhaps it was not so strange at all. I was lonely after my week as a hermit and clearly the remedy for loneliness in Lourdes was to join a work party.

I went to the information office of the Sanctuary, to ask how I could help.

"Help whom?"

"*Les malades.* I would like to help *les malades.*"

The girl at the counter looked at me as though I had asked for directions to the beach. "Did you not come with a pilgrimage?"

"No, by myself."

"Ah, well. Then you must come again, but with a pilgrimage next time."

"But I'm here now."

"Yes, that is evident. But you can't just go and help yourself to an invalid. They already have their helpers, you know."

This was a problem. One notion I had brought to Lourdes with me was that there would be a permanent population of invalids who lived here "to take the waters." Surely the Sanctuary could whip out a directory of malades and set me up with one for a week or two. But the waters of Lourdes are miraculous, not therapeutic. One dip is as good as a thousand (better, probably; a thousand would result in hypothermia). Eventually the girl suggested I try Cité St. Pierre. But there, the woman said sorry, they were already booked solid with volunteers for the year. And that is where matters stood when I went to see my first international mass at the underground basilica.

The Saint Pius X Basilica, as it is properly known, is an echoing, low-ceilinged concrete womb, which the Sanctuary describes—accurately, I would say—as "one of the largest buildings in the world." Indeed, at 14,400 square yards, it's not much smaller than the esplanade itself. It looks more like a sports hall than a place of worship, with its oval form, in-slanting pillars and the velodrome curve of its floor. Though it is neither warm nor intimate, what Saint Pius X has going for it is that it is eminently wheelchair-accessible. The wheelchair-bound can even follow the stations of the cross, the mysteries of the rosary, and the story of Bernadette here, albeit in startling Day-Glo renditions.

They say it seats 12,000, and when I arrived at five to nine, every blessed seat was taken. The wheelchair ranks were stacked, the side chapels jammed. The international mass is one of Lourdes' great set-pieces (the score is available at the bookstore for ten francs), so I should have expected as much. I ended up leaning on a concrete railing, shifting from foot to foot in the circle of Dante's Purgatory reserved for souls who linger too long over their morning coffee.

The standard-bearers for all the parishes in attendance were already parading around the altar as I arrived. Sextilingual announcements were booming out, "Special welcomes today to our guests from Shrewsbury ..." (applause) "from the diocese of Lyon ..." (applause) "from Chicago ..." (riotous applause). Then the music roared in, overwhelming. The robed ones headed for the stage. The show had begun.

And what a show! On either side of the altar, with its looming aluminum Christ, screens flashed translations and highlights, spotlights dazzled the eye, legions of priests modeled their sparkling white and purple robes, censers pumped smoke like dry ice machines. The Youth Corps even *waved their hankies* during the chorus of the Gloria. Had the stage opened up to reveal the Blessed Freddie Mercury, no one would have raised an eyebrow.

A French critic of the sixties, casting a cold eye on *Godspell, Jesus Christ Superstar* and other Christian pop extravaganzas of the era, observed "you don't use holy oil to make mayonnaise." The international mass is pure mayonnaise. Could this have been what Vatican Two had in mind when it

called for "liturgical innovation containing increased amount of spontaneity and informality"? I was trying to take notes, but my coffee and croissant had started to churn in my stomach. At this point, fortunately, the show cut to a commercial break.

Now the video screens showed buff young chaps hammering shingles onto a roof. We were reminded that, thanks to pilgrims like us, new hostels and churches were leaping up all over. Nuns carrying very retro urns began circulating through the crowd to reap donations while the screens invited us "to exchange a gesture of fraternal communion." (Graphic of hands reaching towards each other: *Paix Pace Paz Peace Fried Vried.*)

I flashed a shy glance at the man beside me. Fiftyish, a blue-eyed hawk-nosed fellow wearing a small blue cross on his chest. He extended his hand.

"*Le paix de Christ.*"

He looked me over in a friendly way, trying to pin me down.

"This is your first time in Lourdes?"

"Yes."

"Are you with a group?"

"No."

"*Tout seul?* All alone? In Lourdes?" He shook his head in wonder. "*C'est trop bizarre.*"

He kept looking at my pad, smiling in a way that suggested he knew what I was up to.

"I take it this isn't your first time here?" I asked, in an attempt to divert his attention.

"Twenty years now I have been coming to Lourdes." He gestured to the rows of people in wheelchairs and beds lined up before us. "This is my group. We are from Lyon. My name is Henri."

"Did you all come by train?"

"Yes, by overnight train. We left Saturday night and arrived Sunday morning."

"Isn't that hard on them?"

He shrugged. "They're happy."

A moment went by, then he was at me again.

"Are you a Catholic?"

"No."

"A believer?"

"No."

"Then what are you doing in Lourdes?"

"Just curious."

"*Très bien!*" he said with a laugh. "That is wonderful! Then I hope you have been to the baths? You must go. There's a real feeling of equality there, of humility. Whether you're a believer or not, I think you would learn something. Listen, are you doing anything after mass?"

I was afraid he was going to invite me to bathe with him, but his proposal was more modest.

"If you are interested, I will bring you to see the accueil where we are staying. Just wait till I have taken Communion."

He was back in a moment, smiling as if he had been scoffing paté and crackers. He made a liberal gesture in the direction of the wheelchairs. "*Prenez un malade. N'importe quel malade,*" he said. "Take an invalid. Any invalid." And after a week of scribbling in silence from a guarded distance, I stuck my pen in my pocket and did as I was told. I lucked into a fine, fat old gentleman and the stiff walk uphill to the Accueil Mari St.-Frai where the group was staying taught me why those nuns look so sturdy.

Henri whisked me through the four floors of the accueil, introducing me to everyone we passed along the way: doctors and nurses, clerics and laypersons, sick and well. We popped into the intensive care room, one wall of which was lined with invalids too sick to attend mass: "Georges! Look! It is Bob from Canada. He's come to see you." We stepped out on the rooftop, which is open for soirées and open-air services, weather permitting. As usual, the weather that day was not permitting.

"Henri," I said. "Do you know where I could volunteer to help out?"

"Well, you are welcome to come to us anytime. Just to say hello, or to help, whatever you like. But really, you should ask at the *Hospitalité*."

"The *Hospitalité*?"

THE OFFICE OF THE *HOSPITALITÉ* WAS located in the esplanade near the passage to the Grotto. Some men were standing outside as I approached, laughing and snapping their braces. One, who bore a resemblance to President Milosevic, sported a Spanish flag on his badge. I hazarded a *"Buenos dias."*

"*Buenas tardes,*" he corrected me. "What can we do for you?"

"I want to find out about the Hospitality …"

"*¡Hombre, pase!*" he said, laying a beefy hand on my shoulder. "Come in and meet the boss."

He steered me full-speed through an outer office. The Boss looked up with a grin. He was thick and hale with rosy cheeks and a jutting Teutonic jaw.

"Who is this you're bringing me, Miguel?" he asked in good Spanish.

"This is my friend, Robert."

"From Spain?"

"No, boss. He is from *Ca-na-dá*. He speaks French."

"*Très bien.*" He turned to me. "And you speak English as well?"

"It's my first language, actually. My French isn't so good."

"But you can manage, yes? French is not a difficult language. And we need people who speak English. For how many days are you available?"

"A week," I hazarded.

He rested his chin on his hand a moment, looking me over with a friendly glint in his eye, then scribbled a few lines on a slip of paper and tossed it across the table. It read:

8:30   Men's Baths
13:00   Accueil de Nôtre Dame: Depart Bus Toledo
15:00   Esplanade: Eucharist Procession
19:33   Station: Depart Train Lyon

"Here is your schedule for tomorrow. Miguel, can you make sure Robert knows where to go? And bring him to Pierre for his braces."

My interview was over. The Boss stood up and shook my hand. What had I gotten myself into?

"I'm looking forward to working with you," I managed.

"Oh, you won't be working with me," he laughed. "I go home tomorrow. If you have any questions, Miguel will help you."

Pierre, this week's Number Two, did not think much of Number One's slapdash decision-making process. Tomorrow was Saturday and the next *stage* didn't begin till Monday. Who was going to train me? Couldn't I wait a couple days? And why hadn't I made a proper application from my own country? Where was the letter of reference from my priest? Even as he fussed and clucked, however, he was handing me forms to fill out and peeling off flag stickers for my badge. In five minutes, I was back out in the esplanade, braces in hand. I had entered the service of Our Lady.

All the myriad functions of Lourdes are borne along by the discreet participation of tens of thousands of volunteers. Collectively, they bear the title of "The Hospitality of Our Lady of Lourdes." The Hospitality has two types of members: those who accompany pilgrimages from their home parishes to Lourdes and those who come on their own, ready to fill in where needed. The males among these freelancers assist at the train station and airport during the disembarkation and embarkation of invalids, serve in the men's baths and marshal the daily processions. Women run the women's baths, help out in the accueils and complain that the men get the more interesting jobs.

A period of apprenticeship must be fulfilled before the Hospitality embraces you as a full member. This period is called a *stage* and the apprentice, a *stagiaire*. A stagiaire normally performs a six-day stage once a year, meaning that the Hospitality's personnel turns over at roughly the same rate as the pilgrim population. Each stage includes both on-the-job training in dealing with invalids and class time to study the operation and "message" of Lourdes. You must complete at least three stages before you can request membership in the Hospitality. And while all this may sound rather stiff and hierarchical, it is not. The lowest stage is packed with just-retired gentlemen who may have been here twenty or thirty times as pilgrims, but only now have the leisure to devote a week to a stage. They are perfectly content to share the bottom rung of the ladder with high school students.

A stagiaire is identified by a pin-on badge bearing his or her name, the level of his stage, and little flags to indicate the languages he or she can speak. Flags, naturally, stir passions. The Irish flag, for instance, which the volunteers from the Emerald Isle lobbied hard for, does not indicate fluency in Gaelic; it just shows that the Irish will be damned if they'll wear the Union Jack. My stagiaire friend Miguel couldn't get his hands on a Catalan flag sticker, though his wife, a Hospitality member, wangled one. There are stars-and-stripes stickers too, though I never saw a Canadian maple leaf or a Québec *fleur-de-lys*.

Male stagiaires are easily identified by the ratty old braces, *bretelles*, that dangle over their shoulders. Once, these braces must have been gray and red. Now they are merely dingy. But they serve their purpose, imparting to the wearer a certain dignity, identifying him as a walking information booth, and giving him a place to tuck his thumbs. Full-fledged hospitalers are distinguished by their leather braces. Hospitalers also sport a modest blue and white ribbon with the medal of the Hospitality and, at the highest level of service, a small silver cross. Interestingly, it is only at this level that the hospitaler makes a commitment to the Catholic Church. Up to that point, he or she may be a Buddhist, a Muslim or an atheist (although in fact I met no other non-Catholics in the Hospitality).

From an interfaith point of view, this must be considered a step forward for a body that has not always preached tolerance. In the early twentieth century, the Hospitality was a hotbed of the Action Française, a group notorious for its anti-Semitic, proto-fascist views. Indeed, Lourdes continued to be a rallying point for the most reactionary strain of French Catholicism until after the Second World War. (When the collaborationist prime minister, Marshal Pétain, paid an official visit in 1940, he was hailed for reversing France's anti-clerical laws.) However, since the 1946 appointment to the bishopric of Lourdes of Monsignor Théas—one of the few bishops who had spoken out against the transportation of French Jews—the Sanctuary and its institutions have been models of ecumenism and reform.

If the Hospitality has one distinguishing management principle, it is this: no member may serve for more than three weeks a year. Thus, even positions that one might expect to be permanent, like chief of operations at the train station or marshal of processions, are constantly in flux. This revolving-door policy institutionalizes chaos (the eternal lament of the brancardier runs: "The last fellow told me to . . . and now this fellow's telling me to ...”), but it also ensures that no individual becomes all-powerful or irreplaceable. It also means that everyone gets a chance to try his hand at different tasks. It's a refreshingly democratic and lively system.

The Baths

My first assignment as a stagiaire was to the baths. No visit to Lourdes is complete without a bath. But Lourdes is not a hot spring, so banish any notions of happy pilgrims hymning as they paddle in Jacuzzis. The pilgrims here bathe one at a time with about a minute at their disposal to savor the experience. Not that many want to stay in the water longer: Lourdes' spring-fed baths are normally a bracing sixty-one degrees Fahrenheit (if they go below fifty-five, an alarm sounds and they are shut down). A bath in Lourdes is an austere act of faith and one that offers profound hope to the sick. Every bather has heard of cases like that of Evasio Ganora. Diagnosed with terminal Hodgkin's disease, he found the waters so invigorating that after his bath he waved off his stretcher-bearers, walked back to the hospital and set to work at once helping invalids. His sickness and all its symptoms had abruptly, and permanently, vanished.

The baths are housed in a long, featureless concrete pavilion, with separate entrances for men and women. There are five baths for men, ten for the women, who come in greater numbers and require more attention in dressing and undressing. Entering from the men's end, the pilgrim sees five curtained-off bath stalls. An attendant shows him behind a curtain to a changing area, and instructs him to strip down to his underwear and say his prayers. In the seats lined up against the wall, other men in their underwear are already waiting their turn like clients in a barber shop.

When a pilgrim's time comes, he passes through the next curtain into the holy of holies. This is a room walled with simple gray stone. High on the wall that faces the pilgrim there is a statue of the Virgin. In the center of the room, three slippery steps down, is an oblong trough of waist-deep water. This is the bath. It is long, but not wide, for space is allowed on either side for the attendants who will guide the pilgrim in.

Before the pilgrim can take the plunge, however, an attendant steers him into a corner and instructs him to finish disrobing. (Thanks to my mornings in the baths, I can rattle off the phrase, "Please take off your underwear" in four languages.) The attendant holds up a large blue towel to shield the eyes of the Virgin from the pilgrim's nakedness, then wraps it snugly around the pilgrim's mid-section. "Always *above* the stomach of the fat man!" was my first lesson in this skill, as it is most embarrassing for a pilgrim to lose his towel while being immersed.

The attendant next directs the pilgrim to the top of the steps, where he is joined by another helper. The pilgrim pauses to recite the Hail Mary. Any of the attendants who speak his language pray along with him or, if the pilgrim isn't Catholic or hasn't had much practice lately, fill in for him. Then the pilgrim makes his personal petitions to Our Lady of Lourdes.

There is something deeply touching, and often comical, in these intimate moments. First, there is the physical closeness: wrapping that cold, damp towel around the pilgrim's naked body, taking him by the hand and leading him to the steps. Then, occasionally, the privilege of listening in on his prayers. It happened several times that I ran into a bather later in the streets of Lourdes. As we had first met under rather different circumstances, mutual recognition was never immediate. But when it came, it was accompanied by a warm smile.

I remember one Spanish man, a slight, chatty fellow with a thick beard. When I asked him if he had anything to ask of the Virgin, he told me that, yes, he wanted to pray for the health of his wife and his parents, and also his brother, who hadn't been so well lately, and there was also the trouble he'd been having with his leg since the car accident. . . . I kept motioning with my head towards the Virgin to remind him where his prayers were supposed to be directed, but he seemed quite content to entrust them all with me. Another confiding soul, when I asked him what language he preferred, answered, "French. Although actually I was not born in France, I am from Algeria. In fact, I was born a Muslim. But in life, you know, things happen. ..." Then there was the ancient French priest, a tiny, frail-looking creature with jutting ribs, who stood before the image of the Virgin, joined his hands together and cried his eyes out for five minutes as we all stood by in silence.

Once the pilgrim has said his prayers, the attendants help him down the steps. They guide him the length of the bath to the wall, keeping hold of his wrist and upper arm to prevent him from slipping, then instruct him to bend his knees as though to sit. As he does so, they pull back on his arms, immersing his body in the icy water with a single, clean motion. It is not uncommon for the pilgrim, at this point, to utter a shriek. The attendants then pull him back briskly to the upright position. The one on the left proffers a statuette of the Virgin to the pilgrim's lips, the one on the right, a glass of water. The Holy Mother and Saint Bernadette are summarily invoked ("*Notre-Dame de Lourdes priez pour nous Saint Bernadette priez pour nous*") and the bath is over. The pilgrim is offered no towel for drying, since his startled skin will swiftly shed the frigid water on its own (though some have deemed this a miraculous property of the waters of Lourdes).

Over the course of time, a detailed protocol for the baths has been formulated, though if my brief experience is any indication, not one in three baths run quite as the Sanctuary's handbook envisions. First of all, there are differences among the supervisors. The head man in my bath on the first day (picture Boris Karloff doing John Cleese's impersonation of a Frenchman) was a stickler for procedure. Between baths, he would draw his team together to give us pointers: "Now look here, I want to see you all making the sign of the cross when the pilgrim is at the top step. Here, you understand, *before* he enters the bath. And then, again, as he's getting out . . . Sign of the cross!"

He was also the acknowledged master of complicated cases—the paralyzed and the stricken. Bathing such pilgrims required time, care and expertise. With some there was really no question of dunking them in the water. Instead, they were undressed as far as possible, then administered the water with a damp cloth. But many who looked too sick to get into the bath did so anyway. They were the ones who could settle for nothing short of a miracle; catching a chill was the least of their worries.

So canes were set aside (never to be taken up again?), obese men were hoisted from wheelchairs and their underwear peeled away from flabby white buttocks. Urine and colostomy bags were detached, and tubes clipped with pincers. It took six of us to strap one heavy paraplegic man to a stretcher and bear him into the bath room. Of course it was his stricken legs that he wanted immersed, but the attendants set great store in soaking the chest, so water was ladled over all of the poor fellow's body as he shuddered and moaned.

Such was my first, painstaking morning in the baths. My second, by contrast, felt like a shift on the conveyor belt of salvation. The pilgrims we received were healthy enough to get around on their own and this head man prided himself on turnover. He wanted the next pilgrim ready to go in before the last one was out. This meant that as each bather stood at the lip of the bath, addressing his heart's prayers to Our Lady, the attendants behind him were wringing out a sloppy towel for the next pilgrim.

My fellow attendants were a study in themselves. My companions of the first day performed their duties with operating-room gravity. Trusting in the efficacy of the baths and recognizing that for many of the pilgrims Lourdes was a last resort, they approached their business with reassuring precision. The second-day bath attendants were rougher in their ministrations, like bakers rolling dough, but still they felt the importance of their office and were determined to perform it properly. Problems arose, however, over what constituted a "proper" bath. The Virgin never laid down any rules to govern ablutions.

One quarrel over protocol involved a strapping Spanish boy who told me he had injured his head and wanted to immerse it. When I relayed his request to the French attendants, they refused: "Tell him he can pour water over himself from the pitcher but immersion of the head is strictly forbidden." But the young Spaniard simply brushed off the attendants and plunged his banged-up cranium again and again into the healing waters. Meanwhile, the Irish boy who had come into the bathing room behind him was taking notes. When his turn came, he too proceeded to splash about like a seal in a backyard pool, to the horror of the attendants.

Another difficult pilgrim was a skinny-chested man with a pot belly and a bald head, a man of fifty with a mental age of ten. He was so excited about his adventure that he couldn't stop giggling and dancing as I wrapped the towel around him, and he ended up giving me a cold, wet kiss on the cheek. But when he found himself alone at the top step, confronting the statue of the Virgin, a great fear overcame him. Whether it was the gravity of the ritual or terror of the cold water, he couldn't bring himself to go any further. Finally, the attendants took the situation in hand. Grabbing hold of him from either side, they began first to ease him forward. Before long they were dragging him inch by inch through the frigid water towards the Virgin.

"Sit down!" they told him when they had reached the wall, but the bald man backed away instead, scrabbling with both feet like a cat in the hands of a veterinarian. The attendants hung on; this was all for the little man's good, after all. They tugged him back and forth, trying to put him off balance and, when that didn't work, they laid their hands on his scrawny shoulders to force him down. With one desperate twist, the pilgrim managed to slip away. As he surged up the steps with his pot belly hanging, his cheeks flushed, and the two attendants still grasping for his wrists, he looked like one of Bosch's damned souls scrambling from hell with the demons at his heels. The attendants conceded the battle. The terrified bather reached safety. But then, rather than scamper straight out to the waiting room, he stopped and looked back.

"Is that all?" he asked.

"That's all," the chief replied.

And all the fear rolled off him like water off his goose-bumped skin. He started giggling all over again and wasn't content till he'd given me one final wet kiss.

As things worked out, I served only two shifts in the baths. The rest of the week was spent lifting the sick on and off trains, guiding the blind to the front rows for the international mass and standing sentry during processions. This was probably just as well, as I felt somewhat awkward with all the Hail Marys and signs of the cross that the baths called for. While the baths of Lourdes do not constitute an eighth sacrament of the Church, many treat them as such, and I worried that the presence of a non-believer in this setting might be unwelcome to some pilgrims. Train duty and crowd control had less of an aura of religious mystery about them, and I felt I could participate in them without compromising myself or others.

Even so, there were times when religious observances proved unavoidable. I could hardly be the only one standing in the esplanade as 5,000 pilgrims knelt before the Eucharist. Simple respect and propriety dictated that I bend my knee along with the rest. I even managed to cross myself when the situation demanded, though I had to keep thinking "left to right, left to right" to avoid mimicking the person opposite me and doing it backwards.

The experience recalled a lesson I had learned previously in Japan: that the formal expression of reverence, if it is to be done well, needs to be learned and practiced. Ritual, on the whole, has fallen by the wayside in modern society, but the Catholic Church still knows the value of a well-turned gesture: the bent knee, the sign of the cross, the receiving of the Eucharist. These motions act as a physical shorthand, marking the transition from secular to sacred space and time, and I observed, with not a little envy, the precision, grace, even panache, with which they were performed. Even the ability of the people around me to stand still through long ceremonies without slouching against a wall or stuffing their hands in their pockets impressed me.

It took only a couple of days to go from being a total outsider in Lourdes to being hailed on the street I had become a cell in the organism. I got to know other hospitalers: incomprehensible Michael from Liverpool, whose hand looked like it had been fed into a machine, though that didn't stop him lifting invalids off trains. Fatherly Miguel, who would put his arm around my shoulder and deliver his rambling homilies on life, always punctuated with the question, "¿Sí o no?" (I soon learned that the correct answer was always "Sí, Miguel, sí.") Big English David, who let it be known that he frankly didn't think much of French organizational skills. Sister Agathe, a businesslike French nun who could hardly wait till next year's Jubilee because "Jubilee years are always great years for conversions." The Milanese quintet: Claudio, Luca and Paola, Maurizio and Daniela (Donatella couldn't make it that year), who recalled coming here together years ago as boyfriends and girlfriends, conjuring up a novel vision of Lourdes as a haven of romance. And, of course, Henri from Lyon, whom I met once more at the train station the night his group shipped out. He was ecstatic to see me in my braces and promised we'd meet again, "in Lourdes or in heaven."

A hundred years ago, Zola captured this convivial spirit when he described a pilgrimage to Lourdes as "a few days of hard labor and boyish delight . . . an 'outing' of a number of big fellows, let loose under a lovely sky, and well pleased to be able to enjoy themselves and laugh together." The picture hasn't changed much. The volunteers put in a long day and feel perfectly justified sitting down in the evening over a glass of wine— before trotting off to mass.

What the Hospitality of Lourdes engenders—what Lourdes engenders—is that hard-to-define and harder-to-generate social convergence that Victor Turner, in his *Image and Pilgrimage*, termed *communitas*: "full unmediated communication, even communion . . . which arises spontaneously in all kinds of groups and situations; [*communitas*] combines the qualities of lowliness, sacredness, homogeneity and comradeship; spontaneous, immediate, concrete; it does not merge identities, it liberates them from conformity to general norms." Lourdes frees people from their normal milieu and all its social definitions and sets them into new relations based on equality and a shared sense of purpose.

I admired the *communitas* of Lourdes, and savored it to the extent that I could. I often felt sorry that my participation in it did not extend beyond body and spirit, for it was clear that those around me derived great strength from their faith, and that it was faith that bonded them together. One evening, to my lasting regret, I turned down an invitation to evening mass from a fellow brancardier, a very kindly, retired French gentleman. Perhaps I should have accepted, for he looked quite sad. He thought it would be such fun to get all the boys together for a good prayer.

For a Tooth

Towards the end of my time in Lourdes, the Unitalsi *bambini* pilgrimage arrived. Thousands of mentally and physically handicapped Italian children poured in with their parents and caregivers for a four-day gathering. From the clowns at the train station to the massive song-and-prayer rallies at the Grotto, these days were wholly given over to the children. A giant banner was spread across the face of the Basilica of the Rosary with the slogan, "*Ciao Baby, 99."* (One French woman asked me, in seeming innocence, what the banner was for. When I explained about the pilgrimage she replied, "Ah, how nice. But that *is* a basilica, isn't it?")

The Unitalsi rosary procession began at the center of town and took two leisurely hours to reach the plaza. The people arrived, not in a solid mass, but all in their own sweet time. Children with Down's syndrome holding up their candles. Puffed-out old women in rickshaws holding up their candles. Brothers, sisters, parents, wives and husbands, living each day with the infirmity of someone they loved, holding up their candles. As always there was something strangely moving in the sight of all these people *walking*. Not marching. Not parading. Just walking. Walking slowly enough that no one fell behind. Walking in time to the music and the twilight, which lingered late those June days, till family by family, couple by couple, they had filled the esplanade, the avenues, the grassy median.

Then all at once, it happened. Lourdes really did become Disneyland. "Please, adults, sit on the ground so the *bambini* can see!" came the voice over the loudspeaker. And then fireworks lit up the sky, and the songs —"Whistle While You Work," "Some Day My Prince Will Come," "Supercalafragilistic," "Just a Spoonful of Sugar," all in Italian—came bibbidy-bobbidy-booing over the square. The children screamed and danced and ran around in circles, the ones who could. Who ever dreamed Catholicism could be so much fun?

I sat on the grass with my companions from Milan, watching the basilica turn green, purple and pale blue in the glare of the fireworks.

Behind us, a boy of twelve screamed in terror at each explosion, then laughed as his family reassured him, then screamed again. It seemed as if each time was the first time for him; by the time the next explosion came, he had already forgotten the last one. But his parents never lost patience. "Marco," they told him, "it's only fireworks. They won't hurt you." And Marco would laugh and lean on his mother's arm till the next volley came.

The next day, Unitalsi went home. Seven trainloads full. Ciao baby.

It started in the morning and never ended, but it was easy going for the brancardiers; children aren't hard to pick up. A clown rode around and around the waiting room and the platform in a little red ambulance, squirting mothers with a water pistol, beeping his horn. A fire-blower went striding through the crowd, puffing flames at the kids leaning out the windows of the train. Boy scout troups hauled baggage trucks piled high with suitcases up the platform, then hauled them back again loaded with teenage girls who didn't look in any way chastened by the message of Lourdes. A clown trio—drums, accordion and organ—played the lambada on the platform of the Gare des Malades. The crowd clapped in time as a handsome clown on stilts danced with a middle-aged woman, spinning and twisting her, till in her excitement she almost pulled him down. He recovered his balance just in time, or maybe he had just pretended to lose it.

The band moved into the waiting room, where a middle-aged man with a beard and a big belly started a conga line of children. Some were healthy, others not, but they all played together, and that was as it should be. A tall woman in a blue Unitalsi shirt let herself be whipped around by the music. In her arms, she held a beautiful, wild-eyed girl, with a face dyed deep-crimson on one side. Another girl, perhaps seven or eight years old, sat in a wheelchair, rocking slightly, her forearms rising and falling to a music only she could hear. She was looking in the direction of the conga line, the clowns, the dancers, but did she see them? A woman sat behind her, stroking her shoulder.

We were called out to help load a train and when we came back, the waiting room had emptied. The clowns were sitting in the canteen, rolling cigarettes and looking the same as anyone who's been working hard all day and needs a break, except that they were wearing red noses and orange wigs. Another busload of kids pulled up outside, and the clowns put their working faces back on and headed for the platform. Ambulances followed, and the waiting room filled up again, this time mostly with old people. We eased them onto Lourdes specials, rolled them backwards down the ramp, and set them in rows so they could sit and talk while they waited.

One man asked me how much longer the train would be. I suggested an hour.

"All you do in Lourdes is wait," he muttered.

But most of the crowd was in a good mood. Their holiday wasn't quite over yet. There was a bit of sun today and still a note of *allegria*, thanks to all the children, the noise and the movement. Pierre, the station boss, rolled in and saw a captive audience. Stepping up in front of the thirty or forty ranked wheelchairs, he led the group in an impromptu Ave Maria, first spoken, then sung. He had a lovely strong voice. There were a mother and son beside me, both in wheelchairs. The woman beamed as she sang the prayer. Her son, a man of forty, sat arms akimbo, his head torqued painfully to one side. He was a miniature man, and balding. His tongue stuck out in a way that shocked me at first, until I realized he was laughing.

"He looks very happy," I said to the woman.

"Yes, he's always happy when he comes here."

"Have you been to Lourdes many times?"

"Thirty-four times." She looked at her boy. "Isn't that right, Roberto?"

Whether he understood the question, or whether he was only reacting to the sound of her voice, he made a noise in reply. When she looked back at me she was no longer smiling.

"Every year for thirty-four years. Since his third year of elementary school. He went to the doctor for a tooth. And this happened. For a tooth."

Her voice was full of emotion as she told me this. But it was not angry. It was not broken. It was only a little uncomprehending. For a tooth. How could God let this happen for a tooth? She looked away again. And when she looked back, the smile had returned, the beatific Lourdes smile.

"And you, is this your first time in Lourdes?"

THAT NIGHT THERE WAS an Indonesian delegation at the candlelight procession and so, after Latin, the six official languages, Hungarian and Slovak, most of us heard for the first time the "Salaam Maria."

I went to the Grotto afterwards. The wheelchairs flowed by in their steady stream. The green pixel board spoke on silently to the unheeding pilgrims: *"Kristem. Waar is uw geluk?"* Schoolboys loaded up ten-liter tanks at the taps. Pilgrims waited in line to touch the rock, peer through the plexiglas at the spring of Massabielle, place their candles alongside all the rest. People sat silent on the benches, watching others perform their sacred acts. Some kneeled, as Bernadette had done, and looked where she had looked. The Indonesian pilgrims photographed each other so that in a few days, when they returned to their country and removed with relief their coats and sweaters, they would have a lifelong proof that they had come "in procession," as the Virgin had asked, to receive the blessing of their Lady. Everyone was gathered, brought close by the safety of candles, the community of song, the comfort of a crowd.

At my back, its voice a whisper, a prayer, a song without meaning, the river Gave ran into the darkness.

LOST PILGRIMS

THE CAMINO

DE SANTIAGO

CAMINO.

A track, a way, a road.

The verb in Spanish is *caminar*: to follow a road, to walk.

The Portuguese have their *caminho*; the Italians, *cammino*; the French, *chemin*. It is a Romance word, though its origins are Celtic, which is only fitting, for the *Camino de Santiago* leads the pilgrim to Galicia, the lonely Celtic outpost of Roman Catholic Spain.

Camino.

A track, a way, a road and more. When Christ's words are rendered in French, in Portuguese, in Spanish, he says, *Je suis le chemin, Eu sou el caminho, Yo soy el camino y la verdad y la vida.* "I am the *camino* and the truth and the life." Dante Alighieri, too, at the age of thirty-five found himself *"Nel mezzo del cammin' di nostra vita."* "In the middle of the *camino* of our life."

Camino. Here-and-now yet beyond; spirit yet flesh. Sad that English never took it on, for we have nothing that quite replaces it. "Way" is too abstract; there are no blisters to it, no glory. "Road" evokes concrete, dust and motor oil. You need a car for it. And "path" just runs off the map; taken literally ("a path through the woods"), it is narrow and winding, lacking horizons; taken metaphorically ("the path to enlightenment"), it reeks of sandalwood.

However one translates *camino* it loses in the translation. So let's leave it as it is.

Camino.

SOMETIME ABOUT 1,200 years ago, the first pilgrims began to find their way to the extreme northwest of Spain to pray at the tomb of Christ's Apostle, Saint James, in Spanish, Sant' Iago. How the body of James, who was martyred in Jerusalem, ever came to be buried in the impossibly remote, politically marginal, half-pagan realm of Galicia was not a question that particularly vexed anyone. In an age of miracles, the very wonder of the thing was guarantee enough of its truth. So the pilgrims came, in penitence and devotion, to beg favor or cure or blessing, from year to year in ever greater numbers, until by the eleventh century faith alone had raised the handsome city of Santiago de Compostela to rival Rome and Jerusalem as one of the three great pilgrimage sites of Christendom.

As millions of pilgrim feet tended towards Santiago, they wore roads into the landscape, roads that branched like a fine network of roots to draw Christians from every corner of Europe. In France, the many roads fused into four; and on the Spanish side of the Pyrenees, the four became one: this was the *camino frances*, or French Road, Europe's great trunk road to Santiago.

The Camino was not easily won. Stretches passed through territories contested by the Muslims; there were forests, semi-deserts and mountains to pass; rivers and marshes to ford; wolves and bandits to contend with. To house, nourish, care for, and—not infrequently—bury pilgrims in their coming and going, towns, hospitals, inns and churches sprang up along the way. Yet the Camino never entirely lost its element of danger and hard enterprise. As late as the seventeenth century, the Italian pilgrim priest Domenico Laffi found himself running from thieves, sleeping on the earthen floor of huts, fending off clouds of locusts, and stumbling upon the corpses of pilgrims who had succumbed to heatstroke and wolves.

Satan frequented the Camino as well. How could the demon fail to set snares when he saw so many souls headed for Paradise? So to keep his pilgrims on the paths of righteousness, Saint James became a pilgrim himself, donning the pilgrim's broad hat, cloak, staff and scallop shell. The figure of the bluff, bearded Santiago Peregrino, Saint James the Pilgrim, smiles down on the faithful from scores of altarpieces, niches and church facades along the Camino. No other saint has taken on the characteristics of his devotees to the extent of Santiago.

The surge of faith that built the Camino was at its peak from the eleventh to the thirteenth centuries. It is a time when many of us believe that nothing much was happening in the world. Yet, in reality, the movement of people, commerce, religion and ideas along the routes of pilgrimage was forging a pan-European culture. In time this vigor waned, however, even as the circumstances opposing mass pilgrimage mounted. Power and commerce in Christian Spain headed south with the front line of the fighting against the Muslims. The Reformation shattered Europe's religious unity, while singling out pilgrimage as an idle and superstitious practice. The Inquisition, the endless wars of religion and the Napoleonic invasions made conditions ever less genial for pilgrims. Then, from the 1830s, liberal Spanish governments set out to break the power of the religious orders, shooing the monks from establishments that had served the Camino for centuries.

By the twentieth century, the Camino de Santiago had faded to a shadow of its former greatness. Two world wars, the Spanish Civil War, and four decades of isolation under Francisco Franco looked like the final nails in the coffin. In 1978, the year after Franco's death, the Camino's millennial history touched bottom as a grand total of thirteen pilgrims straggled into Santiago to pay their regards to the Apostle.

Yet even then something was percolating. Franco, who fancied himself a modern-day Santiago, had promoted the Camino as an itinerary for automobile tourism (why walk to Santiago when you could drive?). Grassroots confraternities of Saint James based in Spain and France were charting the foot route once again, producing up-to-date guides for the adventurous. And a new, united Europe was on the lookout for foundation myths.

It took a decade before the first bubbles reached the surface. As recently as the mid-eighties, the Brazilian writer Paolo Coelho (the man who mobilized a tremendous wave of South American pilgrims with his book *The Pilgrimage*) could still portray the Camino as an esoteric and long-abandoned spiritual path. But with the Jubilee of 1993 (Santiago's

Jubilees—or *Jacobeos*—occur in years when the Saint's day, July 25, falls on a Sunday) came a rush of pilgrims that exceeded the wildest predictions. By 1999's Jacobeo, when I walked the Camino for the first time, the revival had come to a full boil. One hundred and fifty thousand pilgrims arrived in Santiago that year on foot (having walked at least sixty miles) or on bicycle (having ridden one hundred and fifty). Such a sight had not been seen since the Middle Ages.

On a hot afternoon that summer, as I sat on a bench in a crowded little park in the town of Los Arcos attending to some blisters, I noticed a very old man whose eyes smiled at me through the furrows of age. I limped over to say hello. He told me that the sight of pilgrims took him back to his childhood, when once or twice a month a gaunt, solitary soul would trudge into town. Then the old man's family and the others would offer the hospitality that was a pilgrim's due: a night's shelter, a meal, perhaps a few small coins. And the pilgrim, for his part, would promise to pray for his benefactors when he reached Santiago. This was the barter economy of pilgrimage as it had existed for a thousand years. But these memories were pages from a faded book: for fifty years or more, from the Civil War until the 1980s, the old man could not recall seeing one single sore-footed pilgrim pass through his town.

And suddenly they were back. Pilgrims galore! Pilgrims bandaging themselves, slapping on sun screen, filling water bottles, laying out picnic lunches, and patching their bike tires. Pilgrims who came from places Saint James never knew: Holland, Germany, England, Ireland, Brazil, the United States, Canada, Japan. But what was one to make of these pilgrims? With their designer sunglasses, denim cut-offs, high-tech hiking boots and spandex bike pants, they did not exude an air of holy poverty. Nor did many of them possess the gravity one expected of a pilgrim. They looked more like participants in a six-mile "fun run."

And why wouldn't they? They were walking and riding through an unspoiled landscape, pausing for refreshment in timeless villages, and meeting other pilgrims from all over the world. They knew that every day, when they had walked far enough, a clean, cheap refuge would be waiting to take them in, and that there would be a place for them to cook or a restaurant nearby with a cut-price "pilgrims' menu." Yes, many of them were suffering the aches that ensued from suddenly, after a lifetime of ease, strapping on a backpack and walking for several hours a day. But there were pharmacies in every village stocked with the best the twentieth century had to offer in the way of blister pads, tensor bandages and anti-inflammatory pills and creams.

The old man smiled indulgently on us all. Did he think humanity had seen the error of its ways and turned *en masse* to penitence? Or was he just getting a kick out of the wide world showing up on his doorstep? As he cast an eye on these bare-legged pilgrims from Brazil, Barcelona, Boston and Basel—who reminded him not a whit of the grimy mendicants of his youth—did he have a hankering to say to hell with Los Arcos and hit the Camino himself? And did he understand the difference between these pilgrims and the ones of old, the difference that lay deeper than Ray-Bans and Reeboks? That these ones didn't really believe in Saint James.

Yesterday's pilgrim went to Santiago, as today's goes to Lourdes, with concrete and practical intentions: to make penance for a sin, give thanks for a grace, fulfill a promise, ask a favor of God. He undertook the long journey to show the sincerity of his faith, and because he believed that praying to the Saint's bones was as close as he could get on earth to whispering in the ear of God. On his way to Compostela, the pilgrim confronted the challenges and temptations of the road and encountered the divine in holy relics, images and sites. These experiences whetted his faith and prepared him for the moment when he would address his prayers to the Apostle. The tomb of Saint James was the grail at the end of his quest, the golden fleece at the heart of his labyrinth.

There still are pilgrims plying the road who, when asked why they are doing the Camino (a favorite icebreaker these days), answer briefly, "For a vow." In other words, they have promised someone—a dying uncle, their mother, their priest, God—that they will make this pilgrimage. Such pilgrims walk far each day and pay little heed to the attractions along the way. They have an errand to run: an errand of the spirit.

The greater number of today's pilgrims, however, even those who profess themselves Catholic, are not on an errand. They have nothing particular to ask or give thanks for when they get to Compostela. Most smile at the notion that Saint James' bones are awaiting them there. When asked why they have undertaken the pilgrimage, they profess a bewildering range of motives. They want to meet people, find God, get some exercise, have time to think, take on a challenge, put off a decision, escape a routine, feel close to Nature, see Spain on the cheap, affirm their old faith, discover a new one ...

Strange pilgrims, indeed.

One might wonder whether to call them pilgrims at all. Certainly, few are cut from the same cloth as the pilgrims of the rue du Bac or Lourdes. With their credit cards, cameras and (God save us) cell phones, they look more like tourists in pilgrim drag. Yet they think of themselves as pilgrims and conduct themselves as pilgrims, and often it is the most agnostic among them who show the greatest pilgrim spirit. Ultimately, drawing dividing lines or setting artificial standards of authenticity diverts from the really interesting point, which is that these people *want* to be pilgrims. They want to have, at whatever remove from medieval

reality, some knowledge of what it means to be on a pilgrimage. They feel that something is lacking in their lives and they have a suspicion that somehow, in walking this very long road, they might find that something.

There is a powerful sense of *communitas* on the Camino, but it differs from that of Lourdes. The pilgrims of the Camino are not a regiment moving in step like the pilgrims of Lourdes, but a ragtag army, all walking the same road to the same city, following the beat of different drummers. If there is anything they have in common, it is this: most of them are interested less in the destination than in the way. So a great transference of faith has occurred. It is no longer Saint James or God or the Virgin Mary that these pilgrims believe in, so much as the Camino itself.

EARLY ON A TUESDAY afternoon, I arrive from Lourdes via Bayonne at the station of Saint-Jean-Pied-de-Port. Tomorrow morning, I will begin to walk the Camino de Santiago for the second time in two years (second-and-a-half, counting the twelve-day hike I made from León to Galicia this June). But where last year I walked at the height of summer in the thick of "the pilgrim season," I fear this autumn crossing will be cold and solitary.

It's a healthy climb to the old, upper town. The main street of Saint-Jean-Pied-de-Port is the Camino; where pilgrims sowed their coin the buildings sprang up on either side. This is the last outpost on the French side of the Pyrenees and the three-storeyed, white-stuccoed mansions are fortresses against the mountain winters. At the very top of the slope, in a 200-year-old house, is the pilgrims' refuge.

I enter the reception through the garden. The hospitaler, a sixtyish man—from Lourdes, it turns out—leans back in his chair, singing a wistful song. Has he been singing all day or did he strike up this perform-ance for my benefit?

"No, I sing for myself to pass the time. Things have been slow the past few days. Too much rain." I take a seat and he shoots a form across the desk to me. Date of birth. Country of origin. Profession. Religion. Motivation for doing the Camino.

Why do I feel uncomfortable checking "None" for religion? Am I worried that the man from Lourdes will take offense? I look over my choices for Motivation: religious, spiritual, *sportif*, cultural. Oh, for an "other" box . . . Spiritual and cultural will have to do. The hospitaler takes the forms with-out a glance and files them in a drawer for some future compiler of data.

"I suppose this is your first time on the Camino?"

"Second. I did it last summer, but I wanted to do it again. . . ."

"*Avec répose*. I understand perfectly. And you'll be staying here tonight?" He beams. "This refuge is like a hotel. Sixteen beds and three showers. In Spain you'll find a hundred beds and one cold shower. And I don't say this from chauvinism."

Ah, the French.

He hands me my "pilgrim's credentials," the passport that will permit me to stay in refuges. It indicates that I am the 4,140th to begin the Camino from Saint-Jean this year. Thousands more will have started from more distant points of France, from Switzerland, Germany, Holland or Italy. Multitudes will have joined the road in Spain.

"Yes, it's been very busy," affirms the hospitaler. "And more spread out than last year, from March right till now. But you can have any bed you want tonight: only two other pilgrims."

Only two other pilgrims? This was a mixed blessing. Good, because it increased my chances for a sleep untroubled by snorers. Bad, because a pilgrimage was no pilgrimage without pilgrims.

I can't say just when the idea came to me that someday I would like to take a long walk. I think it was when I was very young, and the stories

I loved were full of journeys on foot to exotic lands. I never embroidered the idea much. I didn't pore over maps or chart out routes. But it was a strong idea and it never left me. An essential part of its appeal was that it was something *of the past*. Why it was *this* past experience I wanted to live rather than, say, riding a chariot or being a pirate or living in a castle is not easy to say.

My long walk, as I imagined it, was never a hike in the woods or a trek through the jungle (though a journey across the desert held its charms). To be sure, I saw myself passing through forests and over mountains, but there had to be farms and hamlets and towns along the way as well. It couldn't happen here in North America; here had not been lived in long enough, at least not by us. The cities and towns were too provisional, the distances between them, too great. Besides, there had to be other travelers on the road—not so much for the sake of companionship, since I always saw myself undertaking this journey alone, but to provide *encounters*. I've never read Gurdjieff's *Meetings with Remarkable Men*, but the title sums up my ideal of travel (though let's change "*Men*" to "*Humans*").

Every couple of years, I would read something that made this old urge to ramble flare up: *Kim*, Tolkien, Orwell's *Down and Out*, Hermann Hesse, the poetry of Irish monks, the *Fioretti* of Saint Francis, Chatwin's *The Songlines*, Basho's haiku wanderings, Chaucer, Laurie Lee. I wondered whether a walking tour—say around Umbria or the Lake District—might do the trick, but somehow that idea came up short in terms of enterprise. What I really wanted, as I came to realize, was one of those old-fashioned pilgrimages. A good, long walk that was not just tourism, not just looking at things, but a journey with a goal, that would leaven solitude with society.

It was a shame such things didn't exist anymore.

Then one day in 1991 I spotted a book in a remainder bin in London. It was the cover that caught my eye, with its fanciful portrait of a grizzled, medieval pilgrim drinking from a scallop shell. The book was entitled *The Pilgrim Route to Compostela*. I flipped through it for a minute or two, glancing at the photos and hand-drawn maps. I took the book to the counter, paid for it and dropped it in my bag. I never opened it again. I didn't need to. I had already made up my mind to do the Camino de Santiago. I had seen at once that all the elements were there. The long walk. The solitude. The companionship. The goal. The fact that it was very much *of the past*. It was a Catholic pilgrimage, of course, but I couldn't let that put me off. There were no atheist Caminos out there.

I approached the Camino at a walker's pace. Eight years would pass before I took my first pilgrim step. But once I started, I didn't stop.

In the dormitory of the refuge, my companions are comparing notes. One of them is a fortyish man, a mechanic from Périgueux who is in full retreat from Spain.

"I crossed the mountains two days ago. It was horrible. Pouring rain all the way, and the wind at the head of the pass! I could barely stand up. Then I got to Roncesvalles frozen, soaking wet, to find that in Spain they have no bedclothes! Can you imagine? Always there are bedclothes in the refuges in France. I was planning to carry on to Pamplona, but there is no sense if I am to freeze every night. I'll start again next spring."

The other pilgrim is Philippe LeClerc, a lanky student who wears a Madagascar t-shirt and an air of studied eccentricity.

"Have you been to Madagascar?" I inquire.

"No, I haven't. But I love it when people ask me if I have."

He speaks meticulous English, hooking together the parts of speech like engines of a toy train, tying up his strung-along sentences with "And was it correct, the way I said that?" When I say yes, he bursts out with "Ah! My English is so *wonderful* since I am doing the Camino!"

Philippe's loping stride has carried him by one of the famous old French roads all the way from Le Puy, 400 miles northeast. He has walked already the distance that lies before me. When I ask him why he chose to walk so far, he shrugs.

"I had some time …"

His staff leans casually against his bunkbed. A lithe, green bamboo pole, almost as tall as Philippe himself. I take it in my hand, give it a little toss, catch it as it falls. It is an elegant walking accessory: flexible, light and cool to the touch. It lends an air of Oriental mystery to the Camino.

Philippe beams. "Do you admire my cane? It is very *particular*, is it not?"

The last persons I see as I leave Saint-Jean-Pied-de-Port next morning are the Queen of Heaven and her little boy. They are waving *Bon Chemin!* from their niche above the Spanish Gate. Philippe LeClerc and his bamboo cane have already taken the road, so today I walk to Spain and Roncesvalles alone. The crossing of the Pyrenees is a splendid, lonely climb, up beyond the sparse villages with their guttural Basque names—Othatzenea, Erreculuch, Untto—to open hillsides dotted with sheep and shimmering in a thousand shades of green. It's pigeon-hunting season and for hours the only signs of human life are the volleys of shot that echo from far below. Then, up ahead, a striking tableau: a lone figure stands upon a rock, musing over the mountain valley. It's not Philippe. Could it be another pilgrim? A shepherd perhaps? And what does he think he's up to? Posing for a Caspar David Friedrich painting?

As I come closer, I realize that it is no human being at all. Here, in this loneliest of places, the Virgin Mary stands watching her flocks.

ON THE CAMINO, THE FOCUS is not the Virgin Mary. However, the Camino of Saint James is the Camino of the Virgin as well. Stories are told of how she appeared to him in Galicia and later Zaragoza (for according to tradition, James was the Apostle to Spain) and how she still watches his road, guiding the pilgrims' steps. Her queenly image presides over every church and in some she even appears as *la Peregrina*—the female counterpart to the pilgrim Santiago.

Unlike the heaven-descended Marys of modern times, the Virgins of the Camino rose from the earth. Most are *Virgenes encontradas*, discovered Virgins, images that simply turned up one day. Some appeared in tree trunks, others in springs, or caves, or even between the horns of a stag. Often the story accompanies them of how, when the Moors conquered Spain in the eighth century, all the images of the Virgin were squirreled away under rocks or in caves to wait out the time till the Christians had reconquered the land. Then, when that glorious day arrived, each Virgin revealed her hiding place and was restored to her altar amidst great rejoicing. It's a very good story except that the plaque beneath the images always reads: "Virgin and Child. Polychrome wood. 12th century."

So the legends of the discovered Virgins may not be quite literally true, yet they still offer a spiritual and psychological insight. These Holy Mothers were generated spontaneously from the loamy soil of the Spanish religious spirit.

Once, these Spanish lands lay under the rule of the Great Goddesses: Isis, Demeter, Cybele and the other Eastern imports who arrived here on the ships of the Phoenicians, the Greeks and the Romans. The Celts, too, lords of the western marches of the Camino, had their powerful female deities, mistresses of the hunt and the soil. But with the arrival of Christianity and later Islam in Iberia, these tutelary goddesses went into eclipse. It was the turn of Jesus and the Prophet, the saints, the martyrs and the great warrior-apostle Santiago to shine. Through the first, dynamic period of Spanish Christendom and on through the centuries of war against the Muslims, the masculine principle predominated.

Then sometime around the turn of the first millennium, the feminine regained its radiance. Perhaps the light came again from the East—the banners of Mary on the ships of Byzantium, the icons carried back by the Crusaders. Soon the image of a great queen bearing a holy child in her lap was rising up all over Spain. It rose from the soil re-won from the invaders, soil given over once again to domestic life and agriculture. It rose from the woods and from the springs.

The Mother had returned.

Nuestra Señora de Roncesvalles

Once long ago, on the Spanish side of the mountains not far from here, two shepherds were driving their flock home at twilight when suddenly a stag appeared in their path. It fixed them a moment with its great, mute eyes, then skipped away down the mountainside and plunged into the forest, its horns flashing beams of light as it fled.

In the days that followed, the stag with the flickering horns continued to appear at nightfall, always stopping to eye the men before vanishing into the woods. Soon they understood that it was asking them to follow, but they hesitated, fearing it would lead them into danger. At last, on the fourth night, they gathered up enough courage to pursue the mysterious beast.

The stag led the shepherds deep into the tangled woods, running always a little ahead, lighting the way with its horns. When the men fell behind it would stop and snort with impatience until they caught up, then again tear off into the dark. After what seemed hours, the stag reached a glade at the heart of the forest, where it came to a halt. As the fearful shepherds drew near, almost near enough to touch the beast's antlers, it started to pound the turf with its hoof. When it had scraped clear a patch of earth, it caught the men's eyes, seeming almost to nod at them. Then it wheeled and charged away, never to be seen again.

At once, the shepherds set to digging at the spot the stag had marked with his hoof. The loose soil came away easily beneath their fingers, and soon they had uncovered an arch of stone. They dug a little more and found, nestled in the shelter of the arch, a beautiful statue of the Virgin Mary and her son.

Upon that very spot, the church of Roncesvalles was raised to house the miraculous image. And ever since, the people of the neighboring valleys have come in solemn procession each year to pay homage to Our Lady of Roncesvalles.

She is a delicate figure, almond-eyed, Gothic, draped in rich cloth and wearing a crown of burnished silver. She doesn't look like she came from under a rock. High above the altar, beneath the lead canopy that billows up and away from her as if from a gust of hot air, she dandles her son in her lap. The priests chant and lecture and go through their motions before her, but she only has eyes for her boy.

It is chilly in the chapel of Our Lady of Roncesvalles, almost as chilly as outside, where the air is heavy with mist. It is eight o'clock, and apart from seven pilgrims (six more have arrived on the evening bus from Pamplona) and the four priests in their sparkling red and white garments, there are few in attendance for evening mass. It's surprising there are any, for the monastery lies above the highest villages, just below the mountain pass.

The priests look like relics from the early days of the Camino. With the oldest, it's touch and go whether he makes it to the next amen. The service begins with one of them welcoming the pilgrims who have come tonight from Argentina, Holland, Finland, Canada, Andalusia, Galicia and Madrid. We exchange glances. Hey, that's us! The sermon starts on a ringing note, as the priest excoriates the most recent atrocity of the Basque terrorists in their campaign of assassinations. Soon, however, he moves on to more general matters of the spirit and this is the cue for my thoughts to go straying down to my feet. There's always something with the body, isn't there? The stomach, the neck, the back, the eyes . . . After a strenuous day's climbing, what I really want to do now is stretch my legs, lie down, take off my shoes, anything but sit on this hard bench. I know I should be living in the moment, mining the significance of my presence here in this ancient place at the outset of a millennial pilgrimage, but all I can think about is the cramp I'm going to get from sitting in this frigid stone box. The sermon turtles on until, just as I'm making a furtive reach for my shoelaces, the priest says: "And now, will the pilgrims please approach the altar to receive a blessing that has been given since the twelfth century."

We rise, shuffle to the front of the chapel, form an uneven row. The blessing is a long one. It ends with the words: "May the Virgin, Santa María de Roncesvalles, lend you her maternal protection, defending you from perils to soul and body. May you be worthy, under her mantle, to achieve unharmed the goal of your pilgrimage.

"And pray for us when you reach Santiago."

In that instant, every light in the church is extinguished save one: the spotlight on Our Lady of Roncesvalles. There she is, shining upon her throne, above the shabby pilgrims who beg for her protection, above the celibate priests who tilt their squat, balding heads to her and sing in old voices, pitch-perfect with devotion, that most yearning of Christian hymns, Salve Regina, "Hail, Queen."

Santa María de Roncesvalles dandles her son in her lap. And pays us no mind at all.

NEXT MORNING, after three hours walking alone, I hear a voice from behind calling, "¡Hola Peregrino!" "Hello, Pilgrim!"—and I have companions: Mercedes from Madrid, Little Miguel from Andalusia, Big Miguel from Argentina and Timo from Finland. They're a happy bunch. Mercedes is the animator, drawing everyone out with her close questioning. Timo, with his Hemingway beard, is doing the Camino in honor of his sixtieth year. Little Miguel has two weeks for an abbreviated Camino, part on foot, part by car. Big Miguel is a spark of the life force, an artist "by vocation, though not by profession," who emits a non-stop banter that sometimes segues into French or Italian, sometimes peaks into song. The head of his pilgrim's staff, which he uses to conduct imaginary orchestras, sprouts dreadlocks—blue-gold-yellow-red tassels of coarse wool.

"Is this your first time in Spain?" I ask.

"En el mundo," he replies. In sixty-seven years, he has never been out of Argentina. Now, he's making the most of it.

At five, we reach the village of Zubiri. The refuge here is an empty schoolhouse, a rough-and-ready shelter. Everyone wants to go three miles further on, to Larrasoaña, where—as I can tell them from experience—the refuge is as spacious, clean and comfortable as this one is cramped and dusty. But Big Miguel has come down with something. He vomits in the toilet, then flops onto a bunk bed.

"I'll be fine, I'll be fine. You all go ahead. I'll see you in Pamplona tomorrow," he says.

So we continue, arriving with the night in Larrasoaña, where we are the only pilgrims. All of us take a hot shower (a modern pilgrim is a clean pilgrim), then pop out for supper at the village's one, warm, homely restaurant. The cook and his wife sit down to eat at the next table, sharing with us a plate of their own hand-picked mushrooms. And soon Mercedes has begun to talk about Big Miguel, all by himself back in Zubiri. Wouldn't it be nice if he could spend the night with us, in a clean place? If we could all start out together in the morning? . . . With spontaneous Spanish generosity, the lady of the restaurant rises from her dinner and produces her car keys.

"Come on. We'll go to Zubiri and get your friend. Santiago will forgive him for driving three miles."

She and Mercedes leave together, but in fifteen minutes they're back without Big Miguel. Though his bags were at the refuge, he was not. Nor was he to be found at any of the bars in town. Strange. Still, we're all confident that he's okay, that someone is looking out for him.

I don't see Big Miguel the next day in Pamplona, nor any day after. And though, from time to time, along the rest of the way, I ask pilgrims who have caught up with me from behind whether they recall meeting an old artist from Argentina with a staff that sprouts blue-gold-yellow-red dreadlocks, no one can.

Beyond Pamplona, the high Sierra del Perdón juts up in the pilgrim's path. Its hyena's spine is stuck with wind generators. Their fans are pinwheels twirling in the endless currents of wind. My companions of the last two days have already shot ahead, fallen back, dropped out, so I have the way to myself, which is, on the whole, how I prefer it. The past two days of idling away the road have been pleasing. We have laughed and chatted, shared energy food—nuts, chocolate, dried fruit—and stories. Little Miguel has talked about his uncle, a missionary priest who has spent most of his life in Japan. Mercedes, too, has an aunt in a convent. It seems that everyone in Spain has a relative who has taken vows, though invariably it's an older relative. We have talked besides of home and work, family, friends, religion, politics, the past and the future. And therein lies the problem: only our bodies have been here on the Camino. Our minds have been at play in other places, other times. Much as I enjoy the company and much as I am learning from my companions, there is always a voice in my head that says, "You may never be here again, so be here now!"

Already I am up against one of the thorny questions of the pilgrimage: to walk alone or in company? To be the Solitary Walker or the Wife of Bath?

The Solitary Walkers always try to stake the moral high ground on this question, claiming that to walk alone (while thinking, of course, on eternal things) is the holier and more authentic way of pilgrimage. I recall one pilgrim who insisted that he could only stand to walk the Camino in December and January when there was no crowd to trouble his thoughts: "There *was* one other pilgrim last winter," he conceded. "An Italian girl. But I hardly ever talked to her." Sometimes those inclined to monkishness look down their noses on the more gregarious pilgrims, calling them "tourists." Nor is this always mere snobbishness: the noisy torrent of pilgrims that sweeps down from the cities in summer can be enough to try anyone's patience.

On the other hand, one could argue that this "touristic" style of pilgrimage is nothing more than the Canterbury Tales with mobile phones: the fine old tradition of one people and one Church advancing like an army with banners down the road to salvation. In Spain, this style of pilgrimage is called a *romería*, a trip to Rome. The romería is a time-honored custom involving a walk in the countryside to a holy place, enlivened by eating, drinking and socializing, and culminating in a festive religious observance. It is a way of pilgrimage at least as valid and authentic as walking all on one's lonesome and maybe more so: with all the wolves and bandits prowling the Camino in the old days, the medieval pilgrim who valued his life was little inclined to solitude. Today's Camino is the product of the countless noisy, sociable generations who worked together to reconquer and then cultivate the land, build roads, bridges and towns, and extirpate predators of all sorts. To imagine that one can do it "alone" is simply modern arrogance.

That said, this consideration remains: safe passage in solitude being such a hard-won luxury, one has all the more reason to enjoy it—with due humility. There is so much pleasure in being free to walk, to breathe, to pause from time to time and look back over the distance you have covered, and so much to learn from the road, the sky, the human-paced passage of time and distance, that ultimately it seems a shame to spend too many thoughts on anything else. At the end of the day's walk and the stops along the way, there is time enough to be with the other pilgrims.

By midday I have reached the height of the Sierra. Looking back, I can draw a line to Pamplona and then on to the green Pyrenees: my first three days of walking. The line bisects the landscape; the wide world I haven't seen stretches off to the horizon at either hand. I have kept myself going all morning on the promise that I will eat as soon as I reach the top. Now I unwrap my lunch in a gale-force wind. I take shelter in the lee of a stone that marks the former site of the basilica and hospital of Our Lady of el Perdón. Once, there were hospitals in all such places as this, the loneliest and most remote of the Camino, because they were the places where shelter was needed most.

On the far side of the Sierra, a more familiar face of Spain appears: broad, sere, harsh. The houses of the first village, Uterga, are not whitewashed but creamy brown, with flowers and strings of pimentos on the wrought-iron balconies to lend a splash of brightness. A chill drizzle has started to fall and Uterga's church, where I had hoped to take shelter, is locked. As I stand shivering at the entrance, looking over the parish announcements, my eye happens upon a list of names and dates. Every Thursday from September 2 to November 25, two women are scheduled for *servicio de limpieza*, a service of cleansing. Remembering that the nearby village of Obanos is famed for a macabre annual festival in which the wine of communion is strained through the skull of Saint Guillen, I wonder if this *servicio de limpieza* could also be some sort of curious pagan survival. A purification ritual for the local virgins, perhaps?

No, I realize after a moment. It's the church-cleaning detail. Every housewife takes her turn.

Txori and La Virgen Del Puente

The town of Puente la Reina is a point of confluence. Here the road from Roncesvalles is joined by the road from the Pass of Somport—the one a pilgrim would follow if walking from Lourdes. Puente la Reina takes its name from the splendid bridge over the River Arga that some queen or other ordered built long ago.

In those days, a niche in the bridge housed an image of Mary, which bore the apt name of the Virgin of the Bridge. This statue was not easy to reach, so one must assume that the citizens of Puente la Reina welcomed the first visit of Txori. This little bird, of a variety never before seen hereabouts, appeared one day out of nowhere and set to work cleaning the statue of the Virgin with her beak and wings. She fluttered and pecked away until the statue sparkled like new. Then she flew back to where she had come from.

Txori appeared from time to time. There was no telling when she would show up, or how many years might pass before she came again. Sometimes a generation grew old without seeing her—and they counted themselves happy. For as time passed, it was observed that Txori's visits always heralded

disaster. Whether it was war or plague, drought or infestation, the death of a bishop or a king, as surely as Txori came, misery followed. Finally it was decided to move the Virgin of the Bridge into the Church of San Pedro, where she would be safely out of Txori's reach. And there she remains, though I can find no one in Puente la Reina who will confirm that since that day disasters have ceased.

From Puente la Reina, I walk backwards two miles in a torrential rain to see an eight-sided church. This sounds like a foolish thing to do, but if one does nothing foolish, what will there be to write about? When I say I walk backwards, I don't mean literally: I mean that I am walking east, against the flow of the Camino, which is such an unnatural direction after days of going west that it feels like walking into a high wind as today, to compound the sensation, I am.

My destination is Eunate, one of the "Romanesque jewels" of the Camino. It may be only a tiny church, sitting all on its lonesome by the highway, but it is a tiny church of great renown. I failed to visit it last year and was haunted the rest of the way with "You didn't go to Eunate? How could you have not gone to Eunate?" So here I am, head down, walking on the shoulder of the highway, getting soaked to the skin.

Eunate's fame derives partly from its beauty and partly from its eight-sidedness. Octagonal churches—modeled after the Holy Sepulchre in Jerusalem—were favored by the Templars, an order of knights who rose to stupendous heights during the Crusades, initially as guardians of the road to the Holy Land and later as bankers. The Templars played an important role in the development of the Camino, as well as providing the model for such Spanish orders as the Knights of Saint James of the Sword (who sported the very un-Christian motto, *Rubet ensis sanguine Arabum*, "The sword is scarlet with the blood of Arabs"). In 1312, however, at the height of their glory, the Templars were crushed on spurious charges of heresy by a French monarchy that was deeply in their debt and jealous of their power.

Yet the Templars—or those who enjoy dressing up like them—have never quite given up the ghost. "New orders" continue to come into existence and they have claimed Eunate and other numinous locations along the Camino as the setting for "traditional" ceremonies, generally performed on nights of the full moon and involving a maximum of shimmering costumes, animal heads, swords, scimitars, and other knightly or Druidic paraphernalia.

In the end, Eunate comes as advertised. It is compact, elegant, bright and *precioso*. The gargoyles have crumbled over the years, but a few fantastic faces still leer down from the masonry. As for the Virgin of Eunate, she is a worthy guardian of the temple, with her honest, homely Romanesque face. I have no coins to drop in the basket before the Christ child, so I donate my last square of chocolate and sit down to dry off and enjoy the silence.

But no more than five minutes after my arrival, a busload of ten-year-olds comes crowding in. Just my luck. The little church can barely contain us all. The din threatens to bring the ancient ceiling down. Undaunted, the teacher commands silence and launches into her lesson. It's a call-and-answer, full of references to porticos, cupolas and other beasties of architectural terminology that a North American would never encounter short of an undergraduate course. But these kids know their cornices from their finials.

"Very well," says the teacher. "Let's talk about the Virgin of Eunate. What kind of Virgin is she? Gothic or Romanesque?"

"Romanesque," call back fifty voices.

"That's right. And how do we know?"

"She looks serious," calls one voice.

"She has big eyes," says another.

"She's not as beautiful as a Gothic Virgin," chimes in a third.

"Good," says the teacher. "Now imagine Eunate 800 years ago. How would it be different?"

"It would have been painted inside."

"The sculptures would not have been broken."

"There would have been more pilgrims."

"We couldn't have come in a bus."

"Very good," says the teacher. Then she draws the students' attention to the gargoyles, the irregular shape of the dome, and the orientation of the church. She asks them about the Templars and tells them that this was probably not a Templar church at all, but a funeral chapel for pilgrims who died on their way to Santiago.

Then her voice falls. She leaves a space between her sentences so everyone can hear the rain on the roof. "Now pretend that you are pilgrims," she says. "You have been walking all day in the rain. Perhaps already you have walked hundreds of miles on your way to Santiago. This is no easy thing. There have been many dangers along the way. Often you have been hungry. You have suffered from illness. Your feet are sore. Perhaps you have no shoes! There is still a long road before you, but at least you have found your way this far. To be in out of the rain where you can rest your legs for a time, even on this cold stone floor, as you make your prayers to the Virgin; for you, this is as good a thing as lying in a warm bed with a full stomach.

"Probably you are not alone here. There are other pilgrims, on their own long journeys, who have their own prayers to make to the Virgin of Eunate.

"Now I want you all to be perfectly quiet for a moment. Just listen to the silence and the rain. And think of all the pilgrims who have stopped here through the centuries."

And we do.

Nuestra Señora Del Puy

The Virgin of Puy sits in state in her lovely bright palace above Estella, a town long renowned for its devotion to the Camino and its plenitude of religious establishments. *Puy*, in old French, denotes mountain, which is where the Virgin's basilica is to be found. As high as her basilica rises above the town, her image, draped in silver and ringed with potted lilies, rises above her worshippers. I hike up on a Sunday afternoon, between masses, when even the bar adjoining the basilica is closed and only a few of Our Lady's devotees are on hand. They kneel before her to light a candle and offer their prayers at length before paying a more perfunctory visit to her son in his chapel off to the side.

The image of Nuestra Señora was discovered, they say, beneath a tussock by two shepherds in the year 1085. The citizens of the nearest town, hearing of the find, tried to bear her off to their church. But no sooner was she taken from her hilltop than she began to grow very heavy. The further the men carried her, the heavier she became, until finally she weighed so much that not even a team of oxen could budge her. Then it was understood that she wished to be worshipped in the place where she had been discovered. Estella was founded on that site.

Nuestra Señora has worked many miracles, but she is most renowned for her exploit in foiling a church robber in 1640. The thief had slipped in by night and stripped Our Lady of her priceless jewels and robes. But when he tried to make off, the Virgin confounded his senses so that, though he imagined himself striding through the fields, he was in reality pacing around and around the interior of the church. He lay down to rest for the night thinking himself safely hidden in a grove of trees and woke up next morning at the foot of Our Lady's altar, in the grips of the authorities.

The hands of the hapless thief were chopped off. For a time they were displayed in front of the church, nailed to a wooden pole, as an example to all. Eventually a more permanent monument, consisting of a stone pillar with the thief's hands carved on it, was established to commemorate the miracle. It was dedicated: "To the perpetual memory of the stupendous prodigy of the blessed Virgen del Puy."

Or so I have heard. For in our gentler age, the pillar is no longer to be seen.

Estella is my fifth day out from Saint-Jean-Pied-de-Port and it is often around this point that the body lodges its first protests against the unwonted demands being placed upon it. Often, things will hold up for the first few days, fooling you into thinking that walking across Spain will be a breeze. Then everything gives out at once. This shouldn't be surprising when you consider that each day you are taking something in the neighborhood of 25,000 steps, many of them on rough paths or steep slopes, and that your pack has increased your body weight by several pounds overnight.

Last year, I developed a blister on my way to Estella. Just one at first, but that one was enough to make me change my way of walking. The resulting chain reaction left me with new blisters, chafed heels, stiff ankles and aching knees. This year I've successfully countered the blisters with woolen socks, but now instead I find my left shin swollen with tendonitis. Fortunately, one of the pilgrims at the refuge in Estella is a doctor from Denmark. He prescribes a cream and a day's rest.

Little Miguel turns up at the refuge too. Next morning, he is backtracking by bus to Pamplona, where his car is waiting. We share a morning coffee and I see him off. Back at the refuge, I notice the inscription he has left in the pilgrim's guestbook: *Buen Camino a todos los buenos peregrinos y a los malos tambien.*

"*Buen Camino* to all the good pilgrims. And to the bad ones as well."

After my day recuperating, it's on to Los Arcos, home of one of the Camino's rare Black Virgins. Sadly, I arrive in mid-afternoon, off-season, and the cathedral is locked up tight till evening mass. I go to the park where last summer I met my aged, benevolent friend, but there is no sign of him today. There is no sign of anyone. It is two-thirty of a Spanish small-town afternoon and the only souls wandering the streets are dogs and pilgrims.

Shall I stick around? I had hoped to spend the night in Torres del Rio—four miles further on—where last year the Italian hospitaler cooked up a wonderful pasta for the pilgrims. I take all of a minute to weigh a glimpse of the little dark Virgin of Los Arcos against a home-cooked Italian meal. Then I'm off.

In Torres del Rio, however, the hospitaler has gone into hibernation and I have to fend for myself. There is no restaurant in town, only a tiny shop that operates from the owner's front door on the Pythonesque principle of

"You tell me what you want and I'll tell you if I've got it." After a drawn-out process of elimination, I determine that today there are no fresh vegetables, fruit, meat or bread. A box of macaroni, a tin of anchovies and a bottle of corky red wine is what I get for having spurned the Virgin of Los Arcos. At least I didn't have my hands cut off.

Back at the refuge, the Italian hospitaler's smiling, fox-eyed Spanish partner, Geronimo, comes up from the basement to say hello. As I excavate the crumbling cork from my bottle of wine and give my macaroni a stir, he launches into a tirade against the summer pilgrims who expect to be treated like hotel guests.

"They have no regard for other pilgrims, no regard for us. They think they can just snap their fingers, you know? There were two pilgrims this summer, it got to the point where I wrote on their credentials, 'Lacks sincere pilgrim spirit,' so that the hospitalers at the next refuge would know. I tell you, I haven't had a holiday in three years and I'm ready to say to hell with it."

When I tell him what I'm writing about, he brightens up. "Just a second. I have something for you to look at."

He's back in a flash with a special edition of the magazine *Mas Allá*, "Beyond," devoted to "the enigmas of the Virgin." One hundred and twenty illustrated pages of miracles and apparitions ancient and modern. There are crying Virgins, bleeding Virgins, black Virgins, the "holographic" Virgin of Cuba (allegedly projected from a CIA submarine in 1982 with the goal of undermining Castro's atheist regime), to say nothing of *OVNI*, Unidentified Virginal Objects.

"Look at it, but don't take it away," Geronimo cautions, recognizing the covetous glint in my eye.

But I suspect I couldn't take it away if I tried. Like the Virgin of le Puy, the magazine would grow heavier and heavier as I went further from the refuge, till it could be carried no further. And speaking of the Virgin of le Puy, here is an article about other Virgins who share her gift of becoming lead-heavy at will or of returning on their own to places they have been removed from. They are grouped under the rubric "Intelligent Virgins."

It was at this point a year ago that I decided to take a break from the Camino and nip back to Pamplona for the running of the bulls. Of course I had already been through Pamplona but had managed to miss the main event. Day by day, as I walked along the Camino, I could feel Hemingway's ghost and a simple curiosity to know what all the hoopla was about, pulling me back. At last I gave in. My plan was this; I would put in my day's walk by early afternoon, hop the bus to Pamplona, where I would spend the night, then bus back next morning to where I had left off.

All went smoothly. I got my fill of the fiestas, slept on a park bench, and was back on the Camino next day before anyone had noticed I was gone. The real revelation of my jaunt, however, was not the running of the bulls, but the view from the window of the bus as I returned to Pamplona.

There I was, sitting passively, gazing out the panorama windows at the landscape flying by—the distant hills, the mesas rising from vineyards and olive groves—when it struck me that I had walked all this way. Yes, it had taken me days to cover what the bus ate up in an hour, but that was not the point. The point was that I had walked it, and in walking it had gained another knowledge of it than the knowledge of my eyes. I had the knowledge of my feet (and my ankles and my knees); the knowledge of my skin; of my ears and nose; of my mind, that had been alive and thinking in that landscape, not dozing in a metal capsule. I had known this piece of earth at a human pace. In that moment I understood that, despite all our boasts, we have never really conquered distance. We have only found ways to cheat it.

Most pilgrims start the Camino with apprehension. Can I really walk all the way across Spain? It sounds impossible. And in fact, there are some who don't make it, usually because they push too hard and injure themselves. But most pilgrims find by the end that 400 miles isn't such a long way to walk. It just takes time.

The novelty of the experience is a constant topic of conversation. Pilgrims' talk is always gravitating towards aches and remedies, how much or how little to carry, which foods provide the most energy, the wisdom or folly of taking frequent breaks, the best hours for walking. One day, a German pilgrim named Paul, who had had enough of such talk, put everything back into perspective:

"It's just walking!" he said.

And he was right. It is just walking. On the Camino, we relearn the pace proper to our kind. Our bodies and thoughts slow to the speed of the old pilgrims, the wanderers, our nomadic forebears.

Santa María La Real de Nájera

Nájera is one of those improbable frontier towns that at a certain moment of history, through a unique set of circumstances flourishes, then is forgotten forever. The people, having nowhere else special to go, stay on though history has left them behind. Old Nájera is four parallel streets wedged in between the Najerilla River and the huge brick-red rock that abrupts from the plain at its back. It hardly looks like a capital city but for more than a century, as the Spanish Christians drove south into Muslim lands, that's what it was.

Nájera's royal history began on the day when the hunting falcon of the king, Don García Sanchez, went in pursuit of a dove. Don García waited and waited but the falcon did not return. The sun was setting and the red rock of Nájera glowed a deep cinnabar when at last he set off in the same direction as the birds. As he beat his way through the underbrush at the base of the rock, Don García suddenly spotted a cave. Its mouth was the height of a man, and from within, there shone an unearthly light. His heart full of wonder, the king pushed his way through the tangle of vines and stepped inside. He found himself in a high stone chapel. Before him, set upon a primitive altar, was a statue of the Virgin all lit round with candles. The king fell to his knees in prayer and only then did he notice the falcon and the dove, peaceably perched side-by-side, a vase of white lilies between them.

On the king's orders, a sumptuous church was built above the cave. A new chivalric order was founded, too: the knights *de la Terraza*—of the Vase. Don García built his capital here and in time the cave became the pantheon of the rulers of Navarra. Here, to this day, the pilgrim may see Santa María la Real, a great-eyed Virgin, draped in gold and royal blue.

The pilgrims' refuge of Nájera is a beautiful medieval stone edifice on the central plaza and almost as grand as the royal pantheon, with window wells two yards deep and a ceiling upheld by a single beam, cut from a tree such as Spain hasn't seen these five centuries. Taped Gregorian chants soothe the weary traveler. On the wall hangs a small reminder: *El turista exige; el peregrino agradece*, The tourist makes demands; the pilgrim gives thanks.

The hospitaler is a dry little local fellow lodged beneath a cap. He checks my credentials, enters the information in his ledgers, then pushes a box full of 500-peseta pieces at me and says: "Donation?" I conclude that 500 pesetas would be appropriate. As I head out for dinner with Martin, a Swiss cyclist, the hospitaler points at a sign above the door that says: "Refuge closes 10 p.m." When we return at a quarter to, he is pacing outside. We wish him good evening, step through the door, and hear the key grinding in the lock.

"I bet he turns on the music in the morning," says Martin as we slip into bed.

Seven-twenty a.m.: full-on Gregorian chant. I sit up sharply, almost braining myself on the roof beam. Martin is giggling helplessly in the bunk below. And the hospitaler is already safely out the door, like a boy who has thrown a stink bomb into the high school cafeteria.

NO ONE ENTERS LOGROÑO, the capital of La Rioja, without first passing Felisa. She is a legend of the Camino, this matronly woman, with her ramshackle house on the hill, her posse of skinny, yelping dogs, and her own unique stamp for pilgrims that reads: *Higos, Agua y Amor*, Figs, Water and Love.

The dogs perk up at my approach. Not much to get excited about this time of year, so they have to make the most of me. A neighbor calls out from her porch, "Felisa, a pilgrim!" and Felisa comes out of her house at a run.

"*Peregrino*, come and sign my book. Where are you from?"

"Canada."

"Four Canadian girls passed this morning."

"Really?" I haven't heard any rumors of Canadians, but sure enough, here are their names. "How many pilgrims have passed today?"

"Eight," she replies without hesitation.

Felisa's face is fat, friendly and endearingly shrivelled like an apple doll's. She tells me she has lived here for over sixty years, but she never saw a pilgrim before 1988. She's seen every one since. I open my passport for her stamp, take a swig of the water she offers me, and leave a coin on her donation tray: Felisa's an institution worth supporting.

Later, at the refuge in Logroño, I ask the hospitaler how many pilgrims have arrived today.

"Nine," she tells me.

"That's funny. I was talking to Felisa and she told me eight."

"She's right," says the hospitaler after a moment's thought. "One came by bus."

Logroño's co-mayor into perpetuity—thanks to her decisive intervention during the French siege of 1521—is la Virgen de la Esperanza. I go to the Church of Santiago to pay her my regards, but restoration work is underway and she is under wraps. Men in sparkling white space-suits and women in baby-blue overalls swing from scaffolds under klieg lights, caressing the three-storey altarpiece with their power tools. Who knew that art restoration could be so sexy?

I step out of the church and into what appears to be a giant children's board game. Laid into the pavement of the plaza are squares numbered one to sixty-three. They run from one to nine across, then snake back from ten to eighteen, and so on up to the seventh row. Some of the squares are decorated with stylized depictions in metal of famous stops on the Camino. Eunate is here, Puente la Reina, and points yet to come. There is a labyrinth along the way and a prison house. In the sixty-third and final square is Santiago de Compostela.

There are images of pilgrims walking the route, but they leave a web-footed trail behind them. They are geese, in fact, and this gameboard—which I am now pacing out square by square—is the *Juego de la Oca*, the Goose Game. The Goose Game has been played for centuries by children in France and Spain. It is their equivalent to Snakes and Ladders, the players rolling the dice and moving their little goosey pieces in a race to the top. The path is strewn with helpful squares that permit a goose to jump ahead or roll again and others less helpful that compel her to go back or miss a turn. The most perilous square is the fifty-eighth where, even as the pilgrim goose comes in sight of her goal, the Grim Reaper waits to send her back to square one.

The Goose Game can be found in many refuges of the Camino, although the modern board no longer reflects the game's origins. The context has been secularized so that, instead of Santiago, today's goose runs off to Paris or Rio. She dines with her lover, dances flamenco, has her hair done, and works as a waitress or a stewardess.

The Goose Game is not the only children's game that contains a buried Christian allegory. Take a look at hopscotch; if the configuration of the squares reminds you of the ground plan of a cathedral, that's no coincidence. The top square, representing the apse, used to be known as Paradise. One could think of the original Goose Game as a children's version of the labyrinth of Chartres. It teaches that the way to the goal is never straight, that often one is turned away at the very threshold. Chance, of course, plays a role in the Goose Game, but faith and perseverance still win out in the end: even Death just means starting over.

And the geometry of the Goose Game—seven rows by nine—reverberates, like the cathedral of Chartres, with sacred mathematics. Seven and nine are the numbers of earth and heaven, the products of supernatural threes (the Holy Trinity; heaven, hell and purgatory) and earthly fours (the elements, the directions, the seasons).

They are also the numbers of the Virgin.

I WAKE IN THE REFUGE of Santo Domingo de la Calzada with a hangover, courtesy of Däg and Natasha, a Norwegian-Russian couple who gave me the perfect opening last night by asking, "So who is this Santiago?" They had been innocently riding their bikes through Europe en route to Portugal when their hotelier in Bayonne told them about the Camino. Lovely scenery, cheap places to stay, nice people. They aren't sure if they'll go the whole way, depends on the weather.

So who is this Santiago?

Philippe LeClerc was there too, my companion of the first night in Saint-Jean-Pied-de-Port. It seems more like a year than a week since last I saw him. His bamboo staff beside the front door announced his presence. Leaning beside the knobby, hand-whittled staffs of the other pilgrims, it evoked an older, "Eastern" style of pilgrimage. The sort of pilgrimage where the pilgrim simply launches himself into the world, trusting God to steer his footsteps. This was the way of Christ and the Apostles, of the Irish monks and Saint Francis, but it has seldom found favor with ecclesiastical hierarchies. The Church has preferred to keep its pilgrims on straight and well-trodden paths like the Camino, where it can exercise some control over what they see and how they understand it, thereby hedging them from sin, doubt, error and all sorts of dangerous knowledge. Philippe's staff seems appropriate to the new Camino, with its aura of a way of discovery.

But before my head is off the pillow in the morning, the elegant bamboo staff and its owner are out on the road.

It's an hour to the village of Grañon, where last year a friendly bartender gave isometrics lessons to me and a pilgrim from Paris named Richard. She had tips for avoiding stiff shoulders and strained necks from carrying a backpack, but when we asked if she had ever done the Camino herself the answer was the usual wistful no. Those who live along the Camino are mostly content to watch the pilgrims go by.

This Richard moved like a spider on his spindly legs. I thought it would be a challenge to match him one day, stride for stride. In fact, it nearly killed me. Still, matching his steps was easier than keeping up with his doubts. Richard was a questioning soul and he raced along the Camino as though he expected to find all the answers waiting for him in Santiago.

"Things have been happening to me since I started the Camino," he told me. "Things that I am trying to understand. Last week, for example, it was my birthday, and my friends had a party for me at the refuge in the morning. I thought, 'This is fantastic. I have only known these people for a few days, and look at what they are doing for me.' Then later the same day, I almost died. I was by myself, leaning down into a well to get water, when the weight of my backpack pulled me in. I caught myself just in time or I could have drowned. I am trying to understand how such extremes can occur in one day."

As we puzzled over this one, we came to a village with a cross street and arrows that pointed in opposite directions. One read "Camino"; the other, "Bar." We headed for the bar, where the menfolk of the village were gathered, watching the bicycle races on tv.

"Listen," Richard continued. "Do you believe that things only happen when you're ready for them to happen? Because I'm sure that if I had gone on the Camino two years ago, or even last year, it wouldn't have meant anything to me. I've been incredibly self-centered my whole life. I am separated from my wife, I hardly know my child. She may never think of me as her father. It may be too late for that already."

I had never imagined Richard in such a light before now. He had been just another pilgrim, albeit one with incredibly long legs. I wondered why he was looking for the answers to his questions here rather than in Paris. Was it the escape from the familiar that let him see things afresh? Twice already he had interrupted his walk to return to Paris for job interviews, then beamed himself back to where he'd left off, so obsessed was he with seeing this through to the end.

"I have one question. Do you think the Camino can change your life?"

"Maybe, Richard. Maybe it's like you say. It can change your life if you're ready for it to change your life. Otherwise"—and here I could not resist throwing in Paul's line—"otherwise, it's just walking."

"Yes, exactly. If I had done this last year, it would have been just walking. But this year, it's something more."

"What is it?"

"I don't know. I'm just sure I'm not the same person I was even two weeks ago."

I lost track of Richard. He was like so many others I met along the way and took for granted because our paths kept crossing, until the day came when I didn't see them anymore. I wonder if the Camino changed his life. I doubt somehow that it did, or at least not in the sort of once-and-for-all way he was hoping. I imagine him now back in Paris, working at one of those jobs he was interviewing for, living much the same life as before. Perhaps he is putting a little more into his relationship with his daughter.

And perhaps he daydreams sometimes, as he sits at his desk, about waking early, and walking all morning uphill and down on his spindly, far-carrying legs. Of stopping in the shade of a tree for a drink of water and hearing a familiar voice call out,

"¡Hola! ¡Peregrino!"

I SPEND THE NIGHT in the refuge of Belorado, where the hospitaler washes my clothes and hangs them to dry in front of the stove, then welcomes us all to join her for dinner. Sybil was a nurse in Germany, but now she has "retired" to lend her services to the Camino. She has recently finished her own pilgrimage, on foot from Germany to Santiago, then all the way back to Assisi in central Italy. She says she had a hard time convincing Italian drivers that she really didn't need a lift. In one town, the priest coldly informed her that the "proper" way to make a pilgrimage was by car.

"That would have been news to Saint Francis," she laughs.

With time, certain walking rituals become fixed and inviolable. For instance, every morning, within an hour of setting out, I will launch a sudden, frenetic search for my wedding ring, watch, wallet and passport, always in that order. Everything is always where it should be, but because the last three items are kept in different pockets, I must look like I have a mouse in my clothing, as I swat frantically at my chest and thighs.

I sing as I walk, too. Recently, I have noticed that three of my favorite walking songs are about Marys. There's a Brazilian number by Marisa Monte called "Maria de Verdade," and *West Side Story*'s "Maria," and that Billy Bragg song about finding Mary in the dictionary, after Marx and before Marzipan. I keep the beat with my staff, a stick of I don't know what wood that Little Miguel found for me on the way down from Roncesvalles. Evidently some generous soul had sat by the path for a while whittling branches, then left them to be claimed by pilgrims. I'm very happy with my walking-stick. It's light and flexible, with a crook at the top in the shape of a check mark (or a goose's foot) where I can rest my thumb.

A staff isn't a strict pilgrim necessity anymore; the roads are smoother than they once were and one doesn't have to worry quite so much about wolves and bandits. But it feels good in the hand, and it's still useful for testing the depth of streams and puddles or keeping a grip on slippery slopes. A distinctive staff, like the bamboo pole of Philippe LeClerc, is also a calling card. The sight of it leaning outside a bar is an invitation to come in and take a break from the road with some pilgrims.

But on this lonely Camino of October, I have lots of time to sing and few invitations to drink. With a paucity of new thoughts and stimuli passing through my mind, I spend a lot of time calling up the faces and feelings and events of last year. It is remarkable the things that spark memories: a tree, a clump of ferns, a radio transmitter, a misspelt sign. Thus, as I come upon a certain gully on the way to Villafranca Montes de Oca, I remember that I walked this bit last year with John F. Kennedy, and that it was here he found my last year's staff for me. (And what does it mean that it's always someone else who finds me my staff?)

JFK was a school teacher and former punk rocker from Long Island. His name had been a great hit with the Spanish hospitalers along the way. "*¡Qué bien!*" they would say when he signed the register, "That's great!" Then one day a hospitaler said, "*¡Qué pena!*" "What a pity!" That was how John found out that John Kennedy junior had died. John was a cheerfully blasphemous soul. I met him and his companion Matt on their first morning coming down from Roncesvalles and we took turns passing and falling behind each other all the way to Santiago. Matt, though no paragon of virtue, was Catholic enough that he had made John promise not to swear for the duration of the Camino. When, from time to time, John found that promise onerous, he would drop back or forge ahead to swear with me, as he had done that morning.

Thinking back now on these people and things, I can see them becoming a kind of songline; a private songline I lay over the old, communal songline of the Camino. I suppose that if you repeated the Camino enough times, you would have a story for every step of the way that you could sing to yourself as you walked, or tell to someone who loved you, if you could find someone who loved you enough to listen for that long.

It occurs to me that what I'm really doing is making a pilgrimage to my own past.

THE WAY INTO BURGOS runs alongside the N.1, a bleak strip of shrines to the automobile. There are gas stations, truck yards, car washes, garages and every sort of dealer: Opel, Peugeot, Suzuki, Chrysler, Honda, Fiat, Volvo . . . What little grass there is lies on the far side of seven-foot fences. And even if one could walk on the stuff, it wouldn't give much joy. After the variety Nature displays on the Camino, what substitute is that triumph of human dullness, the lawn?

There is a sad undercurrent of nostalgia running beneath this blight. Look at the wildlife on the emblems of the car-makers and groomers. Lions, tigers, seals, sea turtles, elephants, snakes, birds—a Noah's ark of species that will soon exist only as zoo curiosities and hood ornaments.

At the end of the strip, a great factory crouches like a toad. It has windows for walls, allowing us to peek into its sparkling belly. The paradisal grounds that surround it are planted with willow, oak, cedar, even a bonsai cherry, and watered by perpetual sprinklers. Its silver smokestacks puff out immaculate plumes of steam. This industrial Eden is the Firestone factory.

Fire and stone. How fitting.

Burgos is famed not for its Virgin, but for a crucified Christ of such verisimilitude that his hair is said to grow and blood to seep from his wounds. They say that when Queen Isabella (who was renowned for her personal collection of relics) ordered a nail removed from one of his hands as a souvenir, the Christ's arm flopped limply to his side. She hastened to have the nail replaced.

The pilgrims' refuge lies in a shady park on the western verge of the city. In fall, the avenue that leads through the park resembles a movie set of a nineteenth-century sanatorium. At any moment, I expect to see Marcello Mastroianni or Dirk Bogarde come scuffling through the dead leaves in pursuit of some aloof young object of desire. Instead, I find Timo, my Finnish friend from the first days, relaxing with a beer. With so few pilgrims on the road in this season, every encounter feels like a grand reunion. Timo and I enjoy a sybaritic meal in the shadow of the cathedral, dining on local specialties like sheep's brain and sweetbreads. As we leave, Timo cocks an eyebrow at the cathedral and says, "You know, I look at this thing, and I think, For anyone to be inspired to make something so beautiful, there has got to be a God. There has got to be."

It was here in Burgos, my first time on the Camino, that I made up a parcel of the useless items I had been carrying on my back: eleven pounds of shirts, pants and paper that two weeks of pilgrimage had proved redundant. All together, they nicely filled a big cardboard box to send to Madrid for future pick-up. I showed the box around the refuge so that everyone could admire what an idiot I had been, like the reformed smoker who boasts how many packs a day he used to burn through.

"How about it?" I inquired. "Anyone else care to shed a little of the material world?"

I meant it as a joke, but Paul, the German pilgrim, took me up on it.

"The box is going to Madrid? Then please send this too." He handed me a cheap, white, plastic rosary. "The sisters gave me this when I was in Madrid, but I have another now so I don't need it anymore. Please give it back to the sisters, and thank them. It was very helpful."

"Which sisters?"

"I don't remember their names, but you will find them if you ask. They're very famous."

Paul was the sort of holy innocent Dostoevsky might have conjured up, a lost and half-catatonic soul, mild and fierce by turns, who was being led along the Camino by his uncle, a retired school teacher who had decided that a long walk was what Paul needed to get himself sorted out. In short, I couldn't say no. I took the rosary and laid it on top of my spare jeans, knowing it was going to be an albatross. For the three days I spent in Madrid, I carried it around with me, fingering it unconsciously, at each moment hoping and expecting that a mysterious nun would step out of a doorway or approach me in a bar to ask for it. In the end, I left it on the steps of a church.

In the long days of walking, there is time to remember everyone you have ever met, and a few you haven't. One of my partners in this enterprise is Gerald Brenan, the English writer, friend of Lytton Strachey and the Bloomsburys, who came to Spain to stay in the 1920s, and whose works on the politics, literature and culture of his adopted land won him a reputation as one of the most acute observers of the Spanish scene. His memoir *South from Granada* holds a special appeal for me, not only for its charm, but for its revelation that Brenan was a great walker. He speaks with pride of once covering seventy-one miles in twenty-eight hours in the rugged south of Spain, though he confesses that he was held to twenty-five miles a day when he had dysentery.

It's like hearing news of an old friend, then, when I open *El País* on November 5 and find an article on Brenan. Or rather, on his body. For it seems that, although the tomb of his wife, Gamel Woolsey, had space reserved for a second occupant, a few years before his death in 1987 at the age of ninety-two, Brenan signed his body over to the University of Malaga for research. According to one version of events, the writer's decision was prompted by an obsessive concern that his friends and relatives not be burdened with the expense of his funeral. It may be, on the other hand, that Brenan genuinely regarded his body as something whose only worth, once his spirit had left it, was as an object of study.

Whatever the case, the university has found itself unable to make use of Brenan's legacy out of fear of negative press and respect for the principle that a medical student should not know whom he is dissecting, which is difficult to ensure with a corpse as illustrious as Brenan's. And so he remains, afloat these thirteen years in a bath of formaldehyde.

For some time now, Brenan's friends have been trying to pry him away from the university. They hope to see him buried. They lament that they cannot rightly honor his life or grieve his death until a plot of earth somewhere contains his mortal remains. Any of us can understand their feelings because we share a common culture, a culture that has long been in the practice of keeping used bodies near and in one piece, whether in hope of their eventual resurrection or out of sheer, cussed habit. But I wonder whether an observer from another time or culture (Bali, say, where the dead are cremated and their ashes cast upon the sea) might not find this tussling over a corpse queer or even appalling. Would an outsider see fetishism in the desire of Brenan's friends to plant his body somewhere they can go visit it? Or a ghoulish utilitarianism in a society that pickles bodies and carves them up for "the advancement of science"?

The story, in any case, looks to be headed for a happy resolution. The head of the medical department of the university is sympathetic to the cause of Brenan's friends, opining that the author has already made his contribution to science by proving the effectiveness of the methods used to preserve him (though the good doctor confesses he has a hankering to poke around the brain of an intellectual). Someday soon, then, it may be possible to make a pilgrimage to Brenan's tomb. To lay flowers, offer a libation, and sit joyful or pensive in proximity to the vacant frame of flesh that housed his living self, a self once animated enough to walk fifty miles in a day. Till then Brenan's body waits as pure and uncorrupted as the bodies of the saints.

BETWEEN BURGOS and Castrojeriz lies one of the loneliest and most dramatic stretches of the Camino. The villages—Tardajos with its one white-washed street; Rabé de las Calzadas, where the wind whips the leaves around the vacant plaza—look forsaken, abandoned to winter. Beyond them are farmlands scratched into ancient riverbeds and ocean floors. In summer, the fields yield knee-high wheat, but now is the season of burning and turning. Tractors tear up the soil and all the undulating earth for miles around looks like it has been shaved with a dry razor.

Here, I feel myself getting caught up in the Camino again. Perhaps the way until now has been too domesticated. You can hear the silence better in this hard land, these vast spaces. Sometimes I just sit and let the wind drown out my thoughts. At others I see myself from a distance, a small living thing picking its way across the face of the earth.

I catch up with two French pilgrims, Cristal and Florence, and we walk together, heads lowered against the wind. It is too much work talking, and what is there to say in a place like this? We pick our way down the slope called Matamulos, the Mule-killer, to the village of Hornillos del Camino.

The three of us sit on bunks in the refuge, hoping the hospitaler will come soon to turn on the hot water. The topic of horoscopes comes up, and though the women go through the other eleven signs, they can't guess mine. They can't even figure which one they've missed.

"Virgo," I tell them, a little smugly.

La Virgen del Manzano

On the rock above Castrojeriz stand the ruins of a castle. It crumbled, they say, in the same earthquake that shattered Lisbon. By then it had, in any case, outlived its purpose, which had been to repel either the Christians or the Moors depending who was currently in occupancy. Once, for reasons not clearly explained, Santiago himself leapt on his white charger from the heights of the rock. The horse's hoof struck an apple tree as it landed, cleaving it like a bolt of lightning. Within the charred and splintered stump, the townsfolk found Our Lady of the Apple Tree.

Nuestra Señora del Manzano holds a place of honor among the Virgins of the Camino—the Virgins of Spain, in fact—for she was included by Alfonso the Wise in his *Cantigas de Santa María*. This Alfonso (1221 to 1284) presided over the first flowering of learning in the Castilian tongue (though for his poetry he preferred the more musical Galician). He assembled a brilliant court, where troubadours from Provence and Catalonia rubbed shoulders with rhetoricians, musicians, astronomers, mathematicians, translators and scientists. He oversaw the codification of Spanish law and the chronicling of its history. His *Septenario* was an encyclopedic treatment of the seven arts; his *Lapidario* treated stones, their curative and magical properties; he even authored Spain's first treatise on chess, dice and dominoes. But his most personal and enduring literary creation was the *Cantigas de Santa María*.

The *Cantigas* comprise 420 poems written in celebration of the miracles of Mary. Four are devoted to the Virgin of the Apple Tree. The first three relate miracles performed during the erection of her church: a worker falls, but catches hold of a stone by his fingertips; another plunges from a great height, but calls out Mary's name and lands safely; two more builders emerge intact from under a mountain of rubble. By the fourth of the canticles, the church has been built, but remains a health hazard: a beam falls from the ceiling during mass and the Virgin must swoop down to deflect it away from the congregation. Such incidents today would lead to calls for tougher construction safety standards, but in the *Cantigas* they are occasions to admire the vigilant compassion of Our Lady. She is the worker's best hope in a world without hardhats.

This afternoon the church is locked. Maybe they're still putting back that beam. I stop by the refuge to ask if the church will be open for evening mass, but the hospitaler tells me it's shut till next year. Renovations.

"That's a shame," I say. "I wanted to see Nuestra Señora del Manzano."

"Why? Are you interested in art?"

"Yes, but more in the stories. There are so many stories about her."

"Oh, stories," the hospitaler says with a shake of his head. "Yes, yes. The *Cantigas*, the hoofprints of Santiago's horse, all that. But those are only *legends*."

I'm intrigued by the line he draws between that which is worthy of belief and that which is merely legendary. He seems impatient, even mildly embarrassed, with these legends, the way a child feels impatient at his parents' quaint ways of thinking. "We've moved on, for God's sake," I can imagine him saying. "We don't believe in such nonsense anymore."

Yet how many of today's legends were yesterday's truths? Some traditions have survived; some—the Immaculate Conception, the Assumption of Mary—have even been elevated to dogma. But much of what was once believed concerning the miraculous powers of saints, the wonder-working powers of statues or the literal truth of Scripture has been downgraded to legend status. In recent centuries, science and reason have done their best to wring the last drops of the sacred out of matter. I wonder that a religious soul doesn't regret the passing of a time when the world was rife with miracles.

Last year, I walked into Castrojeriz with Joana, a tortured Portuguese pilgrim with stubborn martyr's eyes that said, "Go ahead, burn me." Joana was *exigente*, demanding. When she wanted something, she wanted it at once. If she felt like praying when the church was closed, she knocked on doors until she found the woman with the key. When she was thirsty, she went to a house and asked for a glass of water. When the rest of us were compared to Joana, it became apparent that we lacked confidence in our role as pilgrims. We were bourgeois and self-sufficient, disinclined to "trouble" folks. But Joana knew what a pilgrim's rights were and she wasn't afraid to exercise them.

If she had a question, she asked. I remember her pelting the hospitaler of Carrion de los Condes, a nun, with every unanswered query that floated to the surface of her mind: "Sister, Sister, tell me something. What is the difference between the Orthodox Church and the Catholic anyway? Why isn't there only one church? Do the Protestants believe in the Virgin? Why not? Do you think the Pope is always right? What about the Jews, what do they say about Jesus?"

As we hiked along the one long street of Castrojeriz in the somnolent heat of midday, questions were vexing her like flies.

"Why do I like one church but another no? They is same religion. What's the difference?"

"I don't know, Joana. I never went to church."

"Why do one priest I like, but another I don't like him? They says the same things. But this one I like and this one I hate. Why?"

"Why is the sky blue?" I thought. "Enjoy the scenery."

"I think if you are Catholic every priest should be the same. You shouldn't have one is better, one is no good. I don't know. Maybe I'm not Catholic."

"What are you then? Protestant?"

"How can I be Protestant?" she shrugged. "I have nothing to protest."

After Castrojeriz there is a mesa. It's a steep climb to the top, then a twenty-minute walk across the tableland, and you're looking out over the lunar flatness of the ancient kingdom of León. The sun drops below the horizon as I tramp down the far side, and my way to Itero de la Vega is lit by a sliver of a moon. It's October 31, the eve of All Saints' Day, and far across the fields, floodlight-mounted tractors are still crawling up and down the slopes like sluggish fireflies.

I imagine one of the tractors coming to a sudden halt in the middle of a furrow. The blades are caught on something. The great machine won't budge an inch, forward or back, no matter how the farmer cajoles it. At last he switches off the engine, cursing as he swings down from the cab. Other night-tillers have pulled up to see what the trouble is. They shout advice, hop out to take a look. The farmer drops to his knees and starts to dig at the soil, feeling for the rock, the tree root, the fence post that has jammed his machine.

Ah, there it is! It's not so big.

His fingers go to work, rocking it, easing it from the belly of the earth. His friends lean in, urging him on. With a final tug, the farmer dislodges the object. He stands, and thumbs away the caked mud, then holds up to the floodlights what he has found. It is a statue of the Virgin Mary with her son in her lap.

There is a stunned and wary silence. The farmers drop their cigarettes and cross themselves. One by one, they fall to their knees.

The Holy Mother smiles off into the starry night.

TODAY IS ALL SAINTS' DAY, the day of remembrance. In Spain, this is a national holiday, the day when the living come back to their native towns to visit their dead. A similar holiday exists in Japan. There—in the countryside at least—families to this day will, on a certain August evening, run a trail of candles from their front door to the graveyard to guide the newly dead home. Why does North American culture have no such festival? Are the dead more dead for us? Or is it that we have extended ourselves too far, stretching the ties that once bound us to family and to a certain piece of the earth till they have lost their elasticity?

I bought my lunch provisions last night, in case the shops were closed today. The toothless shopkeeper cackled approvingly as he carved thick slabs of ham and sheep cheese for my sandwich.

"That's right, tomorrow is a holiday. In the morning, we'll all go to church. In the afternoon, to the cemetery. We Spanish are very Catholic. Very devout."

But not very prone to start their devotions early; in Boadilla del Camino, at ten-thirty in the morning, the village has barely woken. And this is reasonable. Surely the dead would want it that way.

The church of Santa María is half the size of the town. My every footstep upon the old wooden floor (an odd feature for a church in Spain) draws a moan. "But that's all right," I tell myself. "I'm disturbing no one's prayers. There's nobody here but me. ..."

I sense my error in mid-thought, take one more look around, and it's only then I really see them.

Nobody here but me? How could I be so wrong? Just look at them. They're on the walls and on the ceiling, in the chapels and at the altar, watching, welcoming, guiding, admonishing: the saints. As long as the saints are with us, no church is ever empty, no pilgrim ever alone. After the windy silence of the plains, they fill the church with a human sound. They gaze down from the walls like the Catholic family ancestors, their heaven-vivid robes giving the promise that somewhere, somewhere, there is a brighter world than the one outside of dusty brown and straw yellow.

There is an expression, "the Communion of the Saints," which I always used to find faintly creepy. But here one sees it in action and it's not so bad. The dead, in the person of the saints, lend a hand to the living. The living pray for the dead to speed them through purgatory and on to heaven. Everyone pulls for everyone else and Jesus and his Mother hear all their prayers. It's the universal church conceived as family and what could make more sense to the gregarious Spanish?

There were saints in my family home, too. They had names like Norman Bethune, Tom Paine, Woody Guthrie, John Steinbeck, Paul Robeson. Robert Burns rated a shrine. My parents were "lefties," and their saints were the saints of the workers' movement and the Rights of Man, the ones who embodied the faith, died for it if need be. The movement even had its own, secular version of the Communion of the Saints: "brothers" and "sisters" pulling together to make a new heaven on earth.

And my own walls? For better or for worse, they are at present saint free.

I stop for lunch near Población de Campos, where a pilgrim pit stop has been laid out next to a tiny thirteenth-century stone hermitage. There are picnic benches, barbecue pits, shade trees. And a bucolic, high-walled enclosure that I don't recognize as the village cemetery until the first car pulls up and a family in their Sunday best piles out. Dad hauls the wreath out of the trunk, Mom brushes the wrinkles out of the kids' clothes, just like this was a real visit to see Grandma and Grandpa. Then they all pass together through the wrought-iron gates. Their car has Bilbao plates, so they've driven a long way this morning. Yet they don't stay long. Five minutes or so, just enough time to say hello. Then they come trooping out, chatting, smiling, and crowd back into the car. Did they come all this way just for that?

For the next half-hour, as I sit in the chill wind, gnawing my way through last night's provisions, a dozen more families roll in. Some have come from as far as Valladolid, Zaragoza or Madrid. Their observances are as brief as the first family's, lasting the time it takes to get everyone lined up, set the wreath just right, offer up a prayer.

During a break in the parade of visitors (somehow words like "mourners" or "the bereaved" don't work here), I venture to the gates and take a peek at the city of the dead. Scanning the tidy, flowering tombstones, I see none that bears the name of an individual. They all are family plots. In death as in life, the family sticks together.

When I pass through the town later, I find the streets lined with the cars of the long-distance travelers. The four bars of Población de Campos are packed and festive with the homecoming crowd. The dead have provided the living with a reason to get together.

Santa María la Blanca

Late in the afternoon, I reach Villalcázar de Sirga, home of Santa María la Blanca.

Last time, I did this stretch of the Camino with Consuela. She was one of my heroes, a stocky, garrulous, down-to-earth, fifty-three-year-old housewife, out on her own for the first time in her life. Words spilled out of her like beans from a sack, but she was always full of questions and motherly interest. When I asked her why she was doing the Camino, she told me it was from "a necessity of the soul" and left it at that.

Consuela suffered more from the heat and the daily demands of the Camino than any of us. To make things worse, she was nearly blind. To read anything, she needed to hold it up an inch from her thick glasses. Still, she was first up every morning, stumping along like she was off to  do her shopping. I had to go hard to keep up with her that day. When we got to Villalcázar de Sirga, we took a stroll around the inside of the cathedral. Neither of us knew to look for Santa María la Blanca. We were just happy to find somewhere cool.

Yet Santa María la Blanca is among the most celebrated Virgins of the *Cantigas*. Fourteen of King Alfonso's songs are dedicated to her miracles and this time I mean to find her. I make a once-around of the cathedral, but can't guess which of the many Virgins she might be. In the end, I ask a guide to point her out.

What, that one?

Plain, plumpish, middle-aged, her right arm missing (the Christ child has lost his head), María the White would attract no attention in an art gallery. But she once drew countless pilgrims to her church, proving again that the most powerful and beloved images of Mary are seldom the most beautiful. Mary is a mother, after all, and who judges their mother by her looks? La Blanca has a mother's smile. She looks like she's figured out your problems already and is about to give you some advice. Looking at her now, her frank, simple face makes me think of Consuela.

María la Blanca performs sensible miracles. Nothing of the showy variety. She guides some lost falconers out of trouble. She restores life to the limbs of a paralytic girl from France. Another French pilgrim she prevents from entering her church till he has confessed his sins ("Don't you dare come in here without wiping your shoes!"). The rest of her miracles fall mostly within her area of specialty: curing the blind.

THE WAY TO SAHAGÚN passes through some of the poorest villages of the Camino. The houses are built close to the earth—low, crooked, hunchbacked. Many are falling to ruin. Trees and stone are scarce here; the crumbling facades reveal the building materials to be mud and straw on a wooden skeleton. As the years pass, and the young continue to abandon the parched land for the cities, these houses will dissolve in the autumn rains.

But the poverty of the towns and the vacant dreariness of the land-scape are set off by the glory of the towering clouds that scud across the sky on the back of the west wind. This harsh wind, which has been blowing in my face since Burgos, must mean winter in northern Spain, because I never felt it last summer. In summer there was only a shy breeze that blew always at one's back. In the middle of a torrid afternoon, when it seemed not a breath of air was stirring, I would turn my face and find it following me, as cooling as a sip of water.

Timo catches up with me somewhere in the middle of this nowhere, and we walk together for a while. He keeps a good pace, jamming his little metal walking sticks into the ground with each step like a cross-country skier. But the road here is gravel, and the *chunk chunk chunk* of the sticks becomes a machine rhythm, like the tick of a clock or the grinding of a locomotive engine. So after a while, I stop to tie a shoelace, and let Timo forge ahead a while. Then I continue with nothing in my ears but the wind.

La Virgen Peregrina

The derelict monastery of la Peregrina, the (female) Pilgrim, broods on its bluff above Sahagún. She looks like a ship of the plains, sailing into the strong wind that blows from Santiago. The Church of Christ is often likened to a ship, a vessel bearing the faithful across the waters of death to salvation. So Mary, as the mother-vessel of Christ and all believers, is both ship and church. La Peregrina adds one more motif to this seamless fabric: Mary the mother, the ship, the Church, is the pilgrim too.

La Peregrina is the female counterpart of Santiago Peregrino, the inevitable expression of the pilgrim's desire to have His Lady always by his side. There is a Biblical model for the Virgin as Pilgrim: Mary's flight into Egypt with Joseph and their infant son. But Joseph doesn't figure in the depiction of la Peregrina. There is only the child, not carried sensibly in a papoose, but balanced impossibly on his mother's left arm.

La Peregrina is life-sized, gracious, a most beautiful Virgin, with weary Andalusian eyes, full of love and wisdom. Her hair is stiff and real, with even, it seems, some strands of gray among the black. In her right hand she daintily holds a pilgrim's staff. The pouch of a pilgrim dangles from around her waist and the seashell and sword-cross of Saint James are embroidered on her garment. In place of Santiago's broad-brimmed hat she sports an outsized crown. One could say she is a little too dolled-up for the road.

This Peregrina is not the only Pilgrim Virgin of the Camino. Another celebrated one is found in Pontevedra, in Galicia. That image (according to tradition, the gift of some French pilgrims) was originally lodged in the Sanctuary of Nuestra Señora del Camino. The one church proved too small for two Virgins, however. Accused of poaching her hostess's devo-

tees, la Peregrina was put out in the street. Undaunted, she set up shop on her own, eventually becoming the patron of the city.

Yet the image of la Peregrina is far from ubiquitous. This is strange, for one might expect that, once the idea of the Virgin as pilgrim had been coined, it would proliferate until every church along the way sported its own Peregrina. Perhaps her failure to catch on derives from the fact that the Camino, despite the considerable number of female pilgrims today, has always been mainly populated by men, and especially middle-aged men, who have put in some twenty or thirty years of domesticity, working and raising a family, and who now long for a manly season on the road. The Camino offers such men camaraderie, a physical challenge, space and time to breathe as they assess their lives and look into their souls, all within a context that is sanctioned by society and the Church.

And where does the Virgin fit into this scheme? She doesn't really. The male pilgrim's preferred companion for the mountains and wide-open spaces will always be sturdy old fellow, Santiago. It is enough to have in the churches of the towns and villages along the way mother Mary's reassuring presence. Like the good wife she is. Mary must tend to home and hearth while the boys go walk about.

Still, female pilgrims increase, perhaps they will take on the Peregrina as a sister, guardian and matron, their own special friend on the road.

"Sahagún" is what time and the Spanish tongue have done to the original name of this place, "San Facundo." In the eleventh century this was the Spanish Cluny, an outpost of the great French Benedictine monastery that for a time eclipsed Rome as the most powerful center of the Catholic Church. Splendid, Cluny-sponsored churches and monasteries sprang up from the plains here, in the lost reaches of northern León, making this a sort of Timbuktu of the Camino.

One of these structures, the Romanesque church of Saint James, has been refitted to accommodate a pilgrims' refuge, a tourist information center and an exhibition-concert hall. The refuge occupies a second floor that has been built into one end of the structure. Red theatrical curtains separate it from the exhibition hall portion, but one can part them and peer down upon the rows of seats. Signs caution pilgrims to be silent during concerts.

Wonderful as this refuge appears at first sight, it has two serious defects. The first is that by summer the windowless sleeping area is a heat trap, a black hole of Sahagún. The second is that the fine arched ceilings make this a natural theater for the snorer. Last year I was shaken about in my bunk by the laryngeal rumblings of a man I dubbed the lawnmower, until at last I slunk down to the ground floor and passed out on a massage table. This year, my luck is looking better. I retire far to the back of the refuge, away from the staccato drip of a leaky shower and pass out cold. It isn't till about five a.m. that I become conscious of the man with the lungs.

I had noticed him earlier—who hadn't?—a grizzled man in road-worn clothes, who carried a tattered old pack. He had stumbled into the dormitory without a word at seven o'clock, sat for a few minutes by himself at the dining table, then gone to sleep on the nearest bed without taking off his shoes. Now, he is coughing. I know at once that it is him. After several minutes of painful, dry retching, his feet hit the floor. He goes lurching through the kitchen like Frankenstein's monster, thumping into doors and walls along the way. A tap starts to run and the coughing gives way to vomiting. He groans and heads back to bed, leaving the tap running. A moment later another burst of vomit comes. This time it splashes on the floor.

I lie there, wondering if there is anything I should be doing to help. I sense from the silence around me that I am not the only one thinking this thought. With drowsy detachment, I observe my squeamishness. My goodness, the shoes on the bed, the running tap, the mess on the floor! A voice inside me is saying: "Why do they let people like that in here? He shouldn't be allowed to interrupt our sleep. He should be in a hospital, not a refuge." Then I take advantage of the not-so-reassuring stillness that follows the sick man's last outburst to sink back into the sleep of the righteous.

Next morning dawns to find the vagrant gone and the refuge echoing with the very sentiments that filled my head last night. The consensus is that the old rapscallion was no pilgrim at all, but some sort of derelict taking advantage of the facilities intended for our use. Scandalous!

Scandalous and also rather curious. For what on earth was the old Camino but Lourdes on parade? In former times, as in third-world countries to this day, pilgrim shrines were the doctors of the poor. The pilgrims of long ago would have sported every illness, disability, disfigurement and distressing infirmity known to man. That was why they were going to Santiago: to be cured. The afflictions of today's pilgrims, strapping specimens that we are in our high-tech walking shoes, are less evident. They are carried in the mind or in the heart.

THE WAY FROM SAHAGÚN to Mansilla de las Mulas sets new standards for flatness and aridity. In the promotional literature, this stretch of Camino is built up as eighteen miles of tree-lined path. The sad reality is a procession of toothpicks whose sparse shade wouldn't shelter a cricket. Work crews are kept busy through the summer, running emergency water transfusions to these parched, wretched transplants.

Six miles along the way, the Hermitage of the Virgen del Peral sits alone in the fields, a minute off the road. And though a minute is a very long time to walk in Spain in July, when I came by last summer I was tempted to see if the little church was open. Of course it was bolted up and there was no indication when, if ever, it might be open again. So I stood in the shadow of the wall, gazing dully back at the sun-burnt road, and before long, another pilgrim happened by.

Toni was thirtyish, from Valencia. He had set out from Roncesvalles last Saturday and already he was even with me. He was averaging over twenty-four miles a day. What was the hurry?

"I have to get to Santiago by next weekend. I'm going back to work on Monday."

They had started to exasperate me, these people who just raced along without seeing anything, doing the Camino just to say they'd done it. This Toni was probably the sort who got up at four-thirty and walked in the dark for an hour with a torch. I thought I'd impart some friendly advice.

"This isn't a race, you know. Why don't you slow down a little and try to get more out of it?"

"You don't understand," he replied. "I made a promise to do this a long time ago. This is the first chance I've had and, with my work, I don't know when I'll get another."

He was right. I hadn't understood. Toni didn't give a damn about the sights of León or Sahagún. He was not concerned with the culinary specialties of Burgos. He couldn't afford to make friends with anyone who couldn't keep his pace. He was a pilgrim, walking 500 miles because he had promised that he would. He wasn't doing this "for the experience." This was an act of thanksgiving, or of penance, or a paying of someone else's debt to God. Suddenly, I felt very much like a tourist.

I wished him *Buen Camino* and watched him speed away. Soon he was a mirage in the landscape ahead of me, though I felt it was the past he was vanishing into.

The Virgin of the Die

The *pulchra Leonina*, they call it, León's beauty, and with justice. The Cathedral of León is a torch carried to Spain from France and, like the Gothic cathedrals of France, it exists above all as a palace for the Virgin, a place so grand and bright and spacious and lovely and glowing with many colors that she will be content to reside there and not go off to answer the prayers of other cities.

Foremost among the Virgins worshipped here is María la Blanca. A most benign Mother, full-faced, Gallic, she stands at the main portal, where the pilgrim enters, serenely pressing the squirming serpent Satan underfoot. The cathedral is hers, but she shares it with a heavy-bellied Virgen de la Esperanza (the Virgin of Hope, or the Expecting Virgin), a sultry Madonna del Carmen and, as every good pilgrim knows, la Virgen del Dado, the Virgin of the Die.

In the high days of the pilgrimage, gambling sharps practiced their trade here, fleecing pilgrims right in the aisles of the cathedral. One day, a pilgrim who had lost his silver flung his die away in anger. The cube hurtled towards the statue of la Virgen del Dado, striking her child square in the forehead. The crowd that had gathered for mass gasped at the sight of blood spurting from the holy face. They turned on the malefactor and carried him to the scaffold (or it may be that he dropped dead on the spot; it depends which version of the story you hear). As for the Virgin, she seized the offending die and retains it to this day.

The refuge of León nestles within the spacious convent of the Benedictine sisters of Santa María de Carvajal. Along with the nuns' quarters and the hundred-odd beds for pilgrims, this citadel houses an elementary school complete with playground and gymnasium. Its strict 9:30 curfew helps to win the pilgrims merit, for if turning one's back on León at 9:30 on a summer night—just as the cool of evening has finally come and bottles of wine are hitting the tables—is not mortification of the flesh, what is?

Last summer, I caught up with JFK here. He had been in León for a day resting off the effects of some bad seafood soup, so he'd had some time to look around.

"You know," he told me, "I've been keeping my eye on this place near the refuge. It looks to me like a whorehouse."

"A whorehouse?"

"I'm pretty sure."

He was clearly tickled to discover such an institution in cultured, Catholic Old Europe and on the Camino no less. It often takes time for us traveling New Worlders to realize that the ancient edifices of European cities house grocery stores, laundromats and banks and not lute-makers or swordsmiths. I followed John's directions to the street of Don Gutierre, which runs up from the aptly named plaza of Saint Mary of the Market. The doors along the narrow way stood open to the street and recorded flamenco music jangled and keened from within. On one door was a handwritten note inviting the passerby to enter without buzzing and I could see a woman just inside sitting on a chair. She wasn't even smoking a cigarette, just looking god-awfully bored. And she had every right to, consid-ering that she and the waiters and the priests were the only people still working at eight p.m. in León.

Last July, the school playground in the courtyard of the convent was a cat's cradle of clotheslines. The refuge was full and several dozen of us slept on the floor of the gym, like so many flood victims. Tonight, there are fewer than ten of us in the refuge. The hospitaler is emphatic that he expects to see us all at vespers tonight with the sisters.

"At one time, 120 monasteries along the Camino were open to pilgrims. Now there are three. This is a rare chance for you to experience the monastic life. The sisters are anxious to share their prayers with pilgrims."

So I haul myself away from the dinner table before the end of tonight's *Quieres Ser Millonario?* (the local strain of the worldwide "Who Wants to Be a Millionaire?" epidemic) and hurry back to the refuge, where the other pilgrims and the hospitaler are waiting. Prayer books are handed round and we are briefed on the order of the readings and psalms for the evening. Then we make our way to the convent chapel where, to my wonder and dismay, the hospitaler leads us up the aisle to the choir itself. We take our places in the second ring of wooden benches, directly behind the sisters. There will be no audience for vespers tonight, only performers.

In the silence that ensues, I scan the faces of the nuns. All I can read there is weariness: this is their seventh round of prayers today, after all. I have a moment to reflect before the service begins that I am about to take part in one of my civilization's most venerable rituals. Benedictine monks and nuns have been calling down the mercy of God upon the world seven times a day since the sixth century. Long ago, kings and lords thought this an industry worth subsidizing, but during the eighteenth and nineteenth centuries, most monasteries of the contemplative orders throughout Europe were dissolved and their properties resold by the state. The effect of this massive "liberation of value" was to produce a new landed class that supported the government, though the land-grab was justified on the fine utilitarian principle articulated by Cavour: "The claustral habit of abstention from work renders labor less respectable and less respected. Monks are not only useless, but actually harmful."

At least when the convent of Santa María de Carvajal dies, it will not be at the hands of the state, but by natural causes. Of the nineteen sisters gathered tonight, no more than a handful look to be under sixty.

The service begins. I am sharing a prayer book with a Dutch woman. We limp through the prayers and readings and songs, trying to keep up in our hobbled Spanish. Then everyone stops and closes their books. A nun with thick glasses rises. Her face is dull, her movements heavy. She looks like she is about to give a report on the convent's finances. But when she opens her mouth, the sound that flows out is sparkling and unearthly. She is singing Salve Regina.

I feel a lurch as the moment goes off its moorings. The concrete particulars—a wooden bench cutting off the circulation in my thighs, a large Dutch woman beside me stifling a cough, a nun whose lips are moving in time with the song—remain in evidence. But equally evident are other things: my life before and after this instant has no reality, substance is an illusion conjured up by the play of light and sound, and there is no place else on earth but this eggshell chapel adrift on the face of the deep.

Then the nun with the thick glasses closes her mouth. The absolutes of light and sound dissolve back into the waters of the phenomenal world. The song has ended and once more I am here on a Sunday night in the convent of Santa María de Carvajal in León.

The nuns, save one, disperse at once, hurrying to snatch a few hours of rest before the next round of prayer. The one who stays behind is the youngest, a lively-eyed woman of perhaps forty-five. She addresses us in a soft, sure voice.

"I know that the Camino exerts demands on the pilgrim. Daily, physical demands. But remember to ask yourself sometimes: 'Why am I doing this?' Try to hold in your mind the reasons for your journey, because I am sure that each of you has deep reasons for undertaking this pilgrimage."

"Remember that Saint James is your companion along the way. He walks with you every day, just as he walked with Jesus in the time of Our Lord. You know that Jesus was always walking the roads of Palestine, speaking to the people, listening to the voice of the Father, and Saint James learned much from the Master. This is something that Christ is trying to teach us by calling us as pilgrims.

As she speaks, her eyes light on us like a blessing. Her voice conducts the electricity of her conviction directly to our hearts. We understand that she has said these words before, perhaps a thousand times, but she is saying them again for the first time. The truth is forever new.

"May I ask you to do one thing? When you get to Santiago, go to the crypt beneath the altar where the remains of the saint are found, and pray to him. This is something few pilgrims do. Just a simple prayer is enough. You can be sure he will carry that prayer to the Father."

Then there is a click and the lights in the chapel go out. The sister's voice continues without a pause, except that now it is the darkness that is speaking. Once again I feel myself going adrift, but this time the light is faint, space has collapsed to the distance between shadows, and there is only sound. Words and faith. The soft, sure counsels of the darkness. Eyes open, seeing nothing, I listen to the voice of the darkness till it says,

"And pray for us when you get to Santiago."

Then I know that it is finished.

I MET CRISTINA THE FIRST TIME I did the Camino. It was in Villadangos del Paramo, twelve miles after León. She smiled so warmly when I passed her on the street that I wondered if we'd met before.

"Have you seen a pharmacy?"

I had, and we strolled that way together. She was a psychoanalyst from Brazil, fit, thirtyish, and in quite a good mood for someone who had, by her own account, been constipated for a week. She told me that she had seen a doctor back in Burgos, but his medicine had given her no relief. Then today, as she was signing the register in the refuge, she noticed that the first-aid booklet on the table in front of her was open to a page about gastroenteritis. Idly scanning the page, she recognized the symptoms it described as her own, though the prescribed treatment was totally different from what the doctor in Burgos had recommended.

"It's unbelievable the things the Camino sets in front of you," she said, shaking her head. "You can always find what you are looking for."

The pharmacy was closed, but we managed to track down the pharmacist and get her the pills she wanted. She didn't feel like joining me for dinner—not surprisingly—but when I got back to the refuge that night, I found her deep in conversation with a wiry, alert Argentine woman.

"Bob, I have just been telling Gabriela here about how I found my sickness described in the first-aid manual."

"It's a Gift of the Camino," opined Gabriela with the air of someone skilled in discerning such things. "When something like this happens, there is nothing to say but *Gracias*. *Gracias* to Santiago for all the gifts of the Camino."

I wondered aloud whether the gastroenteritis was also a gift of the Camino.

"Why not?" she laughed. "I tell you, everything is a gift. Everything is a sign. We only need to be patient and understand what the Camino is trying to tell us. There are no accidents."

"That's true," said Cristina, "and I can prove it. Can I tell you about the dream I had two nights before I left Brazil to go on the Camino? I was in a bar, a nice kind of place, and there was this Oriental woman who was playing the piano and singing. I don't know why she was Oriental, but she was playing a song by—do you know Burt Bacharach?"

"Burt Bacharach?"

"Yes, you know him? Well this song, I knew it, or I knew some of it anyway, but I had never really paid attention before, so I didn't know all the words. All I knew in my dream was that it was a song about the Camino. So when I woke up I checked for the lyrics on the Internet, and when I read them I couldn't believe it. I mean, I had to phone my mother and I was just crying when I told her, because this song exactly described the Camino."

"Which song was it?"

"Can't you guess?"

She had a sly look, as if the answer would be obvious if we only thought about it. We tried out a few titles—"Say a Little Prayer," "Walk on By," "Do You Know the Way to San Jose?"—but none of them hit the mark.

"Do you give up?"

Cristina looked from one of us to the other, letting the suspense build. Then she began to sing a warm and samba-inflected rendition of "What the World Needs Now is Love."

"Of course," said Gabriela, clapping her hands together. "Love is so important. The Camino is full of love."

"No, no, but it's not just that," Cristina insisted. "Don't you know the words?"

Neither of us did.

"Well, the beginning of the song is all about mountains. Mountains and hillsides. Now, at the beginning of the Camino, what are you doing every day? You are climbing hills and mountains!

"Then the next part of the song is about crossing oceans and rivers. Well, I had to cross the ocean from Brazil, and all the time on the Camino we are crossing rivers, right?

"And then she sings about meadows and cornfields and wheatfields. And that's the Camino, too. After the mountains and hills and rivers, it's all meadows and wheatfields for days and days.

"So you see," she said with triumph. "It's the Camino. It's exactly the Camino. In fact, the only thing from the song that I haven't seen yet is the cornfields. Everything else has come true."

I wasn't sure if this was *exactly* the Camino, but it was close enough to shut me up. Gabriela, naturally, was convinced. So we expressed our admiration for Cristina's dream and told her we hoped she'd see her cornfields soon, because it was plain that she was bothered about them. You'd think the rest would have been enough, but no, she wanted to see it all, right down to the last detail.

That night I lay awake, as a team of middle-age bikers snored around me, thinking of Cristina's world of secret signs, where the Camino itself dispenses free medical advice and higher powers speak to us through Burt Bacharach songs; where each of us stands at the axis of a galaxy of meaning and every leaf on every tree has a message inscribed on it just for us, if only we know how to read it. It seemed such a throwback to the Middle Ages, this notion that the world was full of coded messages from

God. It was an idea that fascinated me for the play of the mind it involved even as it appalled me for the casual way it snuffed out the particularity and selfhood of phenomena, turning the world into our own little message board. I found myself torn between wanting to tell Cristina that she was full of nonsense and wanting to wake up tomorrow morning seeing the same world she did.

And then there was Gabriela with her: "There are no accidents." It happened that Gabriela's foam mattress was next to mine, and I wanted to give her a little nudge and ask, "Why do you want to think that your life is all planned out for you? What if there is nothing *but* accidents? What if things just happen the way they happen and then we look for the patterns later? Maybe life is only chance encounters that every so often, when we least expect it, constellate so perfectly you could almost believe that someone planned it that way? Isn't that a more interesting way to imagine life?"

I wanted to ask Gabriela these things, but already her breathing was swift and regular. So I lay awake, trying to guess which Burt Bacharach song she was dreaming of.

I didn't see Cristina the next morning. It wasn't till a few days later that I heard her guts had taken a turn for the worse that night. In too much pain to walk, she had caught the morning bus to Astorga to find a doctor. So the miraculous medical advice hadn't helped after all. Some gift of the Camino.

I thought of her that morning, though. I had only gone about fifteen minutes from the refuge when I stepped out of a little grove of trees. There, silent before me, stood row upon row of shoulder-high corn.

FOR NEARLY A WEEK AFTER CASTROJERIZ, the horizons to the west, east and south have no limits. But all along, the snow-capped Cantabrian mountains are angling in from the north to cut off the pilgrim's progress.

Beyond the old frontier city of Astorga, founded by the Romans to subdue the rambunctious Celts, the land begins to rise. The villages here are built of slate. They are sturdier than those of the plains, but just as derelict. I spend the night alone in the stone refuge of Santa Catalina de Somoza, which the sign above the door identifies as a public school built in 1905. I wonder how many years it has been since this village had enough children to fill its own school. Like so many places on the Camino through Castilla-León and Galicia, this one teeters on the verge of extinction. The revival of the Camino has injected some life into it, but the pilgrimage is a seasonal phenomenon that attracts seasonal labor. I fear the day will come when Terradillos de los Templarios, Hornillos del Camino, Santa Catalina de Somoza and all the rest of these places will be staffed with paid workers from the Spanish Tourist Office whose job it will be to offer pilgrims "the Authentic Camino Experience."

The only heat sources tonight are my body and the electric lights, but the old schoolhouse is so well put together that I feel comfortable. I sit on my bunk for a while, listening to the wind lash away.

In the morning, my feet leave ghost tracks in the powder snow. I peer in the windows of The Cowboy Bar in El Ganso, which overflows on a summer morning with caffeinating German, French and Brazilian pilgrims, but it is closed for the season. Señor Cowboy is probably in Malaga now, enjoying the fruits of his labor. A man standing in the lee of the church laughs when he sees me and raises his hand to nose level: "In Rabanal, the snow is up to here. *Buen Camino*."

In Rabanal, at the foot of the mountains, the snow isn't quite up to here, but it may be before long. The bar presents a cheering scene: seven pilgrims, the first I have seen in two days, are huddled around wooden tables. A fire roars in the fireplace and there are hot empanadas to be had. It looks like a fine place to hunker down for a couple of days, and it turns out that is exactly what these pilgrims have been doing. They tell me there is a big storm coming. The hospitaler and the highway patrol have warned them against trying to cross the mountains. Not wanting to be stuck here all winter, they have called for taxis.

Pilgrims calling for taxis?

I consider climbing up on a table and yelling, "What kind of pilgrims are you anyway?" But I don't, because they're all nice people—two young Spaniards walking together with their old father, an Australian obviously traumatized by this white stuff falling from the sky, a German couple who have adopted a puppy along the way and are more concerned for its welfare than their own ("We don't mind the snow, but Iago's fur is not so thick yet"); and also because they could be right. Maybe the worst blizzard in the history of León is about to descend. I don't need any frozen puppies on my conscience.

So I have something hot to eat and wish everyone a pleasant drive. It's twelve miles to El Acebo, the first village over the pass, so I have no time to loll around. A few hundred yards out of town, the first taxi shoots past, ferrying its load of pilgrims. Hands flutter in the back window. See you in Santiago. A half-hour passes, and a Civil Guard van eases up beside me. There are two officers inside, and one leans out his window.

"Where are you going?"

"El Acebo."

"You know it's *malo* ahead. *Muy muy malo.*"

"I'm from *Canadá*. I'm used to this weather."

The two of them shake their heads.

"I'll stick to the highway. If the snow gets too bad, I'll turn back."

"Do you have a mobile phone?"

"No."

They shake their heads again. Clearly this is the last they expect to see of me until the spring thaw. But this is Spain, after all, where if you want to run in front of a bull, it's your business. They roll up the window and drive away.

The two-lane highway keeps climbing, the wind keeps driving a light mist of snow in my face, and I wouldn't miss this for the world. Today, I really have the road to myself. I reach the abandoned village of Foncebadón, where Paulo Coelho and Shirley MacLaine both grappled with hounds of hell. Today, the only thing howling is the wind. Then an ominous stillness falls as I approach that mysterious way marker known as the Iron Cross.

This is a tall pole, visible for miles, once sacred to Mercury, the god of travelers, now Christened by the tiny crucifix at the top. For centuries, every passing traveler has added a stone to its base, raising a mighty hill of slag in the process. I'm not feeling confident enough in my atheism to walk by here today without pitching my own pebble, but how am I to find one in the knee-deep snow? I reach into my pocket for the only tribute I can make under the circumstances and pray that Mercury likes black chocolate.

Up to now, I seem to have been walking through two days at once: turbulent sky in front of me; radiant sun behind. But suddenly the clouds lower, and I feel myself cupped beneath a great hand. The snow has stopped, the air has turned brown, and the wind speaks in a deep voice. In the Bible, Jesus calls Saint James "the Son of Thunder". It is this Santiago who broods over the mountains today.

Beyond the Iron Cross, in the derelict village of Manjarín, there is a makeshift mountain refuge where, with luck, I will find a meal. A girl sticks her head out when I knock and calls to the hospitaler, "Tomás! It's a crazy pilgrim!" She hurries me in and slams the door behind me. I am struck blind. Only the faintest light ekes in through the one, deep-welled window, and I feel I have been transported back into some scene from the Brontës. A minute goes by before I can make out human forms, four of them, in the darkness. The cats, however, are beyond counting. There is one that will not make room on the bench for me. Another climbing up my shin. The head of a third juts like a gargoyle from a bookshelf. A mewling and hissing whirls around my feet.

But I have arrived in time for lunch. A glass of wine is poured for me and a hearty soup of sausage and cabbage ladled out. When my bowl is empty, it gets refilled. The hospitality is generous, but conversation is entirely lacking. My dinner companions are all in a state of waking hibernation. The only words they utter are threats against the cats.

"Don't you have electricity?" I ask.

"Yes, a solar panel. But on a day like this …"

Then all at once, a pinprick of twentieth-century light pierces the medieval gloom. Tomás has been surfing the stations on his palm-held, Dick-Tracy-style tv.

"Hey look you guys," he calls out. "There's a Woody Allen movie on tonight!"

I offer to pay for my meal but Tomás will not hear of it. The only thing he insists on is that I sign the register. So I leave my hosts to *Bullets Over Broadway* and step back outside, where now the snow is blowing in sheets parallel to the ground. It's put-down-your-head-and-plod time. The visibility is no more than ten yards, but as long as I stay on the highway I can't get lost. Twice I pass small trucks that have skidded off the road and been caught at the brink by saplings. On a day like this, it's riskier to drive than to walk.

It's long after dark when I arrive at the bar-cum-refuge of El Acebo, on the far side of the pass. The hospitaler slaps me on the back and sits me down by the wood-stove, which keeps the place at potato-baking heat. He informs me that his name, Gumersindo, is the longest Spanish name containing no repeated letters. Again, I am fed and plied with wine, then I crawl upstairs to sleep a sleep of blissful exhaustion. The weariness of winter is more easily consoled than that of summer. Next morning, I look out the window to find myself exactly on the snowline. On my left are snow-capped mountains and dark, swirling clouds; on my right, a plunging green valley.

La Virgen de la Encina

In the twelfth century, the Knights Templar stood at the height of their glory. Fernando II of León granted them vast territories as thanks for their role in retaking the west of Spain from the Moor and they were entrusted with the task of settling this frontier, fortifying and governing it. As the symbol of their dominion, they erected the enormous castle whose crumbled mass still dominates Ponferrada.

Unimaginable quantities of timber were needed for the construction of this castle. Soon all the forests near Ponferrada had been cleared, and the knights had to venture ever further into the trackless woods of El Bierzo. One night, a supervisor of the tree cutters was returning very late from his post when he noticed a strange light in the woods. Most men would run from such a sight, but this was a Knight Templar. He hacked his way through the dense brush till at last he came to a giant *encina* oak. There was a long crack in its trunk and the mysterious light was flowing from within. Putting his eye to the crack, the knight saw at the very heart of the oak a tiny image of the Virgin.

He raced back to Ponferrada with the news of his discovery. The next day, he led his fellow knights and the priests to the miraculous *encina*. One by one, they peered into the tree at the sacred image, then fell to their knees and wept like babes. One of the priests declared that the statue had been carved from life by Saint Luke, and it was decided to leave the Virgin inside the tree until a proper sanctuary had been made for her near the castle. Since that time, by virtue of her countless miracles, the Virgen de la Encina has been recognized as patroness of the lands of El Bierzo.

Today, outside her church in Ponferrada, a sign reads: "Let no one enter here without saluting Mary, and saying to her with love: 'My mother, do not leave me.'"

Modern Ponferrada is the Camino's answer to Hong Kong: a mass of soulless high-rises; the great urban vacuum cleaner that sucks the life out of places like El Acebo. It is a rootless place with the air of a giant, open-air refugee camp. At the center of a traffic circle on the outskirts of town stands one of the saddest monuments on earth. Four giant bronze women in peasant dress are gossiping over some bushels of fresh pimentos; the skeleton of a village church rises behind them. The inscription reads:

En recuerdo de las huertas y homenaje a los pimientos de Ponferrada

"In memory of the orchards, and in homage to the pimentos of Ponferrada."

And then, only a few miles beyond the city, small fields where, in summer, women bend to tend their crops by hand, plant by plant; where a man of seventy shouts his mule into motion, then leans a shoulder into the wooden plow.

This region, lying in the valley between the mountains of León and the mountains of Galicia, is El Bierzo: yet another Spanish micro-region, with its own micro-cuisine, micro-customs and micro-climate. Here, two weeks after La Rioja, there are still grapes on the vines. But I feel no inclination to slow down and enjoy the way. Rain keeps coming in bursts and I'd like to catch up with the taxi pilgrims. I resolve to make it as far as Cacabelos tonight, even if it means walking by the highway in the dark. This turns out to be a good sight more dangerous than crossing the mountains of León in a blizzard. After the second near-miss, I haul out my yellow fluorescent rain cape and drape it over my shoulders, if only to make my body easier for the ambulance to locate.

The first time I walked the Camino, I arrived in the town of Campo-naraya just as the church bells were tolling seven. At once, I recognized the tune of the chimes as the Lourdes Ave Maria. I had to stop and lean on my stick, waiting till the tune was done. A little further on, I threw off my pack and lay down by a creek under some trees. I hadn't noticed anyone walking behind me for a long time, but now a woman appeared. Without unhitching her pack, she sat down and introduced herself as Lourdes.

"Lourdes," I said. "Would you believe that just a few minutes ago I was in Camponaraya and the church bells were playing the Ave Maria of Lourdes?"

"Yes, I heard it too. I was in Lourdes before I started the Camino."

I didn't know what to say next. This was clearly a gift of the Camino. But how to unwrap it? Lourdes interrupted my pondering to ask how much farther it was to Cacabelos.

"A couple more miles. Are you staying at the refuge?"

"No, I'm staying at a hotel tonight. The Hostal Santa María. I need some sleep." She stood up. "I'd better get going."

"I'm ready to go too," I said, reaching for my backpack.

"No, you're relaxing. Take your time. We'll see each other up ahead."

But we never did. If Lourdes had any message for me, she got up and walked away with it.

I cross El Bierzo in two days, the mountains of León receding behind me as quickly as those of Galicia rear up ahead. Soon the Camino is threading through the valley of the River Carce on its way to O Cebreiro, the portal of green Galicia.

As I walked this way last year, I heard the thud of running feet and a voice calling from behind.

"Peregrino! Peregrino!"

I looked back expecting to see a familiar face, but instead there was a big, rangy French boy who looked like he had just climbed out of a ditch.

"Peregrino! It's so good to see you. My God, last night I was going to climb O Cebreiro with Sandro and Jacqueline but I get this itch some-times between my legs from my thighs rubbing together so I didn't go with them and we'd had too much wine anyway so I took my sleeping bag to the castle up there for the night and on the way to the top the path is very clearly marked but then I thought it's too boring to take the same way back this morning so I started to take a different path and it kept getting narrower and narrower until it disappeared and I was crashing through the bush like a bear—whaaaah!—and then I came to a river and I was thinking this is it I'm going to drown but lucky for me it wasn't that deep but I still fell down and now I've got this shit all over my pants. I just need to get to a refuge now and wash my face and lie down for a few minutes and then I'll climb O Cebreiro because next month I'll be twenty-five and then I have to be serious and think about a job and getting married and children so I have to do all the stupid things I can before then."

Jean-Baptiste had introduced himself. We walked together the rest of the way to Ruitelán. He did the talking. Perhaps he was an angel, for he had much to impart. "I tell you I make my own rules for the Camino. Number one if I don't know something I ask somebody. Why should I carry a map? they're heavy and anyone can tell me directions and if I'm hungry I go to someone's door and say excuse me can I have some bread and then if there's no refuge I just ask to sleep on someone's grass or in their barn because you sleep better on the grass anyway no lumpy mattress no one snoring no roof but the sky ..."

I ask if he knows what Christ said about the lilies of the field.

"Oh yes," he says, "that's me God takes care of me all right."

The taxi pilgrims are waiting at Ruitelán, the "base camp" to O Cebreiro. At last, someone to talk to. We swap stories over the vegetarian meal prepared by Carlos, an Andalusian shiatsu massage therapist who has set up shop here with his Catalonian partner to tend to the aches and pains of pilgrims.

There is a sunny French girl as well; she has walked all the way from her town in Normandy. Most of the way through France, she tells me, she shunned the beaten path, simply showing up in towns, going to the church and asking for shelter.

"I was never turned down. Sometimes they would let me put my sleeping bag on the floor of the church, but usually they would call around the town and find some family I could stay with and have dinner. Nobody was surprised that I was doing this. They still understand the concept of pilgrimage."

I ask her what she thinks of an atheist making a pilgrimage to the Virgin Mary.

"Why not? Everyone makes their pilgrimage in their own way. I heard of one Dutch pilgrim who stayed with a family in France and they showed him pictures of how medieval pilgrims used to dress. So then he found such clothes, or had them made, and he took them with him to wear in the evenings. Not on the road, you understand. On the road he wore his shorts and running shoes. But at night in the refuge, he would put on his pilgrim's robes. And there was another boy I met who started every morning from the nearest parish church, even if it meant going back miles from where he stayed that night. And then there was this man who never took the road. He had only a compass and he was just using this compass and following the course of rivers. So you see, it's your pilgrimage. You do it how you like."

Taking her advice to heart, I light out first thing next morning. It was fine having company this evening, but the climb to O Cebreiro I want to myself.

The Miracle of O Cebreiro

It's "El Cebrero" in Castilian. O Cebreiro is the name in Gallego, the language of Galicia, which—like Galician culture and cuisine—lies roughly halfway between Spanish and Portuguese. The village at the top of the mountain is nothing more than a church and a clutch of squat, ancient houses, a couple of them with thatched roofs. A monastic community was founded here in the very earliest days of the pilgrimage, but the last two monks packed it in in 1854. Over the course of a century of neglect, the Church of Santa María la Real fell into ruin. The rebirth of the pilgrimage has restored it to use. The other buildings have been refashioned into cozy bars, inns and shops where tourists and pilgrims escape from the weather.

But O Cebreiro's reputation is far out of proportion to its size, for this is the site of the Miracle. Wagner came here to see the "Galician Holy Grail," and it inspired his *Parsifal*. Queen Isabella made a characteristic attempt to possess herself of the miraculous blood, but the mule refused to bear it away from the mountain.

And the miracle?

Once, long ago, a priest was sent to exercise his vocation on O Cebreiro. The assignment was no gift, if you consider the truculent weather that beats away at this mountain-top from year-end to year-end and the isolation of the place, up here among the clouds. The flow of pilgrims in summer tempered the priest's loneliness, but the winters were desolate. Often he celebrated mass in the bone-chilling cold of the tiny stone chapel for no more than two or three worshippers and they so ignorant and rough-mannered that he began to feel that his efforts were wasted.

One morning after a heavy snowfall, while the wind was still bawling, the priest stood at the altar. His lips moved, his hands performed the gestures they had performed so many times, but his heart was empty. He felt alone as he had never felt before, abandoned even by God. He was just raising the Host to the empty church when the doors opened and a peasant from one of the hamlets below stumbled in and sat down. The priest might have been comforted by the company of a fellow Christian, or taken a lesson from the poor man's humility and fortitude. Instead a cold anger flared up in his chest.

"The idiot should have stayed at home," he thought. "Why has he come out in such weather for a worthless scrap of bread?"

The words had no sooner passed the lips of his mind than the priest felt a strange warmth run through his icy fingertips. He looked. Where the holy wafer had been there was now a fragment of flesh. The wine in the goblet had turned to blood.

Some would have it that the priest fell dead on the spot. I see no reason to kill him off. Recently published letters of Mother Teresa reveal that even she, in the midst of her ministry, sometimes questioned the existence of God. Almost every Christian saint and mystic has undergone "dark nights of the soul." It seems to come with the territory.

In any case, the plate and goblet have been preserved. And if the pilgrim looks at the statue of Santa María la Real, she will observe that the Virgin's head is ever-so-slightly inclined; in acknowledgement, they say, of the miracle.

It is warm and sunny in the morning when I start to climb, though snow has fallen through the night on O Cebreiro. The snowline cuts a seam across the slope and above it the clouds settle in. Halfway up, I am overtaken by Sam from Québec, truly a mighty walker before the Lord. I match his pace for a few minutes, then wish him *Buen Camino* and watch him vanish into the mist. I climb the rest of the way in his footsteps.

Near the top, the snow deepens, the fog gathers nearer, and another set of footprints appears out of nowhere. The footprints of the mysterious stranger. I think of the miracle of O Cebreiro and the peasant coming in out of the snow, or the risen Christ joining up with the travelers on the way to Emmaus. Then, a few steps further on, another set of footprints joins the first. One more mysterious stranger! But this one has four legs, and frequently leaves his mark in the snow.

At the summit, the village is still, dreamlike. Then the clouds part and I can see forever, back over El Bierzo to the mountains of León, ahead to Galicia's rolling green hills. For the third time in two years, I am in O Cebreiro. In June, I watched a silk scarf of mist sweep up from one valley, over the village, and down the other side. Now, I see the clean glitter of sun and snow all around me. This is the Magic Mountain. A place you could linger for seven years, hiking in the hills when the sun shines, snoozing by the fireplace when the rain or snow falls, talking to the pilgrims who pass through. A place you could forget to leave.

In the evening, I meet up with Jeremy, the Australian pilgrim, at the bar. Soon, two boys who work for a securities firm in Madrid drop in along with a convivial, fortyish man who goes by J.J.—*Jota Jota* in Spanish. Then in comes Henk, "the Flying Dutchman," with ruddy-faced Gottholt, who has walked from his front door in Germany.

I noticed him earlier, this Gottholt fellow, noticed him with some dismay, in fact, when he claimed a bed in my room (he looked like a snorer). I needed to get caught up on my writing, so I ignored him as he went about settling in. I had a feeling he would talk on and on if ever he got started and evidently I was right, for he has cornered Jeremy, Ancient-Mariner fashion. Out of the corner of my eye, I can see the burly German holding forth from within a cloud of pipe-tobacco smoke, as Jeremy nods mutely. When at last he steps up to the bar, I ask Jeremy what he's been going on about.

"It's his theory of why the shell is the symbol of the Camino. Something about going over the edge. You'll have to ask him yourself."

Ah, so it's the old business of Finisterre and the cockle-shell. Might be interesting after all. When Gottholt returns with a bottle of *orujo*, the local firewater, I ask him to explain.

"Yes," he says, drawing on his pipe, "I have been thinking a good deal about the shell and what it has to do with the Camino and I think I begin to see its meaning. You see, the shell has its outside, which is hard and material, cold. But when we reach the edge, then we have the opportunity to touch the other side of the shell, yes? the underside, the inside, and that is the part that is living. And this is why our Camino cannot stop at Santiago. In Santiago, we are still on the outside of the shell, the material side. We must continue walking to the Atlantic, to Finisterre, because that is the edge of things. That is where we can reach ..." and his knotty hand turns, palm-down to palm-up, "beneath, to where the life is."

Beneath to where the life is. He speaks the words steadily, looking me in the eye all the while with absolute conviction and just the trace of a smile around his lips. I pour myself another shot of *orujo*. I have no idea what he's talking about, but I'm persuaded.

"So what is it exactly that you expect to find in Finisterre?"

"Oh, nothing, nothing," he chuckles wisely. "It's only a joke, my friend."

The following night, after a long and anti-climactic descent from O Cebreiro, I meet up again with Gottholt and Jota Jota in Triacastela. This is J.J.'s fourth time on the Camino, but his first doing it alone:

"The other times I went with the diocese of Madrid—5,000 people. It's very different, because you have to keep a certain pace, you have to move fast. But then, when there are so many of you, so many to talk to, you don't really feel the pain of your feet. It's a powerful feeling to be on a hill and behind you and in front of you there are only people, thousands of people, and all of them singing. I miss the songs. When you walk together with people, you sing and the walk goes faster."

I wonder which way of pilgrimage he prefers: the convivial or the solitary.

"They're both good. But maybe, when you're younger, it's important to have time to talk to people. When you're older, you need more time with God."

Gottholt grabs hold of this point and the conversation strays into questions of whether it is the Father or the Son one speaks to while walking. J.J. claims he talks to the Father, "because it is like talking to my own father, very natural."

"But perhaps," replies Gottholt with dogged logic, "perhaps when you think you are talking to the Father you are really talking to the Son. Remember, the Son said, 'No one shall come to the Father except through me.'"

They follow this line of reasoning for several minutes. I'm wondering why people must always be filling the lonely vastness with listening ears when all of a sudden, Gottholt turns his beams in my direction.

"And what about you, young man? Is it difficult to write about the Camino and walk it at the same time?"

"Yes, as a matter of fact, it is."

"I imagine it's hard to find a balance," he says, narrowing his eyes.

"That's it exactly. I'd say the first time I walked the Camino, I was too involved to see it in a detached way. This time, maybe it's the opposite."

"You must be always thinking about what you will write, hmm?"

"It's hard to avoid."

"I can imagine." He pauses to light his pipe with a mischievous grin. "So then I hope you will do the Camino again someday. Only to experience it next time, not to write about it. Because I think you are standing a little apart, you know? Like you are watching the pilgrims and smiling at them, hmm? And there's nothing wrong with that, we need people to do that sort of thing. But it can't be very nice for you, can it?"

I haven't got an answer ready for this one.

"I don't mean to criticize," Gottholt proceeds. "I know there's more to you than just that. But it's a little true what I say, isn't it?"

He holds me with a twinkling eye for a minute. I tighten my lips. He blows a puff of smoke. J.J. smiles and wonders what he's missing. I can't tell Gottholt he's wrong, because I do feel detached from this experience. But then, what should I attach myself to? There have been so few pilgrims this time, and my encounters with them have been so fleeting. Perhaps I have grown a little solipsistic.

And this is unfortunate, for one of my motives in undertaking the Camino, as in crashing the party at Lourdes, is to escape solipsism. To hear voices that I would never hear in my insulated life at home. To put myself in a position where I am all but compelled to speak to people I would never otherwise speak to, among them people whom I may find irritating to begin with—who indeed may never cease to be irritating—but who have something to impart to me nonetheless. People, for instance, like Gottholt.

I can't quite formulate all this on the spot, and our conversation soon moves on to other topics. But the following day, as I bore into the wind on my way to the monastery of Samos, I'm practicing what I will say on my next meeting with Gottholt. I want to try to explain better where I stand and to thank him for challenging me to stay engaged. I'm looking forward to seeing him shake his head, spark up his pipe, smile that gnomic smile.

When I check the register at Samos, however, his name is not there. So I slosh on through the wind and the rain to Sarria, where he also isn't. Night is falling, and Gottholt is already somewhere ahead, stumping on towards Finisterre, where the life is.

The Virgin of Leboreiro

Before the first time I came to Galicia, I looked at maps, saw its villages strung along the Camino like pearls, and imagined one idyllic node of humanity after another, each with its church, its plaza, its fountain. But for the first few days in pastoral Galicia, one finds nothing of the sort. The villages are no more than eight or ten slate warrens built within shouting distance of one another. There is no city hall or city walls, no plaza, no fountain, not even a bar. The only street life is bovine.

And though Galicia is home to many celebrated Virgins, few of them reside along the Camino. Our Lady seems to have stepped aside in deference to her favorite, Saint James. The only Virgin I hear of in this stretch is the one of the church of Leboreiro, on the way to Melide.

The story tells that once, long ago, a spring suddenly began to flow near the old church. Its waters were sweet smelling and at night a mysterious light shone from it. The villagers began to dig around the fountain, searching for the source of the light and before long they had unearthed a beautiful image of the Virgin. They brought her to the church and built an altar for her there, but every time they left her alone she stole back to where she had been found, as if to say the spring was a holier place than the church. The villagers persisted. A finer chapel was built, and a likeness of the Virgin of the spring was sculpted and set in the tympanum to convince her that the church was hers and that she should abide there. At last, the Virgin allowed herself to be placed in the church, though at night, they say, she still goes down to the pool to bathe.

As one nears Santiago, the villages start to be brighter and more substantial. More of the handsome, Celtic-flavored pilgrims' crosses appear, as well as that Galician trademark, the *horreo*, a raised bin made of stone and wood used to store corn or grain. To look at these solemn and finely crafted objects, one would never guess they had such a prosaic use. They seem more like shrines or tombs. The same goes for the standing stones that mark off property lines like so many little Stonehenges.

The livestock diversifies, too. Besides the cows, one sees straggly-bearded billy goats, real free-range chickens scattered over a hillside, horses that stand in the morning fields gazing in opposite directions like figures in a Magritte painting. There are forests, streams, and broken-down farms, extravagant with moss as Angkor Wat. If the elements of the Camino through Castilla and León are earth and air, the ones proper to Galicia are stone, wood and water.

In the new town of Portomarín (the old is submerged beneath the artificial lake, though when the water is low the church spires poke above the surface), I caught up again with Jean-Baptiste, the breathless French boy. I was bringing my washing in from the line and he was on the lawn of the refuge, looking for a place to lay his sleeping bag.

"It doesn't look like rain tonight so I'll sleep out here instead you know there is that French man in your room who is famous for snoring—aaah!—who needs to listen to that? so tell me someone said you are writing a book about the Camino is that right? then why don't you write a book where you are a kind of guide and you show the people the real meaning you know the secrets of the Camino so they can discover them for themselves because the books now are all so useless nothing but this king did some stupid thing here in the year something something and this church is of this saint and that church is blah blah blah but if I were writing a guidebook listen! I would say for example you are walking down a path and it's the morning maybe and you see a certain tree or else you hear the wind blowing or perhaps you see a cloud and then you follow that cloud and—well—where does it take you?

"Why don't you write a book like that?"

FOR THE FINAL TWO DAYS, I put my head down and plow ahead, making the most of the hours between the winter rains to get one mile and one mile nearer the end. On the last night of my Camino, my only companion is an American woman with a wild and proud head of white hair. Indigo is her name and it has been turning up in the registers for the past two weeks, always a day or two ahead of me. Now I meet her for the first time. As I enter the dormitory, she is involved in the quintessential pilgrim's task of rearranging damp socks in front of a radiator.

She tells me she's sixty-one and has had to take it slow due to a series of foot and leg problems. But she's kept at it, until now, she tells me, after forty days on the road, "I'm almost finished this thing and I still don't have a clue what I did it for."

When I explain the immediate purpose of my Camino, she is delighted.

"I have a friend—a couple of friends, actually—who channel the Virgin Mary. One of them came to Europe last year and she said it was fantastic. She felt very close to Mary here."

"Can I . . . Excuse me, but how do you channel the Virgin Mary?"

"It's not difficult. You just let her enter you and speak through you. I've done some channeling myself, but I decided it wasn't my bag. If I'm going to say something, I want it to be me that's doing the talking, you know?"

"But how can you be sure it's the Virgin Mary?"

"Oh you can tell. By the sort of things she says, for instance."

"And what sort of things does the Virgin say?"

"Oh, very nice things. I couldn't tell you exactly, but I know my friend really enjoys channeling her. You see, I don't believe in the Virgin Mary myself. I'm more of a Jesus person. I find it interesting how the Catholics have gotten rid of Jesus. The Virgin is almost all they've got." As she speaks to me she keeps flipping her socks like pancakes. "But don't you do channeling in Canada? It's very big where I'm from."

I assure her there must be some Canadian channelers out there.

"You know, it's amazing how many Brazilians I've met, and they're all here because of Paulo Coelho's book. Can you imagine? It's ridiculous because obviously he never even walked the Camino. I came because of Shirley MacLaine's book—have you read it? I've met eight or ten Americans on the Camino, all women, and every one of them is here because of her book. You just watch. Next year, there's going to be millions of Americans over here."

I assure her the Spanish will be delighted.

I'm looking forward to walking with her tomorrow morning on the last stretch into Santiago and finding out more about channeled Virgins, but when I get up, she's already gone ahead. I hope her socks are dry.

AND WHAT IS IT LIKE in the end? How is it to arrive?

In the year 1670, when the Italian Dominican friar Domenico Laffi and his friends looked down for the first time from the Monte de Gozo, the Mount of Joy, upon the city of the Apostle, they fell to their knees and launched into a singing of the Te Deum. But they could manage no more than the first two or three verses before they had to surrender to their emotions. They wept until their tears were spent, then descended to the city of the Apostle, singing as they went.

My own response is less ecstatic. I am relieved to be finished and disappointed too. The pilgrimage has ended, and with it the community of the road, the liberty, the joy of walking in the early morning or as evening comes on. The destination, beautiful as it is, has nothing—at least for the non-believer—to match the wonders of the getting-there.

Still, I can say that Santiago is a little like heaven: everyone who arrived before is waiting for you there, and the ones who were behind you soon catch up. Pilgrims find each other, and are reunited for a bottle of wine or two, and talk about how lost they feel, waking up in the morning with nowhere to go.

The medieval pilgrim arriving in Santiago had reached the culmination of his journey. He would view the relics of Saint James: his hat, his staff, the chains that bound him, the sickle that beheaded him. He would enjoy the *abrazo*—the embrace of the statue of the Apostle—even draping his cape on Saint James' broad shoulders and putting his hat on the statue's head. Most importantly, he would touch the holy tomb, kiss it, weep and pray before it, spreading his arms in the form of a cross. Then, assured that his sins had been forgiven, his prayers heard, he would pledge to lead a good life thenceforth.

And us? We go through the motions: a swift *abrazo*, a front-row seat at the pilgrims' mass, a peek through the grating at the Apostle's alleged resting place. Most of us partake of these rituals because pilgrims have always done so. But what does arriving mean to us besides an end to walking? Do we just go home now?

The November crowd is thin. There are no more than ten or fifteen souls kicking around the big refuge in Santiago. Gottholt is off ahead and Timo the Finn is still somewhere back on the road. The only friend left is my staff. I resolve to keep it this time, even if I must lug it by train all over Europe. So I go hunting around the refuge for a place to stash it, just so it won't get "borrowed." The closet beside my bed looks big enough, as long as the door isn't locked. . . .

It isn't. The handle turns, the door opens. And within, green, resilient, firm—yet evanescent as a memory—stands the graceful bamboo staff of Philippe LeClerc.

Our Lady of the Boat

But as Gottholt said, the Camino doesn't stop in Santiago. The real end lies sixty miles beyond, at the brittle edge of things. For although, in death, Saint James' body rests beneath the altar of his cathedral, his stamping grounds in life were by the Atlantic shore. Tradition relates that, as Apostle to Spain, James came even as far as Galicia to spread the word of Christ among the pagans. And it is for this reason that after his martyrdom his body found its way back to this land that he loved and detested.

So once more I go to Finisterre, where the fishing boats still bob and the Virgin still walks on the November waves. And then I make my way up the Coast of Death.

Through the ages, these Galician shores have received many wonders from the sea. It is said that Noah's ark came to rest here. The patriarch founded the town named Noia (which still bears the ark and a dove on its crest), planted Galicia's first grapes, gath-  ered her first vintage, and married his niece Noela to a local baron. Many years later, a ship of another great navigator, Columbus, made land in Galicia. The storm that sepa- rated the Admiral's caravels as they made their way home from his first voyage carried the *Pinta* here with its tales of strange western lands. But the most illus- trious visitor of all was the Virgin Mary, who first set foot on Spanish soil on the rocky shore near the village called Muxía.

There, by the ocean, stands the Church of Nuestra Señora de la Barca—Our Lady of the Boat—all hung inside with bright little model fishing boats. The headland thrusting out into the waters before the church is strewn with boulders, like God's dice. And it is said that one day long ago, Santiago himself sat on one of these rocks, gazing at the waves.

He was pining for home, for Israel. He remembered the great days when his Lord lived and walked upon that distant soil, and He and the Twelve went from town to town preaching and performing miracles. Santiago had spent long years now in Galicia working wonders, healing the sick, proving the might of his Lord against fraudulent priests as he tried to win this stubborn folk from their pagan gods of water and stone. Yet he had saved but three souls. In all these years, three souls.

And lately he found himself missing the aroma of markets over-flowing with dates plums figs pomegranates, the spice-bearing caravans, the palm trees. He missed the gentle lull of the Sea of Galilee as he moored his boat among the reeds. In this land of mist and rain, he missed the stark certainties of the desert. He even missed the Romans and the Pharisees.

Not for the first time, Santiago felt a weariness pushing up through him from his feet to his eyes. And worse, a black self-pity. He had heard that Peter was doing great things among the Romans. That the upstart Paul was cutting swaths through the Greek world. That even the Magdalene had won souls among the Gauls. So why should his light be hidden under a bushel, here at the end of the world?

Lost in these thoughts, he did not at first notice the speck that was growing on the horizon. When he did, he assumed it was only a fishing boat. But no, it was moving too fast. What could it be?

He fixed his eyes on the speck and suddenly he felt his soul growing lighter, lighter, as peace welled up within him. He could see her now, Mary the Virgin, riding in the prow, her face full to the wind. Her bark skimmed the top of the waves and in seconds it had reached the shore. Then Mary drew it from the water like a leaf and turned it over on the rocks with a skill that James the fisherman admired. He tried to rise to greet her, but all the strength had run out of his body, and she came to him instead where he sat on his rock, and touched his hair.

"Man," she said, "I know all that is in your mind and I have come to comfort you and give you strength. Long have you labored among these people, but still their heart is hard. Now it is time to come home to Jerusalem. There, death awaits you, and glory; for you will be the first of the Twelve to sit at my Son's side in the Kingdom of Heaven."

James heard the Virgin's gentle words and was comforted. He closed his eyes and sailed into a little sleep. When he awoke, she was gone.

He stood, and took one last look over the gray Atlantic. Nothing but sky and water. No one could cross it and no one knew what lay beyond. Then he turned and began to walk. It was a long way to Jerusalem.

Behind him, the Virgin's boat remained overturned on the shore. The sail as well. In time, both turned to stone. Today, the sail is called the Pedra de Abalar. Large though it is, it will sink beneath the foot of the pure in heart, though it never budges for the sinful. Nearby is the great stone boat called the Pedra dos Cadrís. It arches high enough off the rocks that a pilgrim can pass beneath. To do so nine times is said to be good for the kidneys.

The Camino de Santiago ends here. There is nowhere to go now but back. I will sit a while on the rocks with the wind pummeling me, and look out over the ocean in the general direction of where I come from. I will try to get "beneath, to where the life is."

THE VIRGIN

AND THE GENERAL

EL FERROL

FOR THE PAST TWO WEEKS, as I have been spooling up the Camino de Santiago with my feet, all Spain, or at least all of the Spanish media, has talked of nothing but the Anniversary: November 20, the twenty-fifth anniversary of the death of *el Caudillo*, Generalissimo Francisco Franco.

Day after day, the editorials have mused over the dictator's legacy. The weekend magazines are having a heyday, pumping out pieces with titles like "The great manipulator," "That phantasm of history," "The face that was seen everywhere," "He was bad, ugly and balding" (a survey of what today's schoolchildren know about the Generalissimo) and the inevitable "Where were you when Franco died?" Tv España raised howls from the Socialists by first scheduling a program critical of the Franco years, then postponing it with the explanation that it was more appropriate at this moment to celebrate Spain's twenty-five years of constitutional monarchy than to pick over what went before.

Once again Franco's face is everywhere. This must come as a shock to the Spanish: the shock of the familiar. For in the generation since his death, most traces that such a person as Francisco Franco ever existed have been rinsed from the nation's face. It is rare anymore to come across a plaque, a statue, a street name, anything that harks back to "that long-ago dictatorship." When one does, the temptation is to take a photo on the chance it won't be there next time.

202

The Camino boasts a scattering of Franco relics, just enough to occasionally jar the blissed-out pilgrim into noticing that he is walking through a minefield of recent history and not some twelfth-century Disneyland. In a cloister of the monastery of Samos, for instance, an inscription reads: "1953. Francisco Franco *Caudillo*, victor of the crusade against Communism, visited this monastery with his wife and daughter." Burgos, the first capital of Franco's "holy war" for Spain, keeps the faith by retaining the old street names that celebrate Franco and other Nationalist luminaries (though I can find no sign marking the street that is identified on my map as the Avenida del Generalísimo). Santiago still has its calle Franco, though ironically the street named for the teetotaling demagogue lies at the heart of the bar district. As for León, it changed its street names only last year. Franco's street is now the calle Ancha, Broad Street, while Plaza Calvo Sotelo, named after the Fascist proto-martyr, has been literally re-Christened the Plaza of the Annunciation, demonstrating that Sotelos may come and go, but the Virgin on her pillar endures. When I ask at León's Tourist Office whether the changeover provoked controversy, the young woman at the desk looks puzzled.

"Why? They are just names of people from the Civil War."

But if they are "just names of people from the Civil War," why change them?

Of all the memorials once dedicated to Franco throughout Spain, the only conspicuous one still standing is a large equestrian statue, situated in—where else?—his hometown of El Ferrol, on the coast of Galicia. Even there, Franco's legacy has proved problematical. The city which during the dictator's lifetime was granted the title "El Ferrol *del Caudillo*" has long since divested itself of that honor. Public opinion there today is neatly split between those who wish to retain Franco's statue and those in favor of sinking it in the harbor. The latter party has dubbed the statue *o burro e o cabalo*—"the ass and the horse"—and recent years have seen attacks by paint vandals and even a pair of bombing attempts. Though these took out a few windows, they made no impression upon the General or his horse.

When I finish the Camino on November 17, I am a two-hour bus ride from El Ferrol. The temptation to see how Franco's hometown marks the anniversary of his passing is irresistible.

But why go chasing after this long-dead and unloved dictator? Because, strange as it may seem, the history of Francisco Franco is intertwined with the history of the Virgin Mary in Spain, and especially with her most illustrious avatar, *la virgen del Pilar*, Our Lady of the Pillar.

The Legend of la Virgen del Pilar

We even have a date for it. It was the second of January, in the year AD 40. Saint James had abandoned the hard-headed pagans of Galicia to their gods of water and stone. He was working his way back across Spain, headed for Jerusalem. He had garnered eight disciples along the way and on this day he was teaching them by the River Ebro.

At that very moment in faraway Nazareth the Virgin Mary's thoughts had turned, as they often did, to the Apostle. "May he have success in his mission," she prayed. She had no sooner spoken the words than Jesus appeared at her side.

"All shall be as you wish," he said. Then he touched her hand, and in an instant she was transported to Spain.

James and his disciples heard a crashing of heavenly cymbals. They were blinded for a moment, as by a bolt of lightning. Then, through clouds of light, they perceived the Virgin, seated on a throne borne by angels. They knelt in speechless adoration. After a moment that seemed an eternity, Mary took from one of the angels a statue of herself, a tiny image carved of wood and set upon a column of jasper.

"James," she said, "have faith! The day is coming when, thanks to your labors, all Spain will hear the Holy Word. Now make a church for me here. Place this image within, that the Spanish people will know that the Mother of the Lord came to their soil in the living flesh. Let it be a sign that her love is greater for them than for any other nation."

With that, the music ceased. The light faded. The Apostle and his eight followers found themselves alone again, in the January chill, by the foggy banks of the Ebro. But now in their midst there stood a little statue of a Virgin on a pillar.

Today, the spot where the Virgin appeared lies at the heart of the ancient Roman city of Zaragoza. In the best of all possible worlds, I would have been in Zaragoza during the second week of October for the festival of el Pilar. I would have arrived a couple of days in advance to call up an old student of mine to act as my guide to the bacchanalia. I would have seen the Virgin pelted with roses by an adoring public as she passed through the streets of her city, then left Zaragoza full of praise, wonder and admiration.

In this less than perfect world, however, where one lives and writes books about the Virgin Mary, I am still in Chartres during the second week of October and don't arrive in Zaragoza until a frigid evening in late November, when the city's body lies stiff and unresponsive beneath a shroud of fog. I have only one night set aside for Zaragoza, barely enough for a glimpse of the place (the *second* place, the Galicians would say) where the Virgin Mary set foot upon Spanish soil. But given the season, it will suffice.

The Virgin's home is the austere Cathedral of el Pilar, the self-proclaimed "first Marian temple of all Christianity." The disproportion in size between the great barn itself and the treasure it was built to house is staggering, for while the cupola over the high altar rises to a height of twenty stories, the statue of the Virgin is no bigger than a doll. Her Baroque handlers, baffled at what to do with something so petite, only managed to dwarf her further by setting her off against an explosive marble sculpture that depicts James and his disciples averting their eyes, one can only assume, from the overbearing taste of an age to come.

Pilgrims come and go by the hundreds. They gather first to pray in the Virgin's chapel, then retreat around the back to kiss her pillar. The pillar is accessed through a golden porthole, and pilgrims must lean down and bend forward to reach it, a posture that leaves their backsides comically protruding. The pillar has been furrowed by centuries of lips, including those of the Pilgrim Pope, John Paul II.

Diminutive though she is, little Pilar is the axis upon which the Spanish sense of a unique Catholic destiny has historically turned; her pillar marks, in the inventive image of one primate of Spain, "the historical and geographical point through which we were inoculated with divine life."

Zaragoza being the chief city of the kingdom of Aragon, the Virgin of the Pillar was the patron of King Ferdinand. How appropriate, then, that Columbus first touched land in the Americas on her feast day, October 12. Later, when the Conquistadors set out to win a new world beneath the banners of Mary and Santiago, the first ship to reach California was "Nuestra Señora del Pilar." The conquerors paid their debt to the Lady of the Pillar with extravagant gifts of gold and jewels. They raised this cathedral over her head and called on Goya to paint its ceiling. Such were the glories of an age when Spain saw herself—justly, it seemed—as the glory of the earth, the nation chosen by the Lord and the Holy Mother to bear the cross to the farthest shores.

But by the turn of the twentieth century, even as other European nations were reaching the apogee of their imperial adventures, most of Spain's far-flung dominions had slipped from her grasp. In 1898, Cuba and the Philippines, the last jewels of the Empire, were captured by the American parvenus, and Holy Spain was left with nothing to support her pretensions, no way to gloss over the fact that she was among the poorest and most backward nations of Europe, plagued by illiteracy, gross inequality of land distribution, strikes, terrorism and political chaos.

It was into this Spain of misplaced destiny that Francisco Paulino Hermenegildo Teódulo Franco y Bahamonde was delivered on December 4, 1892.

If a novelist dreamed up the Freudian tangle of Francisco Franco's roots, his editor would send the manuscript back with instructions to tone down the symbolism. The dictator who would institutionalize the cult of the Virgin as the religion of his regime began his life on María Street. His mother's given name? María del Pilar. Franco's mother was an austere and devout Catholic of the landed nobility. As for his father, Nicolás, he was an easy-living man-about-town with atheist, liberal, Masonic tendencies—just the sort of fellow Franco would spend the rest of his life imprisoning and hounding into exile. Nicolás favored Francisco's younger brother, the athletic, affable Ramón, over puny, adenoidal "Paquito." But the future dictator was cherished by his pious mother, and the two often made the long climb together to the dark little chapel of the Virgen del Chamorro to offer thanks for Francisco's triumphs. Mother and son only bonded the closer after Nicolás Franco took a posting in Madrid in 1912. The rogue had soon set up house with his mistress, abandoning El Ferrol and María del Pilar for good.

By this time, Francisco's military career was already passing from strength to strength. At the age of twenty-seven, he was named second-in-command of Spain's newly formed Foreign Legion. In Morocco, his fearless and patient leadership helped spare Spain the humiliation of being routed from her last colony by tribesmen on horseback. He became the youngest general in Europe at the age of thirty-two and ulti-mately the leader of his nation. The only thing he never managed to do was impress his father. When reporters asked Nicolás how he felt about his son, he would reply, "Do you mean Ramón?" It is said that his profane outbursts against the Generalissimo in Madrid bars more than once led to his being arrested and detained until his identity had been confirmed. In 1942, when the old man died, Franco tried to present him as someone fit to be his father, denying Nicolás's mistress permission to attend the funeral and burying the blaspheming old Freemason in the full-dress uniform of a general.

The facts invite us to read Franco's career as one long, sad exercise in repudiating his unloving father—by demonizing those who lived and thought like him; by polishing his own image as a paragon of abstemious, upstanding, Catholic husband-and-fatherhood; and by exalting his saintly mother, María del Pilar.

THE YEARS OF FRANCO'S youth were years of renewal for the Virgin of the Pillar, as those who yearned for the old Spain turned to her with mystic fervor. Who else could restore the nation's wounded pride, its squandered fortunes? 1905 saw the mobilization of Catholic Spain for her coronation. On this occasion, the Archbishop of Zaragoza proclaimed, "The Virgin of the Pillar is the Spanish Virgin, the Queen of Spain, she who has rescued us from the shades of paganism, she who has saved us from the Moor, she who has saved us from the domination of the French encyclopedists, she who will save us from the errors of modern natu-ralism." It was not the barbarians at the gates he was concerned about, but the ones already within the walls: the radical thinkers of "the Generation of '98" who were calling for reform on the model of modern European states and a farewell to the threadbare dreams of Holy Spain; those same "modernists" whom Pius IX had castigated in the Syllabus of Errors.

In 1908, the call to arms was repeated, as Zaragoza hosted the international Marian conference against "Modernism, the sum and compendium of all heresies." After the conference, in a gesture of mystic nostalgia, Nuestra Señora was wrapped round with a captain-general's sash and the flags of Spain's former colonies were unfurled before her. October 12, el Pilar's feast day and the day when Columbus planted Spain's first seeds in the New World, was thenceforth to be celebrated as *la fiesta de la raza*, the feast day of the Spanish "race."

Political and religious reaction found voice during these years in the right-wing movement *Acción Española*, which championed the concept of *Hispanidad*—the Spanish people's unique Catholic calling. According to the movement's mystical reading of history, the appearance of Our Lady of the Pillar on Spanish soil signaled the national destiny, which was to defend the Holy Church against "the Moor" in whatever form he might appear. The political/religious program of Acción Española found its religious/political echo in Opus Dei, a secretive Catholic brotherhood established in Zaragoza during the same period. Opus Dei's goal, based upon the 999 spiritual insights inscribed by its founder, Josemaría Escrivá de Balaguer, in his book, *Camino*, was nothing less than the "Christianization" of secular society from within. To this end, Opus Dei concentrated on recruiting professionals and the scions of powerful families. At least nine of its members would later serve in Franco's cabinets. Escrivá de Balaguer (who is currently on the fast track to sainthood) was noted for his daily visits to the cathedral of el Pilar and his custom of "always glancing at an image of the Virgin upon entering or leaving a room."

Around this time, Francisco Franco, too, was discerning the presence of the Virgin in his life. The crowning point of the little colonel's military career, his heroic 1925 landing in Alhucemas, fell on September 8, the Nativity of the Virgin. On his return to Spain, Franco's first stop would be to pay homage to the little Black Virgin of Jerez de la Frontera.

I BOARD THE BUS TO EL FERROL ON the morning of November 20, not knowing quite what I expect to find there. But it's a splendid ride over hills and through clouds with fleeting vistas of cities by the ocean. Then the bus rolls through the modern suburbs of El Ferrol, past the naval barracks and the edge of the arsenal, and finally into the well-treed Plaza de España (formerly the Plaza del Generalísimo), where Francisco Franco sits astride his horse. . . .

Resplendent in a fresh coat of salmon-pink paint. I'm already too late.

Anticipating increased police vigilance on the twentieth, the protesters struck on the nineteenth. At midday, the paint guerrillas' white van squealed to a stop in the Plaza de España. While four members of the self-styled "Northwest Popular Assembly" clambered up the Franco monument with paint cans and brushes, another twenty-five set up placards around the base, including one that read *Hai que tirar o burro e o cabalo*, "The ass and the horse must go." By the time the forces of order arrived on the scene (and what is one to make of their twenty-minute response time?) the Generalissimo was clad in shocking pink. The police broke up a shoving match that had broken out between the protesters and some onlookers, and the authors of the deed were transported to the police station, identified and released. The anniversary had been marked.

The mayor of El Ferrol, a Galician nationalist who proposes to convert the Plaza into a parking area, says later, "This sort of thing wouldn't happen if the statue weren't standing where it is." He offers no specifics on where it might better be located.

Now, the late-morning crowds are milling around the Plaza as on any Monday. There are no signs of protests or counterprotests. A police van stands on belated guard near the base of the monument. A few students point from the sidewalk opposite, openly admiring the general's new clothes, and I spot some of the older citizens looking quietly pleased. But most of the crowd studiously averts their gaze from this giant, pink reminder of the not-yet-distant past.

It looks as though I've missed "the action." The local paper offers no hint of any manifestations planned for today. There is only a wreath-laying at the statue, scheduled for the afternoon, and a memorial service this evening under the auspices of the "National Francisco Franco Foundation of El Ferrol." The venue, naturally, is El Ferrol's Church of Nuestra Señora del Pilar.

At lunch-time, I try to draw out the waiter on recent events. He shrugs off my questions. He and his family are not from El Ferrol. They don't know what the people here think. They have no opinions about anything. Not that this stops his wife from warning the children not to go through Plaza de España on their way home from school.

"We always go through Plaza de España."

"Not tonight you don't."

"Why not?"

"Because your mother told you not to."

El Ferrol has many of the characteristics of an extra-territorial settlement. Since the seventeenth century, its *ría*, or fjord, has served as the Spanish navy's principal Atlantic port and arsenal. Thus, although it lies at the furthest reaches of Galicia, it is wired directly to Madrid, whence the orders emanate. Even the city center—a grid laid down in the eighteenth century on the latest rational Enlightenment principles—was planned in Madrid. Franco was born in one of these arrow-straight downtown streets (which the Spanish, captivated by the novelty of arteries meeting at ninety-degree angles, have declared an historical-artistic treasure). In this naval hotbed, the future dictator soaked up the legends of Spain's maritime glory and learned to distrust the liberal politicians and intellectuals who had betrayed the nation, the church and—worst of all—the navy with their schemes to introduce godless modernism.

Today, El Ferrol's book and stationery shops have no postcards to commemorate Franco. Nor does the tourist office dispense any *In the Footsteps of the Generalissimo* brochures. There are no pilgrims to the dictator's hometown, or none whom El Ferrol cares to acknowledge. Perhaps Franco himself anticipated that his legacy would not be honored by his Galician compatriots (whose aspirations to autonomy he so diligently stomped out), for he chose as his place of burial not El Ferrol, but "the Valley of the Fallen," a grandiose mausoleum scooped out of a mountain north of Madrid.

The upshot of all this is that I have to scout around a bit before I find the Franco home, at last, at 136, calle María. It is the only building in this stretch that has no shop at street level, and the windows of the upper floors are blinded. On the first-floor balcony a bombastic metal plaque from the early 1930s honors Francisco and Ramón. (The dictator's dashing younger brother, Nicolás Franco's favorite, brought glory to the family in 1926 by piloting his plane across the South Atlantic and embarrassment to his brother in 1930 when he led an Air Force rebellion against the monarchy.) A second, more matter-of-fact plate, placed by the family after Franco's death, quietly confirms that this was his birthplace. Aside from these modest memorials and that pink monstrosity in the Plaza de España, there is no evidence to implicate El Ferrol in the life of its most famous son.

There is, however, evidence aplenty that Spain has taken up with godless modernism. The window of a bookstore in the calle Real flaunts a whole library of titles calculated to set el Caudillo spinning in his grave: *How to Separate from Your Abusive Husband*; *Your Place or Mine?: Everything Young People Want to Know About Sex*; *A General History of Drugs*; *The Beatles: Revolution in the Mind* and, right beside it: *After the vengeance, the lies, the calumny, the incompetence, Franco: the History*. I suspect that the nonchalance of this juxtaposition—Franco's biography set next to a book about the Beatles, as though the two were in no important way different—would be the worst slap in the face of all for the Generalissimo; worse even than the accusations, the splattering with paint, the being systematically forgotten.

IN THE AFTERNOON, I walk beyond the edge of town to the shrine of Nuestra Señora del Chamorro, where Franco used to go with his mother. Mrs. Franco must have kept herself in fairly good shape, scaling this muddy, rutted hill. At the top, some teenagers are lounging on the walls like giant lizards, smoking and playing music. Not the sort of behavior the Generalissimo would have smiled upon. Inside, the tiny chapel is dark as soot. It's impossible to make out anything more than the rough location of the Madonna. On the wall facing her, there hangs a framed message and a photograph. I turn to the ancient, wraith-like caretaker, who hovers like a bat, sure that I intend some mischief.

"El Caudillo?" I ask.

"*Sí, es el Caudillo,*" she responds. Her brittle voice implies, "As if you'd know anything about el Caudillo."

I wait her out, examining the *ex votos* that have been left for Our Lady, little wax replicas of the body parts she has cured, or been asked to cure—heads, feet, arms, fat legs that look like they've been snapped off statues of cherubs, nipple-less breasts—until finally the little woman wrenches herself from my side to go out and yell at the teenagers. I have just enough time to snap a shot of the Virgin of Chamorro. The flash reveals a plump-cheeked mother in wedding white.

IN THE RUN-UP TO THE CIVIL WAR, Spain's Republican regime launched a full-out attack on the Catholic Church; freedom of religion was declared, crucifixes removed from classrooms, religious orders dissolved and their property confiscated. Divorce and civil marriages and burials came in; state stipends for priests went out. Some of these measures enjoyed wide support, but the suddenness and severity with which they were implemented drove the Church into a corner and led to the disaffection of many who had originally backed the government (it was Swift who observed, "Nothing can render the clergy popular but some degree of persecution"). The process was exacerbated when the government and military were accused of complicity in the burning of churches and monasteries in Madrid and the south of Spain. The "smoking gun" in the scandal was a telegram to Madrid from General Caminero in Malaga that placidly stated, "The burning of churches has started, and will continue tomorrow."

There was nothing terribly new about anti-clerical violence in Spain. There is even an old street ballad that goes, "There were six bad bulls at the bullfight, so the people burnt the churches." However, the paroxysm that marked the onset of the Civil War was horrifying. More than 6,000 priests, monks and nuns died in those first months, most at the hands of self-appointed death squads, many after torture and humiliation. Franco capitalized on the Church's desperation by offering himself as the savior of Holy Spain.

Franco's Nationalist movement and its Acción Española and Opus Dei allies dressed up his bloody coup and the purges that followed as a modern crusade, in which Santiago Matamoros, the "Moor-killer," and the Virgin Mary were drafted for active service. Our Lady of the Immaculate Conception was declared patron of the infantry; el Pilar herself was made protector of the Civil Guard and the Spanish Legion. The whole war effort was "Marianized" (often to grotesque ends, as when the Nationalist "martyrs" were commemorated in her sanctuaries or when Escrivá de Balaguer, the founder of Opus Dei, declared that the war had "a super-natural end. We have to love it."). The rhetoric of the Nationalists revealed, behind the bland smile of their Holy Mother, the face of the Savage Goddess, demanding the tribute of her devotees' blood.

The Nationalists' richest propaganda coup followed a Republican attack on Zaragoza, when two missiles struck the cathedral of Nuestra Señora but failed to explode. What clearer sign could there be of Our Lady's favor? One-eyed, one-armed General Millan Astray, *el Gran Mutilado*, led his troops into the sanctuary of el Pilar, where amid cries of "Long live death! Long live Nuestra Señora!" he touched his cap to her crown, then knelt before her in prayer. The visitor to the cathedral today can still see the erect missiles standing sentry before the chapel of the Virgin.

Post-war, the triumphal forces of Nationalist Spain shared the glory with their heavenly matron. The country remained a European backwater and a weapons-testing ground for the Russians and Nazis, but in Franco's fevered rhetoric Spain had resumed her rightful role as champion of Mary and the Roman Church. General Goma declared that any history of the war should include a chapter "dedicated to the study of the intervention of the Mother of God"; to which the less-discerning Adolf Hitler replied that "it was not the intervention of the Mother of God, but the intervention of General von Richtofen and his bomber squadrons that decided the issue."

Thus commenced a forty-year Marian dictatorship, an unnatural coupling of militarism and Virgin worship. Regulations for the veneration of Mary were among the Franco government's first legislation. Public establishments were required to display her image; officials, to swear they would uphold Marian beliefs. In the schools, students and teachers greeted each other with the jovial exchange:

"Hail Mary, most pure!"

"Conceived without sin."

The mystery of the Assumption, the age-old belief in Mary's ascension to heaven on her death, was elevated to a matter of national honor and government policy. On January 2, 1940, the nineteenth centenary of el Pilar's arrival in Spain, 20,000 youngsters took an oath in Zaragoza "to defend the mystery" even as Franco himself was petitioning Pius XII to declare it an article of faith. Meanwhile, Virgin "research" permeated academia, as the "Spanish Mariological Society" was established with the Virgen del Pilar as its captain.

It was not until the late forties and fifties that opposition to the Generalissimo's Mariocracy began to emerge. (Though in fairness to the

Church, Franco's policy of imprisoning clerics who disagreed with him had something to do with that.) It appeared first among the younger clergy, who sided with the workers and the poor. Finally, in the years following the Second Vatican Council, the upper hierarchy began to openly question the wisdom and morality of cohabiting with fascism. By 1974, the Archbishop of Barcelona was speaking openly on behalf of striking auto workers, insisting, "Capitalists must accept new forms of worker participation."

The Spanish Church had recovered its moral bearings, but much damage had already been done. If Marian devotion in Spain today retains the aroma of a political statement, it is the legacy of her ubiquity in religion, education, politics, public life, and the academic and the military worlds during the Franco decades. In the minds of many, Mary remains linked to the acts of a repressive and widely despised regime.

BY EARLY EVENING, A COLD RAIN has set in. I've taken a wrong turn on the way to the Generalissimo's memorial service, and now I'm huddled inside my non-water-resistant nylon jacket, racing across the empty Plaza de España. If there was a protest or a bombing planned for tonight, it got rained out.

Finally I get myself pointed in the right direction, but by the time I locate the Church of el Pilar it's ten past seven. The doors are closed, the service has started. I pause across the way, under an overhang. If I had been here half an hour ago, I could have taken a peek inside. That was all I wanted, just a peek to see what kind of people would want to remember el Caudillo. But there's no way I can stick my nose in now. They'll just have to mourn without me.

After a minute, I pry myself from the wall of the building and scoot up to the next block. Thankfully, the street to my right is arcaded. Out of the rain now I slow my pace, looking for a welcoming bar. Instead, I find an Internet center. Well, why not? A chance to catch up on my e-mail. It's a typical Spanish Internet spot—not a "cyber cafe," but a game center, packed with high school and university students skilfully racing motorcycles, sparring with kung fu masters, blowing up alien spacecraft. I grab the lone open spot, pop in a hundred-peseta coin for ten minutes of net time and start e-ing.

The first message is to my wife, Michiko; the second, to my friend Dennis. I tell them both how good the Generalissimo looks in pink.

Dennis's message I title *"El burro y el caballo."* There's something liberating about flippancy in the face of a phenomenon like Franco, even if it's a cheap liberation, won without any risks on my part. I'm just getting launched into a good description of the day's events when I become aware of the two oafs breathing down my back. Apparently they want a machine and they've picked me out as someone they can intimidate. One is all but leaning on my shoulder. I shrug him off, then take a glance at my ticker. I've got five minutes left, so to hell with them, I'll take it down to the last second. I go back to my message to Dennis, changing a word here, cutting a comma there.

When the timer on the computer flashes zero, I slowly pull on my jacket. I rummage for some imaginary something in my bag. Then I stand up and make a gracious gesture towards my vacated seat. Showed them. The dapper, moustached gentleman who has been standing too close behind me smiles. He takes a badge from his jacket pocket: *"Tiene identificación? Pasaporte?"*

The police are very pleasant, very sorry to waste my time. But I must understand that these things happen. The dapper one steps outside with my passport to make a call from his cell phone. His younger, leather-jacket-clad partner assures me that he anticipates no problem, but there is such a thing as terrorism in Spain, as I know, and I have been seen outside the church of el Pilar, where, as I know, a memorial service is being held tonight, and this will only be a question of waiting a few minutes while some inquiries are made, nothing to be concerned about …

The older policeman steps back inside. He begins to toss off questions. What am I doing in El Ferrol? When did I arrive? Where am I staying? Do I know anyone here? Where have I been before now? His tone is conversational, as if he just wants to know. He tells me again that there is absolutely no problem, that this is just the sort of thing that occurs, that he truly regrets wasting my time, regrets it so much, in fact, that I must allow him to buy me a drink. As "No thank you" doesn't seem to be an option, I join him beneath his umbrella and take a few brisk steps to the bar across the street.

He greets the staff by name, orders two glasses of very good Rioja and poses a few more questions. He really is a most affable fellow, with his humorous eyes glinting behind his glasses. A pleasure to be detained by. He wants me to tell him about the Camino. He has a friend who has been trying to talk him into doing it for years. And where did I pick up my Spanish? He would love to know English.

"At least enough to read your e-mail," he confesses cheerfully.

Do I speak any other languages? When I tell him that my wife is Japanese, a light-bulb goes on.

"Ah! Then the first message you sent was to your wife! I was wondering. I saw the Japanese name and thought perhaps it was something related to President Fujimori!" He smiles and pats my arm. "A joke, my friend. A very facile joke."

Then he tells me a cautionary tale about a Spanish man in Latin America who was so careless as to advertise on the Internet for someone to kill his wife. Naturally, the police tracked him down and he was sent off to prison. Which demonstrates that there is no security over the Internet, none at all. So one really has to be careful what one writes, because one really doesn't know who might read it. He takes a glance at his watch, then polishes off his wine.

"Well, I will not molest you any longer. I apologize for the inconvenience. But there you are. You have another story to tell about the Camino."

"Thank you."

And with a wave of his hand, he is gone. I flash a sheepish smile at the bartender. She turns her eyes to the television.

THE MORNING PAPER CARRIES a report on Franco's mass. I read it on the first bus out of town.

It was an uneventful service, with barely one hundred people in attendance. Afterwards, the priest of the Church of el Pilar brushed off all questions: "It doesn't matter much to us what the rest of the world thinks." The mayor of El Ferrol, meanwhile, opines that the vandalization of Franco's statue was "the unfortunate but inevitable result of having an anachronistic symbol in a public place." I wonder what would be left of Spain if it rid all its public places of their anachronistic symbols.

The following day, Spain pauses as gravel-throated King Juan Carlos addresses the parliament on the twenty-fifth anniversary of his succession to the throne. I will hear only the first five minutes of his speech, as I sit on the bus to Vigo, before the driver, exercising his democratic rights, changes the station. To that point at least, the king has alluded to neither the Virgin nor the General.

TOTUS TUUS SUM, MARIA FATIMA

MAY 13, 1981

It is the feast day of Our Lady of Fatima. Five-thirty p.m. As he bends spontaneously to caress the girl with the picture of the Virgin pinned to her blouse, the first two bullets whistle through the space where his head had been. But the next ones find him. Now the ambulance must run the gamut of Rome's traffic to reach Gemelli hospital. The victim of the shooting is bleeding profusely from a bullet wound to the abdomen. He has already gone into shock. As the blood seeps from his body, staining his white robes, the same word passes his lips with every breath:

"Madonna . . . Madonna . . ."

The ambulance reaches the hospital in eight minutes. The patient is now unconscious, his pulse almost imperceptible, his blood pressure plummeting. The last rites are administered before the operation begins. Five hours later, though he has lost 60 percent of his blood, it is clear that he will pull through. The bullet has missed his aorta by millimeters, passing through his body without striking any vital organs or causing irreparable damage.

"It's a miracle," the doctors exclaim.

The Pope concurs in their opinion.

From his hospital bed, Karol Wojtyla calls for a certain handwritten letter that has been in the hands of the Vatican since 1957. Popularly known as "the Secret of Fatima," it contains an account of the vision revealed by the Virgin in June of 1917 to a ten-year-old girl named Lúcia dos Santos—now Sister Maria Lúcia of the Immaculate Heart.

The first two "secrets" revealed to Lúcia—that a world war would come, more terrible than the first, and that the Virgin called upon the Pope to consecrate Russia to her Immaculate Heart—have long been in the public domain. But Mary's final revelation, "the third secret," has remained under wraps. For decades, the Vatican's reticence concerning this document has whipped up storms of speculation and rumor. Legend has it that when Pope John XXIII first read the letter in 1960 he fainted. Five years later, his successor Paul VI concluded that the prophecy was not intended for his time and resealed it. What could this letter contain? Nothing less than the precise details of the coming Armageddon, in the opinion of many.

Mere days before the assassination bid, Lawrence Downey, a former Trappist monk, had thrust "the third secret" into the international spotlight. Armed with a water bottle and a cigarette lighter, the determined Australian had commandeered an Aer Lingus jet, threatening to blow it up if the Vatican didn't reveal the Virgin's message. Back in Ireland, the televised rugby matches were interrupted by news bulletins that initially attributed the hijacking to an Islamic group calling itself the "Third Sect of Fatima." The drama came to a bloodless end when French troops stormed the plane on the tarmac in Paris.

Now John Paul has time, plenty of time, to pore over "the secret." He has already perused it once since becoming Pope in 1978, but like his predecessors he set it aside for a future Pope. The events of May 13, the day of Our Lady of Fatima, however, suggest that the future is now, that prophecy is becoming headline.

Were the gunshots in Saint Peter's Square a wake-up call? In the summer of 1981, Solidarity is challenging the communist government of Poland and a Soviet invasion is rumored to be imminent. In the United States, President Reagan is fulminating against "the evil empire" of the Russians as the arms race gathers steam. If the Pope's life has miraculously been spared, it must be so that he can act to avert the disaster that is breaking upon the world.

Before he takes his next step, however, John Paul sends an envoy to the convent of Carmelite nuns in the Portuguese city of Coimbra. From her cloister there, for thirty-six years, Sister Lúcia, the seer of Fatima, has been keeping an eye on the twentieth century. Now the Pope has a few questions for her.

I ARRIVE AT FATIMA STATION EARLY in the evening, step out into the street, and look up and down for the basilica. I've heard that Fatima is a tiny place, so it shouldn't be hard to get my bearings. All I can see for the moment though is a single bar sign, winking like a lighthouse across the way. A stout, white-haired gentleman issues from within.

"*Fátima?*" he calls out to me.

"*Fátima,*" I reply.

"No more buses tonight. It's fifteen miles. Taxi?"

Fifteen miles? That's a pilgrimage in itself. I had been tickled, inveterate budget traveler that I am, about getting the train all the way from Oporto for less than ten dollars, undercutting the bus fare by a pocketful of escudos. Now I'm going to blow my budget on a cab. I duck back into the station to check the bus schedule, but there really are no more tonight. With a sigh, I toss my gear in the trunk of the old Mercedes and we're off like a bullet. I roll down the window and let the night air whistle by. For what I'm paying, I want to enjoy the ride.

This will be my first time in Fatima, though I came very close on a previous trip to Portugal, when I visited Leiria, Alcobaça, Batalha and other nearby towns, but tiptoed around Fatima like that wet spot on the floor. On that trip, I even chanced to see the Pope, or rather the Pope's right hand. It was May 12, 1991, and my future wife and I were visiting the Convent of the Geronimos on the outskirts of Lisbon when we were overtaken by the Papal cavalcade. We weren't aware that the Pope was in town, but there was no mistaking that white glove waving from the window of the limo.

Not being much up on Pope-lore at the time, neither of us knew that the visit was made to mark the tenth anniversary of the attempt on His Holiness's life, or that it was his second pilgrimage to Fatima. The first had come on May 13, 1982, one year after the assassination attempt. That time, he had placed the world under the protection of Mary. On this second occasion, he had come to thank her for "the unexpected changes" that had restored hope to peoples long oppressed and humiliated. The reference to the collapse of the Soviet Union could not have been clearer.

After the ceremony, the Pope placed the bullet that had nearly killed him in the crown of Our Lady of Fatima.

The cab swerves and skims over the gently rolling countryside. The last I heard, Portugal and Greece were running neck-and-neck in the European traffic fatality sweepstakes; my driver looks determined to put the home side ahead. My last time here I kept away from Fatima, mostly because it put me too much in mind of home. When I heard "Our Lady of Fatima," my thoughts reverted at once to the old Our Lady Affattama School at the corner of Victoria Park and St. Clair, where my friend Dougie Walker learned his catechism. The last thing I wanted to see in Europe was anywhere that made me think of the corner of Victoria Park and St. Clair. Fatima, besides, was too modern, and I assumed it would be inconveniently crowded with real, breathing, worshipping Catholics, an idea that held no great interest for me at the time. This time around, after my experiences in Lourdes, I'm ready to give Fatima the benefit of the doubt.

The cab pulls up at the door of a modern, six-storey hotel, in sight of the basilica at last. The driver carries my pack in to the reception and calls to the manager: "Fátima! Fátima! Do you have a room tonight for this young gentleman?"

November hangs over the edge of the semi-official May to October pilgrimage season and to judge by the wallful of keys, finding a room should pose no challenge. Nonetheless, Fátima peruses her selection carefully before settling on Room 407. It's a functional room with a hard bed and a Virgin on the wall. This is my fourth consecutive night in a hotel after a month of bunking down with pilgrims on the Camino. The first night in Finisterre, having my own room seemed an extravagance worthy of an Arabian prince. But the appeal has quickly worn off; the price one pays for privacy is loneliness.

So I take a quick shower and step out to hit the town, only Fatima doesn't offer much town to hit. Unlike Lourdes, with its charismatic old center, Fatima is a modern creation. There was no here here until the three little shepherds (and what is it with shepherds?) started having their encounters with the Virgin. So I console myself with the usual, satisfying Portuguese meal and a bottle of *vinho*. There is no one to approach in the restaurant except two American ladies, and they are deep in conversation, so I head out on my own for a late-night stroll around the sanctuary.

It's a drizzly night. Thirty or forty Ave Maria-singing pilgrims wind their candlelit way across the plaza, a camel train crossing the desert.

Their goal is the open pavilion of concrete, wood and glass that marks the site of the apparitions. A modest affair, it comprises only an altar and a few rows of benches. Inside there is a model of the first chapel that stood here and, in front of it, cased in glass, the statue of Our Lady of Fatima. She is the twin sister of the Pilgrim Madonna I met at the rue du Bac. Bizarre to think that this most simpering of Virgins should harbor an assassin's bullet in her crown.

The pilgrims reach the pavilion. Open to the night, it provides little shelter from the weather, but tonight's visitors, mostly Portuguese and Polish with a few Americans in the mix, don't seem to mind. They are warming themselves at the glowing coals of ritual. The basilica is open late for those who wish to worship in peace, so I leave them to their prayers and go exploring. The basilica is a high, pristine, empty place, too new to have accumulated much bric-a-brac. Up near the altar are the tombs of Lúcia's cousins and co-witnesses of the apparitions, Jacinta and Francisco. Dead these eighty years, they were recently declared "blessed"—the stage before sainthood. John Paul was here, on May 13 as usual, for the occasion.

Out front, five-storey-high posters of the holy children hang like ads for an art exhibition. Their stern, guarded faces overlook a Nuremburgian plaza that could serve as a runway in a pinch. A throne fit for a Pope sits on the landing in front of the basilica, the surrounding area walled in with clear—bulletproof?—plastic. From this vantage point, the outdoor pavilion that houses Our Lady is no more than a splash of light, a gazebo at the edge of the lawn. The rise and fall of pilgrim voices singing "Salve Regina" reaches me as from another time.

Other than that one point of warmth, there is something about this place that makes me uneasy. It's the sense that nothing is accidental here. That from the outset, the millions were foreseen and provisions made for them. It appears that the model of Lourdes was carefully studied and faithfully replicated in the building of the Sanctuary of Our Lady of Fatima, right down to the well miraculously discovered in the middle of the square that allows pilgrims to go home with a flask of Fatima water. But the architecture and layout of Fatima speak a language—perhaps the only language—that one doesn't hear much of in Lourdes: the language of power.

The service at the pavilion is over, but a handful of pilgrims stay on, heads bowed. Somehow, prayer is amplified in this space. You can feel it vibrating in the ceiling, bouncing off the plexiglas walls. A fat, elderly man stands at attention in front of Our Lady, now and then wiping his forehead with a handkerchief. Another kneels on the rain-soaked floor, resting tired arms on the low railing that surrounds the statue. The rapt silence of the worshippers fills this plain little box with an air of sanctity. But the sanctity feels more like something they brought with them than something they found here.

Lúcia of the Saints

Fatima is the name of the Prophet Muhammad's daughter, but Portugal's Fatima was a different lady altogether. It was in 1158, when the south of the country still lay in the hands of the Muslims, that a Christian raiding party, led by Gonçalo Herminques (dubbed *Comemoros*, the Moor-eater) attacked a party of picnicking Arab knights and damsels. After a brief encounter, the Arabs were captured and conveyed as hostages to the court of King Alfonso Henriques. When the King told the Moor-eater to name his reward, the gentle knight asked for the hand of Fatima, the most beautiful of the captives. The King agreed, on condition that the lady was willing, and that she would convert to Christianity. Fatima was and did; but she died soon after. The Moor-eater, heart-broken, retired to the monastery of Alcobaça, and the little country church among the pastures where Fatima was laid to rest took her name.

Here Lúcia dos Santos was born in 1907, the youngest of six children. A precocious girl, she made her First Communion at six, when the usual age was ten. During catechism, as she well remembers, "The priest would call me to his side, and when one or other of the children was unable to answer his questions, he told me to give the answer instead." Her mother was a sensible and serious woman, respected for her skills as a nurse, cook and seamstress: "Everybody knew that what she said was like Scripture and had to be obeyed." Her favorite reading was the lives of the saints, and the first thing she taught Lúcia was the Ave Maria.

Yet there was nothing dour about Lúcia's early years; on the contrary, her elder sisters and brother spoiled her with attention, dressing her up like a doll and teaching her to dance for the neverending round of rural saints' days, harvest festivals and weddings. Lúcia's earliest memories are of pastoral idyls: harvesting corn by moonlight, strewing flowers before the Baby Jesus in the Corpus Christi parade, chatting and singing with her sisters' paramours on Sunday afternoons beneath the fig trees.

All this we know from Lúcia's "memoirs," her many letters written over the years in answer to the prompting and prodding of sundry bishops. These chatty and mostly charming writings provide a vivid portrait of early twentieth-century peasant life. Only sixty miles separated Lúcia's world from Lisbon, but it might as well have been a hundred years. In the urbane capital, the Masonic republican government was busy confiscating church property and imprisoning clergy. Education had been secularized "to stem the spirit of hatred spread by religions." Priests were free to marry, but forbidden to wear their robes in the streets. Christmas had been redesignated "the Day of the Family." One government minister fatuously boasted that in two generations the Catholic Church in Portugal would be extinct.

To judge by Lúcia's memoirs, this tidal wave of change made few ripples on the shores of life in Fatima. Even so, the outside world was impinging on the countryside in another way: Portugal had become embroiled in the First World War. One of Lúcia's cousins was missing in action and it was feared that her brother would soon be called up. She recalls how, "Grown-ups would try to frighten children by saying: 'Here comes a German to kill you.'"

Then, in the period preceding the apparitions, Lúcia's childhood paradise was shaken by a series of misfortunes, misfortunes that recall those of Bernadette. Her father drank and gambled himself into debt, losing a portion of the family property. Her mother became too sick to work. Two of her elder sisters married and the others were sent out as servants to support the family. Lúcia keenly recalls the misery of this time:

"When we gathered around the table at nighttime, waiting for my father to come in to supper, my mother would look at her daughters' empty places and exclaim with profound sadness: 'My God, where has all the joy of our home gone?' Then, resting her head on a little table beside her, she would burst into bitter tears."

Lúcia's escape from these domestic tragedies was in the pastures. From the age of eight, she took over the family's flock. With her younger cousins, Francisco and Jacinta, she spent her days climbing rocks and calling out names to hear the echoes from the hills ("The name that echoed back most clearly was Maria"), singing popular songs and hymns, dancing to the music played by shepherds in neighboring fields, walking in the midst of the flocks "like Jesus in a holy picture." By virtue of her age and dominating character, Lúcia was the natural leader of this little band, as she would continue to be through the events that followed.

The story of Fatima opens with a sort of prelude that takes place in the year before the apparitions of the Virgin. It is an episode that suggests how the war had made the children aware that they belonged to an entity greater than their immediate community, an entity known as Portugal.

One day, as Lúcia, Francisco and Jacinta played in the hills, they saw a strange cloud in the shape of a young man. It was not the first time that Lúcia had seen such a cloud, but what followed was without precedent. Before the children's eyes, the cloud turned into a boy of fourteen or fifteen, "whiter than snow, transparent as crystal when the sun shines through it, and of great beauty."

The young man said: "Be not afraid. I am the Angel of Peace. Pray with me." When they had done so, he vanished. Lúcia swore the other children to secrecy.

A few months later, as the children were taking their siesta in the shade, the angel appeared again. This time, he spoke with urgency:

"What are you doing?" he asked. "Pray! Pray always! Offer prayers and sacrifices constantly to the Lord."

"How are we to make sacrifices?" asked Lúcia.

"Make of everything you can a sacrifice, and offer it to God as an act of reparation for the sins by which he is offended. In this way, you will draw down peace upon your country. I am its Guardian Angel, the Angel of Portugal. Above all, accept and bear with submission the suffering that the Lord will send you."

"It was from then that we began," remembers Lúcia, "to offer to the Lord all that mortified us."

The Virgin first appeared to the children after mass on the thirteenth of May, 1917. On this day, the three had led their flocks to a family pasture known as Cova da Iria. They had just eaten lunch when they saw something that resembled a flash of lightning. As they ran for cover, a second flash came. Suddenly they could see, standing in a tree before them, a woman "who shone brighter than the sun."

"Have no fear. I don't wish to harm you," the woman said.

"Where are you from?" Lúcia asked boldly.

"I am from heaven."

"And what do you want from me?"

"I want you to come here for six months on the thirteenth day of each month at this time. Later, I will tell you who I am and what I wish. . . .

It was Lourdes all over again, save that Lúcia suffered from none of Bernadette's reticence. Her next question to her divine interlocutor was, "Will I go to heaven?"

"Yes, you will," replied the woman.

"And Jacinta?" Lúcia continued.

"Her, too."

"And Francisco?"

"Francisco as well. But he will have to pray many rosaries."

Then Lúcia remembered two local girls who had died recently.

"Is Maria das Neves in heaven?"

"Yes, she is," answered the woman.

"And Amelia?"

"Amelia will be in purgatory till the end of the world."

The woman then asked the children if they were prepared to bear the sufferings that would be sent them by God. When they had pronounced their willingness, she opened her hands, after the familiar manner of the Virgin of the Miraculous Medallion, and released a stream of light that penetrated the children's hearts.

"Pray the rosary every day to obtain peace on earth and the end of war," were the woman's final words. Then she vanished into the eastern sky, leaving jet trails of light behind her.

It all sounds like so much make-believe, the fantasies of a girl brought up on tales of Bernadette. But whatever Lúcia's visions were, they were not a device to attract attention: after the apparition of the Virgin, as after the vision of the Angel of Portugal, she swore her cousins to secrecy. Had Jacinta been able to resist telling her parents, the celebrated secrets of Fatima might have remained secrets forever. But Jacinta could not resist, and Lúcia was singled out at once as the instigator and severely chastised by her mother, who hoped that the whole affair would end right there.

It did not. A month later, on the morning of June 13, a handful of farmers, some of whom had come from as far as ten miles away, were waiting at Lúcia's door to accompany her to Cova da Iria. The second apparition followed the pattern of the first—the lightning, the woman in the tree, the injunction to pray the rosary every day—except that this time, an audience was on hand. Once again, it was Lúcia who did all the talking: Jacinta, according to Lúcia's account, was too timid to address the woman, while Francisco, though he could see her, could not hear her voice.

By July, the third month, the ball was rolling. Three thousand onlookers and a police squadron converged on the Cova da Iria, and though none of them knew it at the time (or for many years afterwards, until Lúcia had received clearance from the Virgin to reveal what she had been shown) it was on this day that the portentous "secrets of Fatima" were imparted. Little did the crowd suspect, as they observed Lúcia and her cousins kneeling in prayer before the Virgin's tree, that the children were gazing into the abyss:

> "Our Lady showed us a great sea of fire which seemed to be under the earth," recalls Lúcia. "Plunged in this fire were demons and souls in human form, like transparent burning embers, now raised into the air by the flames that issued from within themselves, now falling back on every side like sparks in a huge fire amid shrieks and groans of pain and despair, which horrified us and made us tremble with fear."

The vision lasted but an instant. Then, her voice tinged with sadness, Our Lady informed the children that they had seen hell, "where the souls of poor sinners go." She told them it was God's hope that sinners would save themselves by turning to her, but if they continued to offend the Lord, a new war would come, even worse than the present one. If things reached that pass, only one hope for peace would remain: the Pope must conse-crate Russia to Mary's Holy Heart. Without this act, Russia would continue to spread errors throughout the world, causing wars and perse-cutions of the Church. The good would be martyred and the Holy Father would suffer. This was what the Virgin of Fatima foretold. Or this, at least, was what Lúcia remembered so many years later, when the bishops finally coaxed her into committing her memories to paper.

And one more thing was foretold. If the sinners did not repent; if the war-to-come were not averted; if the Pope did not consecrate Russia to Mary, then something truly terrible would follow. Something that, in 1982, is known only to Lúcia and the Pope: "the third secret of Fatima."

IF MARY HAS SAVED JOHN Paul's life, it can only be to this end: that he consecrate Russia to her Immaculate Heart, as the Virgin of Fatima had stipulated.

John Paul is not the first Pope to agonize over the business of Russia. Pius XII, known as "the Pope of Fatima," had attempted to perform an act of consecration during the Second World War. Lifelong diplomat that he was, however, he had not mentioned Russia by name, instead consecrating *the whole world* to Mary's care in the hope that she would take the hint. Clearly she hadn't, for Russia continued in its old ways, sowing errors and persecuting the Church.

John XXIII, in turn, had declined to dedicate the Second Vatican Council to Mary (and by extension the consecration of Russia) despite the urgings of Pope John Paul's mentor, the Polish Cardinal Wyszynski. Good Pope John, and Paul VI after him, still clung to the fond hope that the Soviets could be brought around through diplomacy. But in 1982, with the world teetering on the brink of catastrophe, it is clear that diplomacy hasn't worked. Some even blame the present state of events on the failure of the pontiffs to follow the Virgin's instructions and take a stand against Russia. John Paul is about to redress this failing, inspired by an unlikely source: his would-be assassin.

The man who shot the Pope, Mehmet Ali Agca, has a history of right-wing terrorist activity. Indeed, he had been serving a prison sentence in Turkey for the assassination of a socialist newspaper editor before he escaped and made his way to Saint Peter's Square. It hardly seems likely that someone with his dossier would be working on behalf of communist interests, but from the moment of Agca's arrest, his story has kept shifting. First, he claims to be in the pay of the PLO; then, he is acting alone; the next day, he announces he is Jesus Christ. Finally, he produces from his hat the "Bulgarian connection," an intricate conspiracy with tendrils reaching back to the KGB.

The claim strikes a chord in the Vatican. First, because the Pope and his nearest advisors, the presiding "Polish connection," are by nature suspicious of the Russians. It is no stretch for them to conceive of the KGB eliminating the Pope for political reasons. Second, because Agca's story makes sense on the apocalyptic level. The Russian Communists are playing their usual role as the instruments of Satan, spreading atheism and discord just as the Virgin of Fatima foretold.

Seen from this viewpoint, everything snaps into focus. Political affairs and prophecy are two horses galloping in tandem towards disaster with the world in tow. But there is still hope, for in Pope John Paul the forces of good have a champion uniquely qualified to stop those horses in their tracks. As a Slav, he can penetrate the Iron Curtain, fighting evil on the political front. As a devoted servant of Mary, he can wage war on the eternal plane as well. John Paul's chosen motto is *Totus tuus sum, Maria*: "I am all yours, Mary." He literally wears his love of the Virgin on his sleeve: the letter "M" for Mary is embroidered on all his robes. He has been the first Pope to visit Lourdes and a score of other Marian pilgrimage sites. As a young man, he consecrated his life to the Lady of Czestochowa, the famous dark Virgin of Poland. It is only fitting, then, that the ultimate act of submission to the Virgin, the consecration of Russia, should fall to him.

In June of 1981, less than a month after the attack, John Paul follows the example of Pius XII in consecrating the world to Mary. It is a gesture he will repeat in 1982, on his pilgrimage to Fatima. Still, these are only trial runs. He has not yet made reference to Russia.

The Dancing Sun

On the morning of August 13, 1917, the mayor of Vila Noa de Ourem, the capital of the region, appeared at the door of Lúcia's home in his carriage to offer the children a ride to the site of the apparitions. Instead, he drove them to his home, where he detained them till the next day, hoping they would admit to lying about the apparitions. When the children stuck to their story, he tossed them in the town lock-up and informed them that a pot of boiling oil was waiting for them if they didn't recant. This was a miscalculation on the mayor's part, as nothing was more likely to fortify the children's faith than the prospect of martyrdom. They set about praying for the conversion of the other prisoners and in the end there was nothing to do but pack them all home.

The public, having been deprived of their August apparition, turned out in force for September's. A flood of souls estimated at twenty to thirty thousand engulfed the young seers. Lúcia remembers:

"The streets were full of people who wanted to see us and speak to us. They went on their knees in front of us, begging us to deliver their prayers to Our Lady. Others, who couldn't get close enough, called out from the distance, 'For the love of God, ask the Virgin to cure our son, who is lame.' Another: 'Cure my son who is blind.' Another: 'Cure my son who is deaf.' 'Bring back my husband, my son, from the war.' 'Convert a sinner for me,' 'Give me health.' All the miseries of the human condition were there, and people cried out even from the treetops and the walls, where they had climbed to watch us pass. Saying 'Yes' to some, offering a hand to others to raise them from the dust, we continued forward, thanks to a few gentlemen who opened a way for us through the crowd."

In the face of so much human suffering, the Virgin showed great equanimity. She requested that everyone continue to pray their rosary for the end of the war and commended Lúcia and her cousins for the sacrifices they had made. When Lúcia asked her if she would cure the many sick who had come to pray to her, she made no promises: "Some I will cure; others, no." Then, before she vanished into the east, this: "In October, I will perform a miracle so that all may believe."

Lúcia's mother never accepted the authenticity of the apparitions. For her, Lúcia was simply a fibber, a stubborn girl who had trapped herself and her family in a web of lies. When Lúcia wrote later of the sacrifices she made at this time, her family's indulgence was foremost among them. Now, on the eve of October 13, Senhora dos Santos invited her daughter to mass with the words, "If the Virgin doesn't perform a miracle tomorrow, the crowd will kill us. We'd better confess ourselves and get ready to die."

Thirty thousand camped out that night at Cova da Iria, under the open sky. They were joined in the morning by as many more. Around eleven o'clock torrential rains set in, so that this time the faithful who knelt before the visionaries knelt in mud. Lúcia and the other children were escorted through the crowd to their accustomed places. Then Lúcia asked them all to close their umbrellas and recite the rosary. Immediately, she saw the Virgin in the tree.

"What do you want of me?" she asked.

"That you should build a chapel for me here. I am the Virgin of the Rosary and you should continue to pray the rosary every day. The war will end soon and the soldiers will come home."

"I have many things to ask of you. Cures, conversions ..."

"Some, yes; others, no. All must ask pardon for their sins. They must cease to offend the Lord. He is already so deeply offended."

As Lúcia's colloquy with the Virgin pursued its familiar course, some in the crowd noticed a white mist forming above the tree. Then, abruptly, the rain ceased and the clouds parted to reveal a silvery, pallid sun. It seemed at first to be turning swiftly, sending rays of light in all directions. Then, it was seen to zigzag across the sky and plunge towards the earth, releasing a burst of heat as it fell. According to some, the prodigy of the spinning sun continued for as long as ten minutes. And where the crowd saw only a light display, Lúcia could see the Virgin with Joseph and the Christ child, tracing the sign of the Cross with their hands.

Photographs taken at the scene failed to capture the miracle, but they do show the crowd, kneeling in their 1917 Sunday best, their faces turned to heaven, hats held over their hearts. When it was all over, everyone found their sodden clothes suddenly quite dry.

The Virgin of the Rosary

"The Virgin of the Rosary" is how Mary identified herself in the final apparition. What does this signify?

The title seems harmless, quaint. What pursuit could be more peaceful than the fingering of prayer beads? Ten Hail Marys to each one, while contemplating a Mystery of the life of Jesus and Mary. Yet the rosary has a martial aspect as well. Tradition credits the rosary with the triumph of orthodoxy over the Albigensian heresy in the thirteenth century and with the great victory of the Christian naval forces over the Turks at the battle of Lepanto in 1571. More recently, Austria's release from Soviet domination after the Second World War and the failure of Brazil's Marxist uprising of 1964 have been attributed to popular devotion to the rosary.

In the words of Pope Leo XIII: "The rosary has been established mainly to implore the Mother of God for help against the enemies of the

Christian name." It is, in other words, a weapon in the holy war of the faith against the forces of evil, whatever form they take, whatever name they go under.

DECEMBER 27, 1983
Rebibbia Prison, Rome. Pope John Paul II enters maximum security cell T4. He has come to meet the man who tried to kill him. Outside the cell stand three cameramen, waiting to record the interview. Agca rises as the Pope enters, then bends to kiss his ring. He brings Wojtyla's hand briefly to his forehead in a gesture of respect. Then the Pope and the assassin sit facing one another. The Pope begins to converse in Italian.

"So you are Mehmet Ali Agca?"

"Yes."

"Ah. And you live here?"

"Yes."

"How do you feel?"

"I'm well, well." Agca has been waiting a long time for this moment and he cannot bear any more pleasantries. "I wanted to ask your forgiveness ..."

At once, the Pope draws his chair towards Agca's. He begins to speak quickly in a voice that is too low for the microphones to pick up. Agca listens intently. When he replies, he is almost whispering into the pontiff's ear. Wojtyla closes his eyes and rests an elbow on the prisoner's knee as he hears him out. Agca laughs. The Pope grasps his upper arm and squeezes it. Their conversation continues for some twenty minutes, below mike level.

Then the two rise together. Wojtyla takes Agca's hand. In it, he places a small, white box. At last, his voice can be heard.

"A little gift ..." he says.

Agca opens the box. Inside is a rosary of silver and mother-of-pearl.

The Cult of Fatima

The miracle of the dancing sun made national headlines, bringing Fatima to the attention of all Portugal. Witnesses claimed to have seen it from as far as ten miles away, though whether this makes a better argument for its being a miracle or simply a freak of nature is not clear. If it *was* no more than a natural phenomenon blown out of proportion by the emotions of the moment, then it ranks among the best-timed wonders of history, up there with those timely eclipses of the sun that have made the reputations of so many prophets, conquerors and mountebanks.

The miracle vindicated the seers of Fatima, but it brought little joy to their families. The dos Santos family had to sell off their sheep, since the pasture at Cova da Iria had been stomped bare by the crowds. An endless stream of importunate visitors flowed in to see, interview, touch the children. Then, Lúcia's father abruptly died of pneumonia. When her mother again fell deathly ill, Lúcia's sisters yanked the girl away from the sickbed and told her that if it was really the Virgin she had seen at Cova da Iria, she'd better get down there and start praying. Lúcia did as instructed, and her mother recovered, but remained unconvinced: "Strange," she said. "Our Lady cured me, and somehow I still don't believe it."

In 1918, Francisco and Jacinta contracted the "Spanish flu" that was sweeping the world. Though both survived the initial assault, their weakened constitutions succumbed to pneumonia and both died after agonizing illnesses. Lúcia lived on as the sole repository of the Virgin's messages. In 1921, the Bishop of Leiria arranged a place for the fourteen-year-old girl at a convent school in Oporto. She went off to the home of her Mother in heaven, leaving her earthly mother weeping on the platform of Leiria station. From Oporto, she was moved to Tuy, then to Coimbra. The arduous process of extracting information from Sister Lúcia was underway. Upon each fresh request, she needed to go first to the Virgin or to Jesus for permission to divulge what had been vested in her. Sometimes, permission was granted; others, not. Into the 1940s, bishops were still squeezing Sister Lúcia like a lemon for her secrets, gathering them a squirt at a time. And as the years passed, what Sister Lúcia had to impart grew ever more somber and over-arching. The Virgin of Fatima, who on October 17, 1917, had asked for no more than a simple chapel on the site where she had appeared, was gradually revealed to be pregnant with dire warnings for all mankind.

As for the cult of Fatima, it grew fitfully during the early years; this despite the military coup of 1917 that installed a regime less hostile to Catholicism. There were still powerful anti-clerical forces at large, who threatened pilgrims and blew up the first chapel on the site. More critically, the Church itself was reluctant to lend support. Many in the ecclesiastical hierarchy were dubious about the visions. Many more were scared of them. Fatima represented a spontaneous eruption of popular faith of a sort not readily controlled or channeled, an outbreak of *communitas* that could easily turn against the Church. The parish priest of Fatima, recognizing the bifurcation of popular and institutional worship, asked Lúcia in anger: "Why are all these people going to prostrate themselves in prayer in the middle of the fields, while here the living God of our altars, in the Blessed Sacrament, is left all alone, abandoned? What good is all this money left under a tree, when the church repairs can't be finished for lack of funds?"

It was only following a new military coup in 1926 that government and church joined hands to marshal the forces unleashed in Fatima. (Indeed, it was not till 1930 that the Portuguese Church declared the apparitions authentic.) In 1928, as the basilica rose from the leveled landscape of the Cova da Iria, Portugal officially dedicated itself to the Sacred Heart of Mary. Our Lady now had a political function: to preserve the nation from atheism and communism, while blessing Portuguese-style colonialism and fascism. From 1932 to 1968, this unholy union of Virgin and State was presided over by the monkish technocrat, Antonio Salazar. Salazar, like Pope John Paul, credited Mary with saving him from an assassination attempt. Impressed by the Virgin's complaisance, he sought out other ways for her to serve him. The cult of Fatima proved a handy political tool, permitting the failings of the government to be blamed on an insufficiency of rosaries prayed. And when things went poorly in the colonial wars—as they generally did—the people could be called upon to refill the coffers of the national shrine.

Francisco Franco took lessons from Portugal, dragooning the sad-eyed Lady of Fatima into service in Spain. Nor was Our Lady's political activism confined to Iberia, not after 1948, when the Bishop of Leiria posed for *Life* magazine with the envelope containing Lúcia's handwritten "secrets" on the table before him. The Army of Mary, a right-leaning international organization "dedicated to the war against atheism, the greatest heresy of all time," chose Fatima as their seat, and Our Lady of Fatima won a name as the most inveterate of cold warriors.

The stridently political tone of Fatima inspired dismay among many Catholics. Pope Paul's visit to the shrine in 1967 was viewed as both a setback to the ecumenical movement set rolling by Vatican Two and an unfortunate endorsement of a totalitarian regime. Evidence that Rome itself had gone into damage control over the visit can be heard in Vatican Radio's commentary: "Pope Paul purified devotion to Our Lady in Fatima. He swept away the atmosphere of secrecy, of political and social exploitation, of false mystery, of whisperings and gossip. In his discourses the Pope made no mention of the mysterious Fatima that intellectuals have used to put forward their own ideas under the cover of Our Lady."

Fifteen years later, with Portuguese totalitarianism a closed chapter, Pope John Paul II feels no need to apologize for his devotion to Our Lady of Fatima.

MARCH 25, 1984

Saint Peter's Square. It has been said that this is the darkest moment of the Pope's journey. The prospect of all-out war between the superpowers, leading perhaps to nuclear annihilation, weighs heavily on his soul. Only one solution seems to offer itself.

He has requested the cooperation of all the bishops of the world to pray in unison for the conversion of Russia. At this moment, it is said, there is even a bishop *in* Russia—not by chance—to ensure the efficacy of the prayer. The statue of Our Lady has been airlifted in from Fatima. The Pope has spent the night in prayer before it, and now he follows it in procession through the square. Kneeling humbly at the feet of the Virgin, he addresses to her words that are, by Vatican standards, singularly clear: "Especially, we entrust and consecrate to you, Mary, those peoples and nations *that have particular need* of this consecration." The die is cast.

Is John Paul's statement direct enough to satisfy the Holy Mother? Will she hear, this time, humanity's cry *de profundis*? Consulted later, Sister Lúcia says yes. This act of consecration is just what Our Lady had in mind. It is an extreme act the Pope has taken. Some bishops have been openly lukewarm towards a gesture that smacks, it is hinted, of mumbo jumbo. There is nothing to do now but watch and hope.

Lúcia's Memoirs

As drizzle turns to rain in Fatima, I equip myself with an umbrella and set out to see what pilgrims see here: the hills where the Angel of

Portugal appeared to the children and the tiny, well-kept houses of the seers, out in what is still the countryside. They are charming, evocative, and quite deserted. This is the time of year when Fatima withdraws into its shell. There is no pageant, no bustle. I slog back to town, find a shop with a good stock of Portuguese pastries to tide me through the afternoon, and settle down with Lúcia's memoirs.

They make a good read. Lúcia has an enthusiasm and attention to detail that bring the old country customs, the songs and the festivals to life. She also knows how to conjure the heightened reality of the world of childhood. Or is it that she has never left that world? Perhaps she stopped growing at the age of fourteen, when she entered the convent, for often she seems to be writing not so much of herself at ten, as in her own ten-year-old voice. Of course, childishness is not necessarily a bad thing in a visionary; it may allow her to see right through walls the adult world has built. Lúcia's childishness, however, seldom shows that sort of penetration. More often, it is a precocious sort of childishness that sounds all-too-eager to graduate to adulthood.

Lúcia loves to cast her actions and those of her cousins in an exalted light. She cannot resist the pose of a martyr, as when she reacts to her mother's accusation that the apparitions were fabricated: "My sisters sided with my mother, and all around me the atmosphere was one of utter scorn and contempt. Then I would remember the old days, and ask myself: 'Where is all that affection now that my family had for me just a short while ago?' My one relief was to weep before the Lord, as I offered Him my sacrifice." Writing twenty years after the fact, Lúcia is still nursing her wounded *amour-propre*; she has not learned to empathize with her mother's ordeal. Of course, no one is perfect. Lúcia's flaws can be endearing, if sometimes in an irksome way. She reminds me of my housewife friend Consuela, from the Camino; a warm, talkative soul, bubbling over with memories and stories. What a burden it must have been for Lúcia, keeping all those secrets for so many years.

The problem is that the world does not regard Lúcia as a memoirist, but as a lightning rod for the divine. And the divine messages she transmits are no harmless behests (stamp a medal, build me a chapel, drink this water), but politically loaded prophecies of doom. By granting credence and recognition to these visions, the Church has sent the world into a tizzy. Reading them over, I can only question the wisdom and discretion of the body that let matters get to this point.

The theology of the visions alone ought to make them suspect in the eyes of the Church, for they reduce the Christian faith to a forced diet of prayer and sacrifices, proffered in the faint hope of appeasing a wrathful God. Our Lady of Fatima is the picture of helpless resignation, like the wife of a violent drunk, who warns her children not to make their father angry because there's precious little she can do to protect them. Not since the Middle Ages has Mary stood so nakedly as the shield not against the hardships of the world or the wiles of Satan, but against the heavy hand of God the Father himself. Jesus, mercy and love-thy-neighbor all go missing in action in the spiritual wars of Fatima.

And though, as I read Lúcia's memoirs, I try to give her the benefit of the doubt, to enter into her mental world, I find she tests the limits of credulity. With Bernadette and Cathérine Labouré, it is easy to believe that they related only what they *saw*, whether one believes that their visions were "real" or not. But Lúcia's descriptions of the appearance and the sayings of the Virgin seem so hackneyed, such a farrago of Lourdes and Sunday school, that I'm ready to side with her mother in thinking that the whole business was make-believe.

Or at least until I come across this passage, a marginal correction Lúcia has written for a book on Fatima: "Chapter Seven, page 64, says, 'small earrings.' I didn't see any earrings. I remember a golden cord which, like a brilliant sunbeam, seemed to border her mantle. It was reflected in the space left by the mantle as it fell from the head to the shoulders, shimmering in the light which enveloped Our Lady's whole person in undulating variations, which momentarily gave the impression of small earrings. I must have been referring to this when I gave that reply." The hyper-reality of this description calls to mind the acuity of that other unlikely visionary, Cathérine Labouré, and just about persuades me that Lúcia, like her spiritual sisters, did see *something*.

Even so, my willing suspension of disbelief has been lifted, and without it, I suddenly feel as if I am looking at that Rorschach silhouette that is either a goblet or two faces kissing. I find myself reading an entirely different story of Fatima, more *Turn of the Screw* than *Song of Bernadette*: a dark little parable of three children grappling with the nightmares of the adult world.

This story begins in the moment when the Angel of Portugal tells the children to "offer prayers and sacrifices constantly to the Lord" in order to bring an end to the war. The children's response to the command is "to offer to the Lord all that mortified us." This idea, that by taking suffering on oneself, the suffering of others can be alleviated, is basic to Christianity. But in the minds of the children it assumes a stark and absolute grandeur. From this moment, the fate of Portugal rests on their young shoulders. Their smallest action, their every choice must be seen in the light of a sacrifice and act of reparation "for the sinners." They have adopted the logic of the flagellant.

This is particularly true of Jacinta. She eats the bitter chestnuts rather than the ripe ones. She abstains from water on a hot day or drinks from a dirty pool. She turns down fresh figs and bunches of grapes that are offered her. She grips nettles in her hand, or strikes her legs with them. At every crossroads, she chooses the way of self-denial and pain in the hope that her small self-sacrifice will satisfy the choleric Father in heaven.

One mortification that all three children share is "the rope." This is a rope that Lúcia finds one day and ties to her arm. When it starts to hurt, she suggests to the others that they fasten bits of it around their waists as a sacrifice to God. They divvy it up among themselves and get into the custom of wearing it always, though it causes them such "terrible suffering" that the Virgin instructs them in her September apparition to take it off at night. Francisco is on his deathbed before he finally removes his, fearing that his mother will find it and be angry. Jacinta, likewise, only surrenders her rope to Lúcia when she falls ill. According to Lúcia: "Her cord had three knots, and was somewhat stained with blood."

As Jacinta descends into this nightmare, her character is transformed. The child whom Lúcia had once characterized as happy and capricious gradually becomes gloomy and judgmental. Lúcia says:

"When I saw her deep in thought, and asked her, 'Jacinta, what are you thinking about?' she frequently replied: 'About the war which is coming, and all the people who are going to die and go to hell! How dreadful! If they would only stop offending God, then there wouldn't be any war and they wouldn't go to hell!'"

Later, when Jacinta falls sick, visitors come to her bedside. Lúcia reports:

> "When people asked her questions, she answered in a friendly manner, but briefly. If they said anything that she thought improper, she promptly replied:
> "'Don't say that; it offends the Lord our God.'
> "If they related something unbecoming about their families, she answered:
> "'Don't let your children commit sin, or they could go to hell.'
> "If there were grown-ups involved, she said:
> "'Tell them not to do that, for it is a sin. They offend the Lord our God, and later they could be damned.'"

Looking back, Lúcia describes Jacinta as "a holy person who seemed to be in continual communication with God. All her actions seemed to reflect the presence of God in the way proper to people of mature age and great virtue. I never noticed in her that excessive frivolity or childish enthusiasm for games and pretty things, so typical of small children." Lúcia is speaking here in her voice of a precocious ten-year-old; but this only means that she is echoing the voices she has heard in the adult world around her, voices that speak of Jacinta not as a child mired in life-denying depression or traumatized by visions of war, but as a model of holiness. They are the same voices that are heard today advancing Jacinta's candidacy for sainthood.

What instructive saints these children will make. One day, Jacinta asks Lúcia, "What are the sins people commit for which they go to hell?"

Lúcia, for once, is at a loss. "I don't know! Perhaps the sin of not going to mass on Sunday, of stealing, of saying ugly words, of cursing and of swearing."

"So for just one word, then, people can go to hell?"

"Well, it's a sin!"

Later in Lisbon, where Jacinta was taken for a last-hope operation (two of her ribs were removed using only local anaesthetic), she was asked if, in any of the apparitions, Our Lady had mentioned what sort of sins offended God most. "Sins of the flesh," responded the nine-year-old. Her reply was duly noted by the adults around her.

But what could this phrase mean to Jacinta? "Sins of the flesh" were only another of those phantoms of the adult world, like the alcoholism of Lúcia's father, or the war that had taken Jacinta's older brother, or the painful, wasting disease that was about to claim her own life. Only one thing could have been clear to her: that there were dark forces abroad in the world. Forces dimly understood, yet capable of destroying families and striking down children. How could one account for such terrors? It must be that God was angry. The only hope, then, was to seek the protection of the Holy Mother and try to make amends to the Father, lest in His wrath He sweep all of wounded, sinning humanity into the abyss.

IN THE YEAR AFTER John Paul's "voodoo" ceremony in Saint Peter's Square, Mikhail Gorbachev becomes head of the Soviet Union. Soon the Soviet forces are withdrawing from Afghanistan, as Solidarity stages strikes throughout Poland. In 1989, the USSR holds its first multiparty elections; Solidarity is victorious; the communist governments of Czechoslovakia, East Germany and Romania collapse; the Berlin Wall comes down (there is a chunk of it near the basilica in Fatima, erected in 1994 as a thank-you to Our Lady). A scant seven years after Pope John Paul consecrated to Mary "those peoples and nations that have particular need of it," the Communist party of Russia is dissolved.

All of which makes an extremely powerful argument—either that the prophecies of Fatima are true or that prophecies, given sufficient credence, can be self-fulfilling. Could Pope John Paul's mere faith in the prophecies have changed, or accelerated, the course of history?

After the assassination attempt and the revelations that proceeded from it (including, it is said, a personal vision of "the dancing sun" experienced during his convalescence), Karol Wojtyla altered the Vatican's Soviet strategy from one of conciliation and detente to one of hard-nosed opposition. Unlike Pius XII, whose resistance to the Nazis reportedly took the form of exorcising Adolf Hitler's photograph, John Paul leaped into the fray of history. He identified himself fearlessly with political and trade union movements that would have been anathema to previous Popes, while promoting an ethic of non-violent resistance. It may be that his actions were sufficient in themselves to make his prayers come true. Yet without his prayers, could he ever have acted with such bravery, such decision?

MAY 13, 2000

John Paul makes his third pilgrimage to Fatima. The occasion is the beatification of the *pastorinhos*, Francisco and Jacinta. This is their first step on the road to sainthood. Sister Lúcia is among the 600,000 in the audience.

One of Lúcia's fondest memories is of her First Communion. Her sisters staying up all night to make her a white dress and a wreath of flowers. Going into the kitchen of the house to bow to her parents and ask their blessing. Her brother carrying her to church so that her dress will be spotless. Then running to kneel before the altar of Our Lady of the Rosary. But most of all she remembers her mother's words: "Ask the Lord to make you a saint." Eighty-eight years later, Lúcia is almost there.

Later that day the Vatican puts an end to six decades of speculation, as it releases without fanfare the "third secret" of Fatima. The great revelation is not a schedule for Armageddon after all. It reveals no dates, no names, no Savior, no Antichrist. Only the vision of a Pope being murdered.

Lúcia tells of "a bishop robed in white, whom we understood to be the Holy Father." He traverses a great city, half in ruins, praying for the souls of the corpses he passes on the way. Then, in the company of other bishops, priests, monks and nuns, he scales a steep mountain towards a great cross. He falls to his knees at the foot of the cross, and is set upon by a group of soldiers armed with guns and arrows. The soldiers kill the Pope, then turn their weapons on the rest of the crowd. Angels collect the blood of the martyrs.

And that is all.

The sense of anticlimax is palpable. Is *this* the earth-shattering "third secret of Fatima"? This crude sketch, painted from a child's palette, of armed men cutting down clergy and civilians, as if the twentieth century hadn't already seen enough of that? The Church has anticipated the world's disappointment. The "secret," it explains, is to be read symbolically, as a vision of "the struggle of the atheist systems against the Church and Christians."

But the real secret of Fatima that is unlocked this day is another. It is the secret of why Pope John Paul made of himself a chisel to break the stones of the Berlin Wall: he recognized in Lúcia's sacrificed pontiff an image of himself. The similarity between the Pope shot in Saint Peter's Square and this one, murdered on a mountain, may not seem so obvious to every eye. But for John Paul, the likeness was striking enough to make him change the course of history.

Fátima Nunca Mais?

Before I came to Fatima, I spent a few hours playing snakes and ladders in the vertiginous streets of Oporto. I made a purchase in Livraria Lello, a sumptuous *fin-de-siècle* bookstore, and found myself a restaurant with a view of the river Douro. Some students snatched up the table beside me. It was nice to see that they made their statements not with designer-label jeans or sunglasses but with books. One brandished the latest by Jose Saramago, the author who recently brought this bibliophile nation its first Nobel Prize for Literature; a girl sported the Portuguese edition of Salman Rushdie's *The Ground Beneath Her Feet*; one fellow, evidently a retro type, had his Nietzsche under his arm. I decided to leave my book about Fatima in its bag.

But now I'm ready to look it over. *Fátima Nunca Mais*, Fatima, Never Again, is the work of the controversial Padre Mário de Oliveira. Expelled from the military chaplaincy in the 1960s after praying for the right to autonomy of Portugal's African colonies, imprisoned by Salazar in the 1970s, de Oliveira is today a media personality and the author of a score of books. The occasion for *Fátima Nunca Mais* was a televised debate on the question, "Do you believe in the apparitions of Fatima?" De Oliveira's frank "No" provoked what he describes as "an (almost) national scandal. Never had such a thing been heard on television, much less from the mouth of a Catholic priest." By the summer of 2000, the book had gone into its tenth printing.

A sample of chapter titles indicates the tone of the whole: "Fatima: an Inferno of bad taste"; "From the God of Fatima, deliver us, O Lord!"; "There is no secret of Fatima"; "Fatima: the glory of our nation, or its shame?" In the chapter "I, Mary, mother of Jesus, have nothing to do with Our Lady of Fatima," de Oliveira attacks the imperialist bias of the cult:

> "And what was the role of Fatima, and of Our Lady of Fatima during the sad and bitter years of the dictatorship in Portugal, and, above all, during the terrible years of the Colonial War in Africa? Could we have maintained, during so many years, without a popular revolt, three fronts in this war without Our Lady of Fatima, without the pilgrimages to Fatima, without the vows to Our Lady? How many gold necklaces, how many rings and

watches, how many candles bought and stupidly burnt, how many millions and millions of offerings for prayers, religiously paid for by soldiers and their families, poured, during these tragic years, into the coffers of the Sanctuary of Fatima?

"Meanwhile, neither Our Lady of Fatima, nor her still-living seer had a single word to say against the real genocide that was the Colonial War; not a word of solidarity and sympathy for the poor Africans who were fighting for their more-than-legitimate right to autonomy and independence."

De Oliveira's vigorous rhetoric goes down well with a pitcher of young Portuguese wine and a port-drowned flan. Nothing like good, old-fashioned religious polemic. But even as I read, a voice in the back of mind keeps asking, "Why are you enjoying this so much?" And I have to admit that it is because Padre de Oliveira is saying what I want to hear. His is a strong, Catholic voice supplying me with pretexts—sound, well-reasoned, historically grounded pretexts, but pretexts nonetheless—for not liking Fatima. But could it be that the real causes of my dislike are more subjective? The bland, modern surroundings; the over-calculated Sanctuary; the terrible weather; Lúcia's being too obstreperous for my taste; the Virgin's cloying smile. Perhaps it all boils down to the fact that Fatima is not Lourdes.

In that case, I must ask how Lourdes would have struck me if I had first arrived there on a dank November day when the pilgrims were few and far between.

The fact is that I liked Lourdes because my heart went out to the pilgrims and because I felt what it was to be a part of what went on there. Could it be that if there were pilgrims in Fatima now, I might manage to overlook all that I find depressing and eerie and false about this place? Would the tide of their simple, human priorities—ailments, doubts, longings—wash over, if not wash away, the evils of the past? Pilgrims do have that gift of turning a place from what it is into what they want it to be. It isn't fair to pass judgment on Fatima without this crucial evidence. For now, however, there is no work for me to join here, no pilgrims to fraternize with, nothing to be gained by staying longer. I leave Fatima after only three days.

Fátima—the hotel manager, that is—is surprised when I return the key to room 407.

"I thought you were staying a week."

I could explain that the air of her town is too heavy with prophecies. That a Virgin who opens up hell to the eyes of a seven-year-old is not to my taste. That I find myself longing to run off to Lisbon and join a Masonic lodge. Instead I say, "I'm sorry, but maybe I'll be back. In summer next time."

JUNE 13, 2000

The President of Italy announces that a pardon has been granted to the Pope's intended assassin. Mehmet Ali Agca will return to Turkey to serve the nine years remaining on his prior prison sentence. When he has done his time, Agca says, "I want to retire to a quiet life of prayer and repentance."

Italian prosecutors express their regret that now they will probably never know whether Agca acted on his own, or whether he was only the final link in a larger conspiracy involving an Islamic fundamentalist group or the KGB. A chief Vatican spokesman indicates, however, that the Pope welcomes the pardon: "He has been insisting on this for some time."

For his part, Agca has no doubt who bears the ultimate responsibility for his actions: "The devil put the gun in my hand. Nothing happened by chance. Sister Lúcia knew all along that it would happen."

In July, Agca surfaces again. This time, he has written a letter from prison declaring a "culture struggle" against Rome. "Pope John Paul is a good man," he writes, "but he should retire and go back to Poland. The Vatican is the headquarters of the devil."

AVE

STELLA MARIS

BARCELONA

Christmas is coming to Barcelona.

In the pedestrian mall of Portal de l'Angel, neon blazes through the drizzle. Artificial stars shed five-pointed light and electric angels gaze down from on high. Only twenty-five shopping days till Jesus' birthday! Jewels, delicacies, rare scents, fine garments; all the gifts of the Magi, plus Japanese cameras and American computers tempt the cell-phone toting crowds from the windows of the fancy shops.

And although Barcelona's Christmas won't be white, there is definitely a north wind blowing: a dozen guerrilla Santas armed with grappling hooks scale the face of the Cottet Building; holly wreathes the Corte Inglés department store; from a movie marquee, the Grinch grins down. Even City Hall is merrily walled in with conifer branches from God-knows-where. One expects at any moment to see city employees appearing with hoses to flood the *plaça* in the deluded hope that it will freeze over.

Of course, I feel quite at home with this "American-style" Christmas: a dash of North Pole, a splash of Bethlehem. It's just not what I had expected of Barcelona, ancient capital of Latin Mediterranean culture, where until recently Saint Nicholas was still better known as a saint. But who am I to spoil their fun?

Later tonight, I leave for Italy and the final leg of my pilgrimage. First, I'll be visiting friends in Milan, the ones I met last year in Lourdes. Luca and Paola have just returned from Nepal with their adopted child, Ramesh, and on Sunday I will attend his baptism. When he has me off to one side, Luca, who likes to see me squirm, will ask: "So if you don't believe in Jesus, what is Christmas to you?"

It's an interesting question. I came up against it a few years ago in Japan, where my role was often more cultural ambassador than English teacher. I had shown my class a videotape of Dr. Seuss's *How the Grinch Stole Christmas*. They loved the story, the music, the animation; but they were a little puzzled by the ending. What caused the Grinch's change of heart? Why did he bring all the toys and Christmas goodies back to the Whos instead of dumping them off Mount Crumpit?

"Because now he understands the spirit of Christmas," I said. It seemed as much explanation as anyone should need.

They digested this information for a moment. Then one careful hand went up.

"What is the spirit of Christmas?"

"Well. The spirit of Christmas …" What *was* the spirit of Christmas? "Well. It has to do with giving. With the joy of giving …" Realizing that this phrase was lifted from a toy commercial that had appeared in the video, I changed tack. "Or sharing, really. Christmas is a time when you share things—gifts, of course, but also love—with your friends and family. But the true Christmas spirit is more than just sharing with your friends and family, it's sharing with . . . everybody."

My students nodded, but I could see they were dubious. How could you share with everybody? Who would want you to anyway? In their culture, a finely graded scale of obligations was observed. An unmerited or immoderate gift merely embarrassed the recipient, while sticking him with an unasked-for indebtedness. This business of sharing one's love and possessions with "everybody" must have struck them as rather profligate behavior.

Yet it is what Christian and post-Christian society has set as its standard for 2,000 years. That radical dictum of Jesus Christ—"Love thy neighbor as thyself"—bedevils our consciences still. Even for those of us who live without God and Christ and Mary, the message remains, so basic to our beings that we assume the whole world shares it. It has been resold in new bottles by socialists, liberals, trade unionists, existentialists, democrats, pop psychologists, Frank Capra and Charles Dickens. We learn it by osmosis from our high culture and our low, from our newspapers and our textbooks. Some even endeavor to live by it (and not only Christians). The rest of us are at least a little civilized by it. And every year, just around Christmas, everyone buckles down and tries to put it into practice. Then the chests of the charities swell, the larders of the food banks are restocked, blood is donated and time volunteered.

Once this annual orgy of goodwill has passed, some grumble as they count up the expense; others wipe their brows and feel content that they have paid their tithe for another year; some keep on giving, though perhaps at a lesser pitch. And some, there must be some, experience what the Grinch and Scrooge and Ben-Hur and George Bailey and the Little Drummer Boy experienced (and what I never even attempted to explain to my class), which is *epiphany*.

Epiphany. That moment when the unbeliever's eyes open for the first time on a truth so dazzling, so self-evident, that all doubts and questions melt away, the restlessness of the heart is stilled, and life's labyrinth is revealed as a shining path: only follow, and you will reach your goal. The first Epiphany, of course, was to the Wise Men, who knelt with their gifts around the cradle of Jesus and saw before them the way, the truth and the life made flesh. It is another ideal, another chimera, that has been handed down to us from Christianity: this yearning for the moment of absolute clarity that illuminates a lifetime.

To get back to your question then, Luca, I suppose this is what Christmas is to me: the wholly unreasonable yet ever unvanquished hope, harbored in the heart like a guilty secret, that someday, from somewhere, clarity will come.

But here I am in the Ramblas, that wide, vibrant dry riverbed that channels Barcelona's crowds down through the old city to the harbor. At the foot of the city, majestic atop his column, Columbus looms through the mist. The great mariner, the captain of the *Santa María*, gestures beyond the new civic aquarium and the IMAX cinema to the gray Mediterranean.

"Look West, Barcelona!" he seems to say, "West to the future! to your destiny!"

Except that the port of Barcelona does not face west. It faces southeast, leaving the Admiral pointing in the general direction of North Africa.

As I turn into the Paseig Colom a balmy breeze sets the palm trees a-swaying. It's hardly weather to turn a Canadian's thoughts to Christmas. More like a May evening by Lake Ontario. I duck up a side street and find myself in the little plaza before the Basilica of Santa María del Mar—Saint Mary of the Sea.

This is a courtesy call. I had intended to spend this day not in Barcelona, but in the jag-toothed mountains two hours outside the city, at the monastery of Our Lady of Montserrat. Perhaps the most famous of the "Black Virgins," *la Moreneta* has welcomed pilgrims to her shrine for more than a thousand years, since the day she was discovered in a crevice among the rocks by . . . I think you can finish the story. Her specialties are easy childbirths and happy marriages, and a visit to her shrine is an indispensable ritual for Catalonian newlyweds. But an earthquake has damaged the shrine and I haven't been able to determine whether it has reopened or not. Meanwhile, my friends are expecting me in Milan. I have no choice but to give Montserrat a miss this time and content myself with a day in Barcelona. No great penance.

True to her name, the basilica of Santa María del Mar stands close by the harbor, so close that the ancient church she was built over bore the name Santa María de las Arenas, Saint Mary of the Sands. The present basilica, which dates to the thirteenth century, has from the beginning been Barcelona's church of the working man and especially of the fisherman and mariner. Here they would light a candle to the Virgin before setting out on the deep and after a safe return.

Out of the gusts of the Barcelona evening, I step into a pure, bright, arching space: simple yet not stark; devoid of the usual Baroque bombast; peaceful. A rehearsal for a harp recital is underway. I take a seat, and feel the weight of the world lift softly from my shoulders and dissipate in the airy vault. As I lean back, it strikes me that Santa María del Mar has an ominous shape for a seafarer's basilica: she is a giant, overturned boat.

Having gathered myself, I launch into my customary "cathedral stroll," poking my nose into the chapels as I go. I'm nearly alone here this evening. Only a handful of worshippers kneel in prayer. An informal audience has gathered near the altar, where the harp rehearsal proceeds in stops and starts. Other idlers like myself perambulate, slowing as they pass each chapel, pointing, admiring, looking for all the world like the window-shoppers in the Portal de l'Angel.

The perimeter of the basilica is scalloped with chapels, each lodging its saint. In one of the first is a replica of Our Lady of Montserrat. Like other medieval Madonnas, la Moreneta is crowned and holds the infant

Jesus. Her maternal hand hovers above his shoulder lest he tip. I'm a little bashful at not having made the trip out to see her shrine: "Sorry, Montse," I mouth. But she doesn't mind; she's forgiven much worse.

As I continue my circuit of the basilica, more Virgins pop up. There is Our Lady of the Rosary, telling her beads. Our Lady of the Olive, with fresh-cut sprigs at her feet. Here is Our Lady of the Immaculate Heart, and there, of the Immaculate Conception. I find Our Ladies of Dolores, Carmen, Pilar and Esperanza, who remind me of the Dolis and Carmens and Esperanzas I met along the Camino. Our Lady of the Court is here to serve the mighty; Our Lady of the Destitute, the poor. Our Lady of Remedies offers succor to the sick. And Our Lady of Cervelló? I don't believe we've met. . . .

It's starting to dawn on me that this basilica is a nest of Virgins. There are no less than fourteen incarnations of Mary lodging here beneath the mantle of Santa María del Mar. They occupy more than a third of the chapels. The Lord Jesus, by contrast, has only one chapel to himself, while father Joseph must split one with Saint Eulalia.

And how different each Virgin is. Medieval queen and Renaissance lady; Baroque maiden and Andalusian widow. Mary by turns is regal, meek, serene, grief-stricken, loving, stern, insipid, fearful. In most representations she is, before all else, a mother—waiting for her child's birth or mourning his death; holding him in her arms or on her lap—though sometimes she stands on her own.

There are clearly some popular favorites in this array of Marys, as the offerings of flowers or candles evidence. It reminds me of Notre-Dame de Paris, where two months ago I saw the rainbow-gowned Lady of Guadelupe, matron of Mexico, aglow in the bonfire of candles that burned at her feet. The chapels that stood on either side were vacant and gloomy, but hers was alive with fire and prayer. A modest disclaimer had been posted nearby, in deference perhaps to all the other Virgins and saints in the cathedral who hadn't had a candle lit to them in years. It read:

There is but one Lady, the Virgin Mother of God,
to whom men and women sing throughout the world,
from whom every Christian asks protection.

But if there is "but one Lady," why was everyone flocking here, neglecting all the other Marys?

The history of the Virgin of Guadelupe is instructive. Her special appeal to the indigenous peoples of South America is based on the fact that, at the height of the Spanish conquest, she revealed herself as a dark-skinned woman, surrounded by Aztec symbols of divinity. She

appeared, that is to say, as one of the people. So although she was "the Virgin Mother of God," she was not quite the same Virgin Mother of God as the one of Lourdes, or the ones of Montserrat, Fatima or Chartres. She was the Virgin of Guadelupe, the Virgin of Mexico and the Mexicans, who had appeared uniquely to them, in a form they would recognize, speaking the language they spoke. All Christians are welcome to worship her and seek her protection, but still she is *theirs*.

There is no other figure in Christianity as protean as Mary. God the Father is forever ancient and bearded. The saints have their stock features: James in his pilgrim's garb, Peter with his keys and tonsure. Even Jesus—the adult Jesus—for all the different ways he has been understood through history, retains his distinct face and his rooting in a particular place and time. But the hue of Mary's skin changes easily, as do her features, her garments, her age. She can adopt any form, so long as it is the form of motherhood. She becomes the Mother of all by being the Mother of each.

As for the namesake of this church, María del Mar, I have not encountered her on the landlocked route through France and along the Camino. But last summer, of course, we met in Finisterre, at the end of the world, in a church that was named Saint Mary of the Sands, just as this one once was. María del Mar is the Virgin who watches over fishermen and sailors, snatching them from the waters of death when all hope seems lost. She is also called *Stella Maris*, the Star of the Sea, the North Star. As Stella Maris, Mary for centuries has guided the sailors of Spain and Portugal over the oceans and back home again. In thanks, they have raised shrines to her on the farthest beaches and harbors and stony littorals.

It is quite possible that Columbus himself stopped at this church to pray to María, Stella Maris, upon returning from his initial Atlantic voyage in 1493, for at that time, their Catholic majesties Ferdinand and Isabella were holding court in Barcelona. By the then-sandy shore, the returning hero docked his ship (not the *Santa María*, which had broken up in the Western Isles, but the *Niña*), before making his triumphant progress to the royal palace, bearing treasures that could not be bought even in the Portal de l'Angel: exotic fruits, strange beasts, parrots in every color of the rainbow, gold . . . and six natives of the distant isles.

I would like to relate something of these six, the first ambassadors of the "New" world to the "Old." I can find, however, no word of them. Not their names, or ages, or sex, nor how they were clothed for their royal audience, nor how they comported themselves. One can only try to imagine what they might have thought or felt as they were paraded through the noisome streets of the old port. They left no trace of themselves and no further mention is made of them, save for the plaque in the Cathedral of Barcelona that commemorates their baptism.

The Stella Maris whom I saw walking on the waves in Finisterre was a handsome local woman, dressed for the weather. But the presiding Virgin of Barcelona's Santa María del Mar is not salty in the least. In fact, she is a typical Gothic Madonna, with a crown on her head, a royal gown, and a sweet French lilt to her hips. A little model of a caravel has been placed at her feet, but it isn't fooling anyone. This Lady has never set foot in a dinghy, much less put out to sea.

And as it turns out, this is not the original Santa María del Mar. The first met a gruesome end in the Spanish Civil War. In July 1936, at the outbreak of hostilities, the basilica was stormed by rioters. As crowds of locals stood by and watched, tombs of long-deceased noblemen and clerics were pried open, sacred images defaced and shattered, priceless ecclesiastical hardware melted down. Then the basilica itself was set ablaze with Santa María del Mar still inside. The fire roared and smoldered for eleven days (which gives us some idea of how much there was to burn) until nothing remained but bare chapels, stark walls, a charred ceiling: the very "minimalist" look we so admire today.

One can only marvel once again at the hatred Mary has inspired over the ages.

The historian Owen Chadwick warns against reading too much into anti-clerical riots: "An infuriated mob would like to batter down palace, or Houses of Parliament, or castle. But these homes of government are too stoutly defended for crowds with sticks and pistols to attack. The mob must wreak its wrath on something which is helpless, is regarded as public property, and is associated with government"; hence, an assault on the churches.

And yet it was remarked in Spain, during the Civil War, as in other wars and revolutions, that anti-Church violence took on special venom when the Holy Mother was the target. In that very month of July 1936, the monks of Our Lady of Montserrat were massacred. In Seville as well, the Virgin of the Macarena (recently the inspiration for a most indecorous international hit song and dance) only escaped the war because an old charwoman, on hearing that the church was to be burned down, wrapped her up, took her home and tucked her into bed. ("And where did you sleep?" she was asked later. "Oh, while Our Lady was with me, I slept on the floor," she replied.)

Who was Mary to those so set on destroying her? The handmaid of the landed gentry and the capitalists? The camp follower of the fascists? The opium of superstition, who kept working men and women from liberating themselves? Was she the light of mercy itself that they were trying to extinguish? Or was she simply the holiest thing the mob could lay its hands on?

The churches in Barcelona and throughout Republican Spain remained closed for the duration of the war. But when the fires had spent themselves, Mary returned. Things would never again be as magnificent as before, but Mary's roots are humble and she is more at home in a hovel than a mansion. Her overturned boat of a church got a sweep and a scrub. The chapels were spiffed up, the old statues and images replaced. A Gothic Virgin who had escaped the general destruction was called in to play the part of María del Mar. Maybe the canons of the church thought they could switch her for a more nautical Mary when the opportunity arose, but this one seems to have grown into the job. Today, the palace of the Virgin is warm again, safe, bright and full of music. True, the people this evening are up at the Portal de l'Angel, shopping for their secular Christmas. But should they choose to return, this place will be waiting for them.

A   M A D O N N A

O N   E V E R Y

C O R N E R

R O M E

Jubilees and Indulgences

They've been coming by the trillions since January, genuflecting at the places holy to Peter, Paul and Mary; breaching the sacred doors that open only once every twenty-five years; swarming to the Pope's public appearances in the consciousness that each one could be his last. But the year of Rome's twenty-sixth Jubilee is winding down. There are acres of vacant seats for the evening prayers in Saint Peter's Square. The special pilgrim buses ply their routes three-quarters empty. The volunteers in their "I was a stranger and you welcomed me" t-shirts have precious few strangers to welcome. Rome belongs, as much as it ever does, to the Romans.

The oldest pilgrim guides to Christian Rome date back to the sixth century. After the conquests of the Muslims had taken Jerusalem off the pilgrim map, Rome came into its own as Christendom's chief center of pilgrimage. Many of the pilgrims were recent converts, won by the Roman Church from the heathen and Arian Christian tribes of northern Europe, and for these new Catholics, Peter was the king of Saints and Rome a fabled city. From the beginning, pilgrims brought home talismans and relics: strips of cloth they had lowered through *confessio*—vents in the tombs—to touch the holy cadavers or flasks filled with sacred oil from the memorial lamps. Today's pilgrims go home instead with postcards, crosses, rosaries and plenary indulgences.

Indulgences? Didn't they go out with Martin Luther?

Not at all. True, they are no longer for sale, as they scandalously were in Luther's day, but they can still be had. Indulgences are the currency of Grace, used to reduce one's term of suffering in purgatory, and the Catholic Church is God's banker, conferring them upon all who perform a prescribed act of faith, such as a pilgrimage, in the proper spirit. Indulgences are good for greater or lesser periods of time, depending on the act of faith performed, but a "plenary" indulgence is highly prized, for it wipes a sinner's slate clean.

Plenary indulgences were first offered as an incentive to the Crusaders (it was not only the Muslim warriors who expected to go to Paradise if they died). But Pope Boniface VIII, in declaring the inaugural Roman Jubilee for the year 1300, decided to extend the privilege to pilgrims. The traffic to Saint Peter's city had been flagging for years, as the feet of Europe headed for the upstart Camino de Santiago, but the prospect of winning a plenary indulgence drew a crowd of two million. Dante attended that first Jubilee and thought well enough of it to immortalize it in his *Inferno*, where the sight of souls being whipped by demons reminded him of Jubilee crowd-control practices. The contemporary state of affairs is not so grim, though I can't say I regret having missed this summer's crowds, which were doubtless worthy of Dante's pen or Fellini's camera.

But the pilgrims around me clearly haven't come to Rome just to take advantage of a once-every-twenty-five-years special offer. (If an indulgence was all they wanted, they could get it closer to home by visiting any of hundreds of specially designated "pilgrimage churches" throughout the world this year.) No, the pilgrims are here to see Rome, the city of the Popes and the martyrs, of Paul and of Peter; the capital city of their religion. Of course, here, as in Paris, the pilgrims jostle with tourists; but to a greater extent than in Paris, their paths overlap, the difference between pilgrims and tourists in Rome being less in what they see than in how they see it. Thus, while both pilgrims and tourists flock to the Colosseum, the tourist identifies almost automatically with the Roman spectators, while the pilgrim empathizes with the Christians who were thrown to the lions. Likewise, the tourist's beauty spots—Saint Peter's Square, the Sistine Chapel, the Catacombs and the Pantheon, to name a few—are, to the pilgrim, places of devotion as well.

But there are also specialized pilgrim itineraries that venture to sites the tourists seldom see and one of these is the visit to "the seven churches." The visit is a mini-pilgrimage to some of Rome's most venerable basilicas that was popularized in the sixteenth century by Saint Filippo Neri. As the seven churches are scattered around the perimeter of the old city, this was traditionally a two-day jaunt that combined masses and confessions with picnics in the *campagna*. Today, buses cover the route in a matter of hours without benefit of wine and minstrels.

I decide to join the seven churches loop in the hope that it will help me tap into the pilgrim spirit, for after three days in Milan being spoiled by the warmth of my friends and their families, Rome feels lonely and daunting. So I start at Santa María Maggiore (Neri's final stop, but close to my hotel) and work my way around San Pietro, San Giovanni in Laterano, San Paolo fuori le Mura, Santa Croce in Gerusalemme, San Lorenzo, admiring all that a pilgrim is meant to admire, wondering particularly at Santa Croce's assortment of Holy Land bric-a-brac (three fragments of the true cross, two thorns from Christ's crown, three chips off the marble column where he was flagellated, a joint of Saint Thomas's doubting finger, and the entire horizontal cross-beam, now a little worm-eaten, of the Good Thief's crucifix), and trying to make some human contact.

But before I make it to the seventh church, my well of admiration is running low. I must be suffering from aesthetic overload, having seen too many beautiful things in the past two months. Also, the concrete desert that has been laid over Filippo Neri's idyllic *campagna* is wearing down my feet and my soul. And in any case, I'm still not meeting anyone. This Jubilee business is just too reminiscent of, well, tourism: the pilgrims tootle about in their buses, disembark at the holy places, follow their guides around in greater or lesser states of inattentiveness, take the inevitable photos, buy the postcard of Saint Thomas's finger (and maybe some bath soaps, herbal tea or liqueur; the brothers who run these places are very enterprising). Now and then, I get a chance to exchange some pleasantries with a pilgrim, but soon he's back on his bus and off to the next stop, leaving me to gaze mutely at objects. Under these circumstances, with the pilgrims skittering about the big city like water-bugs, the sense of *communitas* is spread very thin.

And this is not what I had hoped for at this stage of my journey. I'll be going home soon and, after disappointments in Fatima, Zaragoza and

Montserrat, I'm hoping to encounter something living. I want to see again the sparks of ancient devotion flying in the air, to feel the stillness of prayer fill the space around me. Somehow, chasing pilgrim buses doesn't seem like the way to find that. I have a hunch that the place to experience Jubilee fervor is not among the pilgrims to Rome, but among the Romans themselves; that I need to start asking not, "Where do the worshippers go in Rome?" but, "Where do the Romans go to worship?"

Street Corners and Altars

Once, one could have answered this question by standing at almost any street corner in Rome and looking up.

They are called *Madonnelle* (singular, *Madonnella*), the images of the Virgin that populate the streets of Rome. Usually they are set high on walls, most often at street corners. Some are painted in fresco, on wood, or on canvas; others are sculpted in marble, stucco or terracotta, or figured in mosaic. Some are no more than photographs of Virgins purchased from souvenir stalls. A few have artistic merit, but the majority are conventional, sometimes crude, portrayals (not that aesthetic judgments weigh too heavily with worshippers; results are what count). Some of the Madonnelle are ornately framed by angels and cornices and lit at night. Many are set behind glass, which preserves them from the elements but makes them difficult to see or photograph.

Although there are still a few medieval and renaissance Madonnas around, most of those we see today date back to the seventeenth and eighteenth centuries. There are, by one recent count, 637 of them—which is a terrific number, for old Rome is not such a vast city—but in the nineteenth century there were more than 2,700. At that time, interestingly, only about half of the images portrayed Mary, the remainder being dedicated to Christ or the saints. The fact that the Virgin figures in virtually every image that has survived to the present day demonstrates yet again her staying power.

The Madonnelle continue a tradition that reaches back to pagan times, when shrines to various gods and goddesses stood at crossroads throughout Rome. These shrines often bore the inscription *Posuerunt me custodem*, "They placed me here to watch," indicating that their role was to safeguard the city and its citizens. After the triumph of Christianity in the fourth century, this job was taken over by Christ, the martyrs and Mary. The street-corner icons fulfilled other functions, too. They were time-savers, allowing the busy housewife or tradesman to make a swift nod towards the holy image when there wasn't time to attend mass. The candles that burned before them by night served as Rome's only street lights till the late nineteenth century. Most importantly, they soaked up an excess of devotion. All of the images of Mary above all the church altars weren't enough for the Romans. They wanted their Mother present in all places, at all times, to watch over them, and, of course, to answer their prayers.

Inevitably, certain Madonnelle acquired reputations as wonder-workers. It shouldn't make any difference, one might think, whether one prays to the Madonna on this corner or that one: there is, after all, "but one Lady" to whom all prayers are directed. But then, by the same argument, there is only one lottery and it shouldn't make any difference where you buy your ticket; yet there's always a line outside the shop with "Million Dollar Winner Sold Here" posted in the window.

One illustrious Madonnella was the Madonna della Pace, an image who first drew attention to herself by bleeding when struck by a stone. In 1481, Pope Sixtus IV, anxious to avoid war with Florence, led a procession to her street corner to beg her intercession. She granted his prayer and received in return her own little church, making her one of the many Madonnelle to be relocated from a street corner to an altar. Another was Santa Maria del Pianto, Saint Mary of the Tears, so named for having once wept upon witnessing a murder. A fierce argument had broken out in the street below her and one of the antagonists stood poised to kill the other. At the last moment, the man who was about to be stabbed cried out: "Madonna, have mercy on me!" The attacker was so moved that he dropped his weapon and embraced his enemy—who coolly knifed him in the ribs. The sight of this treachery moved the Madonna to bloody tears that continued for three days.

The Madonnelle reached the height of their fame in the years 1796 to 1798, when the terrified citizens of Rome were awaiting the arrival of Napoleon. The prodigies began on the ninth of July, 1796, when the Madonnella of the Via Archetto was seen to move her eyes. In the days that followed, ever-greater crowds, which soon included the Pope and his cardinals, crowded into this obscure alley to see the miracle repeated. According to one witness, it was when the worshippers kneeling before the effigy, reciting her litanies, reached the invocation to Holy Mary that "she turned her eyes from one part of the crowd to the other, casting a loving gaze over all the people." One empirically minded observer scaled a ladder with a compass in hand to measure the movement of the Virgin's pupils.

Before long, an epidemic of eye-shifting Madonnas had swept the city. Everywhere, Madonnelle were rolling their eyes, raising them to heaven, weeping. The Madonna of the Via Baccina caused a bunch of dried lilies to bloom. Pope Pius VI proclaimed  days of fasting and penitential processions before launching a canonical inquiry into the phenomenon. The tribunal concluded that twenty-six Madonnelle had expressed their love and mercy to the Roman people in one miraculous way or another, and the Romans showed their gratitude to these Madonnelle in their usual manner, by detaching them from the walls and setting them up in their own churches. A few can still be seen in their original posts, however, including the Madonna Addolorata of the Piazza del Gesù, who bears the following inscription, dated 1796:

> "His Holiness, Pope Pius VI, concedes to all of the faithful, of both sexes,
> two hundred days of indulgence, which may be applied to souls already in purgatory,
> for each time they devoutly recite the Litany of the Most Holy Mary before this sacred image."

In the end, the Virgin only succeeded in delaying the arrival of Napoleon's armies, as her treasures from the Sanctuary of Loreto, along with countless other invaluable papal possessions, were sold off to satisfy the rapacious terms of the Treaty of Tolentino. Despite it all, the French occupied Rome in 1798, and the eighty-year-old Pius VI was arrested under the name, "Citizen Pope," and imprisoned in France, where he died a year later.

Sad to say, devotion to the Madonnelle is fading. It is rare to see flowers or candles before them anymore, much less worshippers reciting the litanies of the Virgin. When I stopped on busy streets to take photos of Madonnelle, Romans would often glance up to see what on earth I was shooting, then pause to admire a knick-knack of the civic furniture so familiar to them that they had stopped seeing it. And an even surer sign of obsolescence than mere neglect: a few Madonnelle have been "museumized" for the Jubilee, tagged with generic identifying plaques.

Can a correlation be drawn between decline in devotion to the Madonnelle and a rise in Roman anxiety levels? For according to the *Osservatore Romano*, official daily of the Vatican, a full 60 percent of Romans admit to feelings of insecurity that verge on the neurotic. "The quality of life in Rome," according to this survey, "is affected not so much by fear of particular criminal acts, as by the psychological insecurity of the citizens, their fear that at any moment, anything could happen." This sort of urban malaise has likely been a constant of Roman life since the days of the Caesars. But surely, the Romans felt more secure when they had, at least, the Madonnelle to watch out for them.

The Romans have almost always been under the eye of one female divinity or another. Starting in 204 BC, when the Senate called the Magna Mater to Rome from her home in Pergamum, the capital welcomed goddesses from every corner of the world. On that first, celebrated occasion, the Great Mother was credited with rescuing Rome from Hannibal, just as Mary would later be thanked for saving the city from Napoleon, Hitler and various other scourges.

Strangely, Rome's first Great Mother took the form of a small, dark stone, a meteorite that had fallen from heaven and was never formed into any image. This fact is both ironic and appropriate: ironic, in that Rome was destined to become the capital of the image, applying the naturalism of Greek art to Christian subject matter, championing the use of icons against iconoclastic Byzantine Emperors, and ultimately leading the late Gothic and Renaissance world in its quest to reproduce the human form;

appropriate, because in 204 BC, the Virgin Mary, Queen of all images, had yet to been born.

Marian Rome begins with Santa Maria Maggiore. One fourth-century August morning, the Virgin marked the site of her future basilica with an unseasonable snowfall. Every fifth of August to this day, a flurry of white rose petals cascades from the ceiling of the church to commemorate the miracle. The building of the basilica actually commenced during the papacy of Sixtus III (432 to 440), in joyful recognition of the decision of the Council of Ephesus to confirm Mary in her title of *Theotokos*—Bearer of God. The fact that the Council had taken place in 431 indicates the precociousness of Rome's Virgin worship. As for the location of the basilica, one can only assume that Mary knew what she was doing when she chose the site of a former temple to the mother goddess Juno for her own place of worship.

Of course, Santa Maria Maggiore is a treasure chest, and her greatest treasure (greater even than her celebrated crib of Jesus) is the icon of Mary known as *Salus Populi Romani*, the salvation of the Roman people. The image is one of the many dispersed around the Christian world that are said to have come from the hand of the Evangelist Luke. Legend has Popes as far back as the seventh century parading the holy image through the streets of Rome to call down the Virgin's mercy in times of plague and war. The tradition has not died, and it even reached a belated climax in the Marian Year of 1954, when Pius XII proclaimed the universal queenship of Mary. The declaration was solemnized when Pius crowned the Salus Populi Romani in Saint Peter's Square before a crowd of half a million worshippers and the massed banners of the 760 most renowned Marian churches of the world.

And Santa Maria Maggiore is only the greatest of Rome's churches dedicated to Mary. There is also Santa Maria in Trastevere, whose twelfth-century mosaics, inspired by Saint Bernard's sermons in Rome on the Song of Songs, portray Mary as the Bride of Christ and Queen of Heaven; Santa Maria in Aracoeli, founded on the spot where, according to legend, the Emperor Augustus was granted a fore-vision of the Madonna and Child; Santa Maria in Cosmedin, home to Rome's oldest mosaic of the Virgin, not to mention the Madonna degli Sportelli, renowned for her jack-in-the-box performance in 1672 (the priests had been unable to unlock the little doors [*sportelli*] in front of her image, but during the singing of the Gloria, at the words, "Let us adore thee," they flew open wide); and Santa Maria Rotonda, consecrated in 609 (only

after Gregory the Great had shooed the old pagan gods from the premises says the legend) and better known as the Pantheon.

According to *Roma Santuario Mariano*, the most complete authority on the subject, there are over 250 churches, oratories and sanctuaries dedicated to Mary in the Roman diocese—and that's not counting fourteen pages of Marian churches that are no longer in existence. There is even a Marian counterpart to Filippo Neri's visit to the seven churches with thirty-one stops on its itinerary. Visiting a church a day for a month wins the pilgrim a seven-year indulgence.

But I don't want to fall back into doing the rounds of Rome's churches, admiring bones and marble. I feel like the Madonnelle have brought me a little closer to where the life is. I'm going to stick to my outdoor research.

La Madonna della Rivelazione

The Sanctuary of the Madonna della Rivelazione sits on a hill above the busy Via Lauretana, at the southern reaches of the city. It is just opposite the beautiful old monastery of Tre Fontane, which was built on the site where the Apostle Paul lost his head. This juxtaposition of Tre Fontane and the Sanctuary of the Madonna reflects a symmetry in the lives of their founders; for just as Saul the Jew, when asked by Jesus, "Why do you persecute me?" became in a twinkling Paul the Christian, so Bruno the Protestant, when confronted with the same question by the Virgin Mary, became Bruno, champion of the Immaculate Conception.

The complicated spiritual odyssey of Bruno Cornacchiola began when, as an Italian combatant in the Spanish Civil War, he was converted to Protestantism by a German. He returned to Italy so embittered against the Catholic Church—and particularly the doctrine of the Immaculate Conception—that he started planning to kill the Pope. Before he could put his plot into action, however, he took a walk in the woods near Tre Fontane and met the Virgin Mary.

"Ora basta!" she scolded him in the tones of an exasperated mother. "Enough already! Stop persecuting me!" Once she had finished raking her prodigal son over the coals, her tone softened. She told Bruno to pray for the conversion of sinners and the union of the Christian churches. In the months that followed, as she continued to appear to Bruno, the visions received considerable press. Bruno's eventual return to the arms of the Church was accompanied by a surge of cures and conversions, and a new devotion was born.

At the top of a flight of mossy steps, on the edge of a eucalyptus forest, the Sanctuary of the Madonna has a sylvan air to it. One can see why urban rats would want to escape here and ample parking space is provided for them. The simple, whitewashed chapel, big enough to seat a hundred, brims with fresh-cut plants and flowers. The statue of the Virgin robed, not in the usual Virgin blue, but in the green of Roman pines, stands in a grotto, between what appear to be giant stalks of asparagus.

It is lunchtime, and worshippers keep ducking in for a minute or two, fitting a moment of silent prayer into their day. The odor of flowers and the sight of Our Lady in green make for a welcome relief from the grind of Rome—at least until two tour buses pull up. Evidently the Madonna of the Revelation has made it onto pilgrim itineraries. The crowd that rolls out of the buses sports distinctive, skilfully knotted yellow silk scarves. Even as pilgrims, Italians know a thing or two about style.

I make a prompt getaway to the garden behind the chapel, where a passage has been cut through the hillside. Its ceilings are tiled with Sacred Hearts, its walls plastered with family photos, plaques, water colors, letters that plead for mercy or give thanks for favors. It's impossible not to get caught up in these dramas, posted here in all their raw immediacy. Some are dated this morning. Are they public testimonials or private letters to Mary? Both, it seems:

"Help Stefano escape this nightmare."

"Bless my sister and give me a little nephew soon."

"I don't know how things will turn out in my love life. God will decide for me. But I pray you not to make me suffer more."

"Thank you for helping Alberto find the courage to face this terrible sickness."

This is the bulletin board for the community of those who suffer, believe and care. The thankful leave testimony that there is hope; the desperate expose their wounds with trust. There is a heart beating here, or many hearts, rather. Many hearts who, through the weeks and months and years, follow their discrete, eccentric ways through the labyrinth of the city, intersecting nowhere except here. They always find their way back here, to this still center.

La Madonna Del Divino Amore

"Signore. Signore, scusi …"

Today is December 8, Feast Day of the Immaculate Conception, a national holiday in Italy. At eight o'clock in the morning, the firemen of Rome will raise a ladder to the statue of the Immaculate Conception that stands atop a pillar in the Piazza di Spagna and place a bouquet of flowers in her outstretched arms. But now it's 5:15, and I have just completed the overnight pilgrimage from Rome to the Sanctuary of the Madonna of Divine Love, nine miles south of the city. It's chilly and I'm tired, but I've found myself a nice stone step to sit on and a well-placed post to lean against. Warmth is radiating from the core of my being, and my spirit has almost worked itself free of the body when a hand grasps my shoulder and summons it back.

"Signore, scusi …"

"Cosa?"

The young man wants to know if these are the steps to the bar. Poor guy. Five thousand people to pick from, and he wakes up the one who doesn't have a clue.

"Bar? No, I don't think so. Toilets, maybe …"

He looks dubious, then heads up the stairs anyway. So what did he need to ask me for? I lapse back into a fitful sleep.

The Madonna del Divino Amore is, in the words of scholar Matilde Passa, "a discreet Madonna. She has never cried, never rolled her eyes, never bled. Even her first miracle was not portentous, but simple, country-style." That first miracle occurred in 1740, when a pilgrim on his way to Rome was laid into by a pack of wild dogs. The attack occurred at the foot of a tower on which was painted a fresco of the Madonna and

Child beneath a dove, symbol of Divine Love. The man called upon the Madonna to save him and at the last moment the dogs veered away, presumably to bite someone else.

The miracle was indeed unpretentious, but then so are most people's prayers. Within ten years, the pilgrimage had grown to the point where a sanctuary had to be erected to welcome the worshippers and house the holy image, which had been detached from the old tower. The Sanctuary of the Madonna thrived for more than a century, due in no small part to its location: just far enough from Rome to feel like a real excursion, but still within a day's walk or ride, and with plenty of picnicking opportunities along the way. It's the sort of pilgrimage the Spanish would call a *romería*, except that it didn't go *to* Rome but *from* it.

By the 1900s, however, the Santuario del Divino Amore was long forgotten. A journalist described it in 1930 as looking like a village after a sacking. Yet it was precisely at this juncture that Don Umberto Terenzi was appointed rector. At first, Don Umberto regarded his new post as one to wiggle out of as quickly as possible. He could see no future in shepherding this derelict parish. Then one day he flipped his car as he was driving back from Rome. None of the vehicle's occupants was injured and the positive-thinking young priest took this as a sign that the Madonna del Divino Amore had plans for him. He would remain in her service till his death in 1974.

Don Umberto threw himself into restoring the fortunes of Divino Amore. Within a decade he had established new nursery and elementary schools, an orphanage, an order of nuns and a rail link to Rome. Then, once the groundwork was laid, the Madonna herself took over. In 1944, when the occupying Nazi forces commandeered the sanctuary to serve as a military command base, it was decided to ship the image of Our Lady to Rome for safekeeping. Somehow, word of her pending arrival spread and she was welcomed to the city like a returning heroine. The crowds that swelled into her temporary dwelling, imploring her to put an end to the war, were so great that she had to be installed in the spacious Basilica of Sant'Ignazio. It was there, on June 4, 1944, that the citizens of Rome made three vows they hoped would win their Lady's favor: first, to reform their lives; second, to enlarge her Sanctuary; third, to perform some notable act of charity, details to be determined at a later date. Despite the wishful nature of the first vow, and the "future considerations" clause attached to the third, the Madonna gave the Romans the benefit of the doubt. Four hours later, the Nazis were on their way.

A week after the German withdrawal, Pope Pius XII joined the faithful in the Basilica of Sant'Ignazio to confer upon the Madonna del Divino Amore the title of *Salvatrice dell'Urbe*, Savior of the City. The designation was a conscious echo and renewal of the Salus Populi Romani that had been worn for twelve centuries by the Madonna of Santa Maria Maggiore and a very distant echo of the accolades bestowed two millennia before upon a featureless black stone from Pergamum.

The Mother had saved Rome once again.

After the war, the pilgrimage to the Sanctuary of Divine Love came back to life. The nine-mile walk is a summer event—there's one every Saturday night from Easter till the end of October—but one more has been added, just for me, on the eve of the Feast of the Immaculate Conception.

I have high hopes for this little pilgrimage. It will gather the Roman faithful together in a living body. There should be a warmth about it and enough exhaustion-induced euphoria to make the participants open and approachable. If I'm lucky, I'll team up with a group. Maybe I'll even find myself a Virgil. (A Beatrice would be asking too much.)

I arrive at Porta Capena, south of the Circus Maximus, at half past eleven. There must be a couple of thousand pilgrims waiting, candles ablaze, for the pick-up truck bearing the image of the Madonna to rev its engines and lead the way. Hymns and Ave Marias are breaking out like brushfire and the blinking blue lights of the police escort lend a festive note. A little after midnight, we start to move, heading past the Baths of Caracalla and out the city gates. Within moments Rome is behind us, not that anyone looks back. There's nowhere to go now but forward, in the train of the Madonna. It's a clear, mild night, and the way is along an ancient Roman road, walled on either side. A lovely night for an all-night traipse, if it weren't for that unctuous character with the megaphone who is leading the prayers and songs, telling everyone what they should be thinking and feeling and generally acting as host and master of ceremonies for the pilgrimage. I can understand that he is performing a function, but couldn't he just sometimes leave everyone to their own thoughts and prayers? I'd like to talk to some of my fellow walkers—not all of them are singing and praying along—but the volume of the loudspeakers is set at a conversation-killing level.

We carry on until two, when the procession takes a break at a filling station, and the picnic baskets are broken out. Bottles of wine, fruit and monster *panini* appear, then disappear, as the pilgrims transfer weight from their shoulders to their stomachs before the second half of the walk. I stroll around the crowd, looking for a friendly face without any luck. This is starting to look like a long evening. Then I notice that some of the pilgrims are starting out early, evidently hoping to put some distance between themselves and the sound truck. Not a bad idea. I manage to squeeze ahead of the pack just as Father Megaphone calls the faithful to their feet. From the top of the next hill, I look back at the tightly packed mass raising their candles in the air behind the Madonna.

But I still can't find anyone to talk to. When I sidle up to three college-age girls and ask if they've done this before, they erupt in a giggle. Serves me right; I should pick on someone my own age. These ladies here look friendly. And they are. For a minute or two. Well, maybe these gentlemen. Or maybe not. Everyone I speak to has mastered the urban art of cheerfully responding to questions or comments without encouraging any more. Each pilgrim group is quite content to remain in its own oyster shell. This is no Camino. But at least I understand now the role of the megaphone-man: he's here to lend cohesiveness to a group that would never cohere on its own, like those messages you see on the big screen at sports stadiums, ordering everyone to "Make Some Noise!"

There's nothing for it but to plod on beneath the moon and stars, trying to enjoy the smells and the sounds of the night, hoping the hours pass swiftly, wishing I hadn't worn the new shoes I picked up for that baptism in Milan. When I cast my mind back, no moment of the walk stands out. Or one: sometime, very late, the pilgrimage passes a seniors' home where a few of the residents wait to cheer us on from a balcony.

It's after four o'clock when I catch up with a group of Filipinos. Initially, they are as cool to my approaches as everyone else, but when I tell them I am from Canada, one of them cries out, "My sister lives in Vancouver!" and the connection is made. There are ten of them in all, eight of them women who are working as domestics in Rome. For the rest of the way, they ply me with oranges, pineapple-on-a-stick, and detailed questions about Canada's working conditions and weather. When I ask how many times they've done this pilgrimage, they can only shake their heads. "Many, many!" they laugh.

And then, at long last, the Sanctuary of the Madonna del Divino Amore pops into view. With its faux-Chagall aquamarine windows, it looks from the distance like a fish-tank or a high-concept disco. This is the new chapel, the one that was promised the Madonna back in 1944. The Romans, accustomed to viewing things from the perspective of eternity, were fifty years building it, but are still pleased with themselves that they got it done in time for the Jubilee. As we approach, I realize that the complex has a lawn for a roof. It has been burrowed into the hillside below the old Sanctuary. I also note that the mall-size parking lot out front is filling up fast, meaning that if the pilgrims don't hurry, they'll conclude their all-night walk with an unseemly race for seats. Tonight, the last shall not be first; the last shall stand.

From the inside, the fish-tank looks more like a university lecture hall: wide, bright and sterile. The stained-glass windows and white sweeping curve of the place are daring, but a bit much at this hour. The fluorescent glare makes for a rude awakening. The Madonna would have been wise to look over the building plans back in '44, before she sent the Nazis packing.

The church is built to accommodate 1,000 seated and 1,500 standing, but by the time the priest steps up to the mike, it's full well beyond capacity. Feeling I should leave room for the faithful, I have taken a seat near the back while my Filipino companions claim places near the altar. But before very long I have surrendered my seat and then my two feet of concrete window ledge. Stragglers keep pushing in and before I know it I'm sitting on the floor looking into a forest of legs. That's when a small, sensible voice in my head asks, "What on earth are you doing here?"

I pick myself up, stumble back into the night, find a place on the steps. And am just starting to doze off when a hand grabs my shoulder and a voice says: *"Signore. Signore, scusi ..."*

People continue to pass me on their way up the stairs as I drift in and out of sleep. After half an hour or so, it occurs to me that no one has come back down, so I rouse myself to make an inspection. And behold, at the top of the steps, there *is* a bar. Of course there is a bar, this is Italy. It's a lovely bar, too, suffused with the aroma of fresh brioches and espresso coffee, and crowded with noisy pilgrims. How sensible, to take a little restoration after a long walk.

But aren't these people missing mass?

No, they know exactly what they're doing. They are the purists; content to take a pass on the fishbowl because they're waiting on the real thing ("the real *pastasciutta*" as my friend Luca would say): six o'clock mass in the old chapel.

It's tiny, compared to its olympian successor, but the eighteenth-century chapel is genuine. It's standing room only, but the kind of standing room that makes you feel warm and close to the people around you. Instead of glare, it has glow. The original image of the Madonna del Divino Amore is here, shining amid the usual welter of clouds and angels, and old women shoulder their way through the press of bodies, getting as close as they can to be sure she can hear them. Parents hoist bleary-eyed children onto their shoulders. The genial priest, yet another Filipino, manages fine without a microphone. In a corner by the door, there is a wooden box with a stack of paper, some pencils, and the message, "Whoever wishes to ask something of the Virgin, fill out a paper and put it in the box."

Off the main chapel are the Madonna's rec-rooms, three chambers chock-a-block with ex-votos, photos, sacred hearts and thanks for favors received and miracles performed. Best is the tribute from the crew of the dirigible *Italia*, who nearly came to grief when they went down in the Arctic wastes as they attempted to reach the North Pole in 1928. The radio went dead and all attempts to revive it over the course of several days failed until one of the crewmen, Biagi, prayed to the Madonna del Divino Amore. At once, the radio whistled and cracked, rescuers arrived, and the crewmen survived to present the headphones to the Madonna.

As for Mary's giftshop, it doubles as a trophy room, the glass cases bursting with prizes dedicated by sportsmen. The bicycles of racing champs dangle from the ceiling and the walls are hung with the jerseys of soccer heroes. The most recent gift comes from Roma hero Francesco Totti. In a photo on the back of the Sanctuary's monthly bulletin, Italy's scoring king hands over a framed sweater to the rector of the Sanctuary, while his beaming mother receives a rosary.

I stand through the service in the old chapel. The hymns rise and fall like convection currents, generating enough warmth, human and divine, to drive the chill away. The gesture of peace is given and received with kindness. Day is breaking as I stroll into the tiny plaza outside. In an hour or so, the firemen will be placing their bouquet in the arms of the *Immacolata* and later the Pope himself will speak at the foot of the pillar raised by his predecessor, Pius IX. The narrow streets near the Spanish Steps will be jammed with tens of thousands of pilgrims and Romans, and the sparks of devotion will be flying. These are things I had wanted to see.

But right now, the pilgrims are filing out of the old Sanctuary of the Madonna del Divino Amore, carrying their children, holding hands, standing in sociable knots before they all go home for a rest. The first birds are singing. Out beyond the little square, the fields and lazy hills are turning from gray to green as day arrives.

I see no hurry to get back to the city.

The Presepio

So let's finish in the country. We are looking down as from a low-flying plane upon a village outside the walls of Rome, sometime in the eighteenth century. Daylight is failing. There are candles in the windows of the houses and the workshops of the small-craftsmen. Farmers are heading in from the orchards, and some of the locals are already enjoying a drink at the trattoria. But the baker still rolls his dough, the smith hammers at his anvil, the cobbler mends his shoes. The women are setting tables and calling the children to dinner, while on a hill near the village, a herdsman leans against some ruin of antiquity, playing his flute.

So far, no one has noticed the angels.

Sometime soon, they will. When they do, they will drop their work, set down their glasses, take their children by the hand and gather in wonder around the doors of the stable, where already some shepherds and three men dressed in rich and fanciful garb kneel in the straw around the mother, the child, and the befuddled old father. For the first moment they will stand in silence. Then they will drop to their knees one by one, already obscurely conscious that all has changed and nothing will ever be the same again.

For now, though, the angels hover unnoticed, sounding their soundless trumpets, and life goes on as it ever has.

According to tradition, the first *presepio*—also known as a *crèche* or nativity scene—was made by Saint Francis for Christmas, 1223. He constructed it inside the grotto in Greccio where he spent the last years of his life as a way to bring home to the local peasants the humility of

Christ's birth. The idea seems natural today, but in its time it was part of the revolution instigated by Francis that brought Mary and her Son down from their thrones in heaven and re-imagined them as a humble woman and a child born in a manger. In the presepio, the Queen of Heaven became again the maid Mary. From Francis's inspiration sprang a tradition that is still vital after nearly eight centuries. Indeed, thanks to the presepio, Rome remains virtually Santa Claus-free. Hosanna!

In this season, the elliptical Piazza Navona is crammed with presepio stalls. There are boxes full of shepherds, cows, kings, camels, haybales, cats, centurions. Pick out a cozy manger and furnish it as you please. The cheap figures are made of plastic these days, though still hand-painted, if one can trust the vendors. The expensive ones—which can be very expensive indeed—are made of wood or terracotta, and garbed in rich cloth.

The churches have started breaking out their presepios, too, though Saint Peter's won't go on display till after I leave the city. Fortunately, Rome's most impressive manger scene is on view all year round at the Basilica of Saints Cosma and Damiano, near the Colosseum. This teeming masterpiece of *l'arte presepistico*, a product of eighteenth-century Naples, occupies an ample stage. The life-like figurines are made of wood and ceramic. According to the literature, they include "11 orientals, 49 women, 26 shepherds, 20 black persons, 8 children, 23 men, a blind person, 2 people who are sleeping, and a family with a newborn child." Formerly, the work was shown in the basilica, but the theft of some figures convinced the church custodians that it should have its own exhibition space, on the far side of a sheet of glass and a ticket booth.

But right now I am uptown, at the Sala del Bramante in the Piazza del Popolo, where the twenty-fifth annual presepio fair is being hosted. There are one hundred on display from all over Italy, but especially the South. Some are the products of presepio schools, while others have been made by individual artists who have placed their business cards beside their creations. One aisle features presepios sponsored by international embassies, from Portugal to the Philippines.

It's a slow night and near the closing hour, as the girl at the front door has been kind enough to remind me. As I pass between the banks of presepios, glancing from side to side, it strikes me that while a few lean towards modernity and abstraction, the vast majority seem to endorse the view that Jesus Christ was born somewhere in Southern Italy before the onset of the industrial era. Even the most conspicuous exception to this rule, a space-age Nativity made of fluorescent plastic, sets Christ's birth in the future rather than the present. There are, in other words, no Vatican Two inspired creations replicating the dreary outskirts of today's Rome; not the faintest stab at "relevance." Saint Francis's aim in building the first presepio—to remind the worshipper of the poverty of Christ's birth—has been superseded by a pining for a lost Arcadia.

I come to the piece I described at the top of this chapter, with its shepherds and angels and Roman countryside. It is entitled not "The Nativity of Christ," but *Roma Sparita*, "Vanished Rome." How much effort and love the artist has poured into recreating the world of the peasant and village-dweller. Clearly, pre-industrial life is the sacred that he means to celebrate. The birth of Jesus has been squeezed into a very small corner of the pastoral panorama.

There is barely time to take a peek into the rear exhibition room. An older man in a dark suit, the only other visitor left, is standing before one of the displays, shaking his head with gentle laughter. The presepio before him is whirring and buzzing. When he steps away, I move in to take a look. Once again, the view is of a pastoral landscape seen from above, but this landscape is filled with laborers, all frozen in the middle of their tasks. The piece is entitled, "Presepio in motion: 1700s Neapolitan," and when I press the button on the panel in front of it, every figure instantly sets to work. Grapes are crushed, wood sawn, corn ground, mortar mixed, knives sharpened, mills turned, fish scaled, prosciutto sliced. The only figures in the whole scene who don't have a job to do are the Holy Family, tucked away in their grotto.

For the thirty seconds that the motor runs, a lost world of skilled and meaningful work comes back to life. The chaotic Rome outside, where "at any moment, anything can happen," gives way to another kind of society, one full of people who know each other, work with their hands and see the fruits of their labor. A human community that revolves around the cycle of the seasons and the mystery of life and death embodied in the still, silent epiphany of a father, a mother and a child.

Then the hum of the motor dies. The busy figures grind to a halt. The water stops running. And through an open window, the growl of the traffic steals in.

A GREAT

TREASURE COMES

FROM THE SEA

LORETO

THOUGH I AM, in most respects, irreligious, I am a confirmed fatalist when it comes to hotel reservations. If there is meant to be a room for me, there will be and I'm pretty sure that there will be no room for me in Loreto on the night of December 9. So there's no point racing to get there. I'm getting tired of hotels in any case. Tired of trains, too, so I pass on the morning departures, have lunch with my friend Raffaele and catch the 1:30.

The tracks head northeast from Rome, picking the path of least resistance through the vertebrae of Italy's mountainous backbone. Ancona is fogged in, but five minutes from the city the train breaks through the mist and I can see the Adriatic, a stone's throw from the window and ahead, the lights of the coastal villages twinkling in the twilight. Twenty minutes later, I'm stepping off the train at Loreto station. I hoist my backpack, wonder whether to hop on the shuttle bus until it settles my internal debate by driving away, then walk uphill to the town in the gathering night. This is my last stop, the end of a long journey. In a few days, I will be in Paris again, admiring Notre-Dame's Nativity scene with its Jean-Paul Gaultier-garbed magi looking like extras from *The Road Warrior*. Then I will fly back to Canada. But first, this. First, the *venuta*.

The walls of Loreto's cathedral are the walls of the town. One minute you are outside, facing a seemingly impregnable citadel, the next you are in the flood-lit Piazza della Madonna, Loreto's stage for religious set-pieces. The elegant bell tower and the facade of the sixteenth-century church stand at the south end. In the center is the fountain where barefoot pilgrims once washed their feet before entering the basilica. The majestic Renaissance arcades of the papal apartments run along the west and north sides and on the east is a row of spanking new, confession-box style souvenir booths, where I purchase a cheap Madonna of Loreto medallion.

The maritime air is crisp with anticipation. Already the crowd is assembling. There's a constant to-ing and fro-ing from the adjoining streets as groups check in to make sure they haven't missed anything yet, then head back to the noisy, cheery bars and restaurants. Mobs of pre-adolescent choirgirls and boys tramp up and down the piazza behind the banners of their villages. The girls from Giarre, wherever that may be, have set aside their Ave Maria and taken up the chant of "Ba-ba-ba Ba-Barbara Ann." There are deckchairs set up along the barriers by seasoned pilgrims, who want to reserve the best spots for when the Madonna passes. Above the piazza, a jumbo screen broadcasts the action from within the basilica, as over the loudspeakers a Fatherly voice croons hymns, details the schedule for the evening, and reminds us all to keep an eye on our valuables.

Much as I'd like to dive straight into the church, I shall first pay a courtesy call at the hotels. What with 800 young singers and their parents, several hundred armed forces pilots, a whole contingent of Red Cross nurses *and* the fact that the vigil has fallen on a Saturday this year, I expect there will be no room at the inn tonight. But it won't take long to find out, as the town of Loreto is little more than a few tents huddled in the shadow of the great church-fortress.

"Good evening. Do you have a room?"

"For tonight?"

"For tonight."

"Are you joking?"

"I should have made a reservation?"

"You should have made one last December."

Eventually I find a place where they will hold my pack for the night and let me check in tomorrow noon. That's reasonable. I can suffer for my art through one more roofless night. Besides, my guidebook to Italian festivals assures me that the festivities go on till three with bonfires, songs and traditional food and drink. I'm confident I'll find enough music, grappa and good company to get me through till the morning. As for tomorrow, there will be plenty to keep me alert: the pilots' mass, the fly-by of the *Frecce Azzurri* …

But now it is time to visit the house where the Virgin Mary was born.

It is said that Saint Nicholas of Tolentino was kneeling in prayer before the window of his cell when he saw the Holy House approaching. It was three in the morning of December 10, 1294, and Nicholas was not yet a saint but only a brother so his whoops did not go unheard.

"Brother Nicholas! Now is the time for silence!" griped a voice from the darkness.

But Nicholas only whooped the louder. "A great treasure comes from the sea!" he cried. "A great treasure comes from the sea!"

The monk who had chastised Nicholas shuffled to the window to see what he was raving about. He ground the heels of his palms into his puffy eyes and peered out over the still, moonlit Adriatic. "I see nothing," he grumbled.

"Put your foot upon mine," said Nicholas. The brother did so and at once he could see it too. A squadron of angels was flying high above the sea. Some blew trumpets, others sang hosannas, but most of them had their shoulders set squarely beneath a small brick house. Up on the roof-beam of the house sat the Blessed Virgin with the infant Jesus in her arms.

"Now do you see the treasure that comes from the sea?" cried Nicholas. "It is the house of the Virgin Mary!"

Within moments, the rest of the monks were tumbling over each other to step on Nicholas's foot and see the miracle. The church bells started ringing all on their own as the brothers piled into the chapel to thank the Lord and the Holy Mother for the inestimable grace that had been visited upon them and upon Italy.

It was three in the morning of the tenth of December, 1294, as the angels lowered their sacred cargo gently, gently to the shore near Loreto. This was the night of the *venuta*—the arrival of the Holy House.

IT WILL BE UNDERSTOOD that so sacred a structure as *la Santa Casa*, the Holy House of Mary where the Virgin was born, where she received the angel of the Annunciation, where she raised the boy Jesus, and where, after his death, she met with the Apostles—could not very well be left behind in the Holy Land after the evacuation of the Crusaders. Who knows what indignities the heathen might have visited upon it? That is why the Lord sent his angels to carry it to safety. But the angelic transport of the Holy House from Nazareth to Loreto was no direct flight.

At first, the angels had set it down on the Illyrian coast, facing Italy. But the locals did not show the house sufficient regard—a shame they bear to this day—so the angels airlifted it again, this time across the Adriatic. Still, the flying house took time to find its place. The first location turned out to be too heavily forested, leaving the pilgrims (of course, there were pilgrims from the very start) vulnerable to bandits. The angels relocated the house to a more open area, but this site was owned by two wicked brothers, who divided the pilgrims' gifts between themselves. Once more, the angels moved the house, this time plunking it down right on a public road, where it would be accessible to all and the property of none. It has not budged since, though over the centuries its outer walls have been sheathed in marble to keep relic-hungry pilgrims from chipping the structure away a pebble at a time. Also, a great cathedral has been built to enclose, Russian-doll style, the marble casing that encloses the Holy House that enclosed Mary who enclosed Jesus.

The line-up, several hundred deep, starts at the doors of the basilica. Everyone wants to set foot in the Holy House tonight, to touch or kiss the smooth stone of the inner walls, to contemplate the fireplace where the Virgin prepared meals and the bowl the Christ child ate from, to kneel and pray to the dark Madonna of Loreto as pilgrims have done these seven centuries.

As early as 1375, Pope Gregory XI was conferring indulgences upon "the great multitudes of the faithful" who flocked to the Holy House. For the next four hundred years, Loreto went from strength to strength, becoming not only the world's most frequented Marian shrine, but the richest and most illustrious. From the fifteenth century, Loreto (and its bulging treasury) was placed under the direct authority of the Popes, who transformed it into the religious second city of Italy, erecting splendid papal apartments and dispatching a procession of Rome's finest artists to embellish them.

Loreto's location on the Adriatic coast was not insignificant: in the sixteenth century, the citadel of the Madonna stood as a figurative and literal bulwark against the hostile dominion of the Turks, the "evil empire" of the day. When the allied Christian forces sank the Sultan's armada at the battle of Lepanto, the victory was attributed to the intercession of Our Lady of Loreto. The Christian commanders came to kneel before her and Christian prisoners liberated after the battle brought their galley chains, which were melted down and used to make gates for the basilica and the Santa Casa.

The list of luminaries who paid tribute to Our Lady is a who's who of popes, saints, emperors and kings. Queen Cristina of Sweden relinquished her royal crown and scepter to the Madonna. Though Louis XIII of France didn't come in person when Our Lady granted his prayer for an heir, he sent a *bambino d'oro* of the same weight as the infant. Other pilgrim noteworthies included Cervantes, Stendhal, Montaigne, Tasso and the Marquis de Sade. Galileo came, as did Descartes, who credited the lady of Loreto with inspiring his "method." Pedro de Villa, a mariner from Columbus's first voyage, arrived in 1493 to fulfill a vow made by the crew in the midst of an Atlantic storm. A dutiful Mozart went home with religious trinkets for his mother, while the father of Goethe paid a local girl to go on her knees around the Holy House for him (and kept an eye on her to be sure she didn't try to short-change him).

The flow of pilgrims and wealth was interrupted only by the visit of Napoleon, who came not to worship, but to despoil the sanctuary of its fabulous treasures. On arrival, he found that the Pope had already spirited most of the prize pieces away to Rome. (He could have saved himself the trouble, as he ended up selling them all to buy off the French.) Nevertheless, the Corsican helped himself to anything that wasn't nailed down, including even the statue of the Madonna of Loreto. It was displayed for a time in the Louvre under the rubric: "Oriental wood statue of the Egyptian-Judaic school."

Yet all these celebrity pilgrims were only the froth tossed up on the unending waves of the humble—the millions whose lips consumed the statues, whose knees wore parallel grooves two inches deep into the pediment around the base of the Holy House, carving the marble like butter. They came from everywhere, but Central Italy and Illyria especially could be counted on to send out their annual pilgrim delegations, as regular as trains to Lourdes. Several times a year, to the cry *"Viva Maria!"* pilgrim convoys of *ciociari* put out, covering the 400 kilometers to Loreto in five days. September to December was prime season for the *cecchi*, the peasants of Loreto's own province of Le Marche, who came in festive dress with minstrels and colorful ox-carts. The most distinctive pilgrims were the Slavs, primarily Croats and Slovenes, whose homeland

had briefly hosted the Holy House prior to its flight to Italy. They would circle the house on their knees from early morning till far into the night, weeping and crying, "Return to us, O beautiful Lady, return to us with your house!" Out of respect for the Slavs' devotion, and sympathy for the depth of their loss, the custodians of the sanctuary allowed them to sleep in the arcades and the open rooms of the papal apartments.

An art gallery occupies these same apartments today. Alongside its more distinguished pieces, it displays a sampling of small, crudely painted panels from the eighteenth and nineteenth centuries depicting miracles of the Madonna. The panels run a gamut of violent, sometimes gruesome, incidents. People are shot, pierced with swords, run over by carriages. They fall from trees, from ladders, down wells. Walls collapse on them. But thanks to the intervention of the Madonna, they all survive to give thanks through these paintings, pictorial testaments for a largely illiterate age. The artists are identified solely by the name of their lost profession: they are *Madonnari*, "Madonna painters."

The most characteristic souvenir brought home by pilgrims to Loreto in olden days, more distinctive by far than any scallop shell or water bottle, was a tattoo. The shoemakers of the village doubled as tattoo artists, pricking Madonnas, Sacred Hearts and crucified Christs into the flesh of the faithful. The bearer of a tattoo proclaimed his submission to the Virgin and placed himself under her constant protection. This painful and infection-prone business continued—to the scandal of society's progressive forces—well into the middle of the twentieth century.

Tonight, however, I see no one sporting a fresh tattoo. Nor is anyone shuffling on his knees around the Holy House, or weeping, or singing. Even in Italy, even on the night of the *venuta*, today's worshippers are cloaked in the uniform of bourgeois decorum. They laugh, and jingle the change in their pockets, and check their cell phones for messages. When their turn comes to pass through the doors into the House of Mary, they cross themselves. They pass their fingers over the stones, offer up a quiet prayer to the dark Lady above the altar, take a good look around, then exit by the far doors.

One longs for a bit of old-fashioned emoting.

FLAVIO STANDS AT THE DOORS of the basilica, alone with his cigarette. He's the first airman I've spotted. Tomorrow they'll fill the center pews of the church for mass, then promenade about the piazza arm-in-arm, the cream of the Italian air force, feigning not to be conscious of how sharp they look in their caps and uniforms.

"Excuse me, you're a pilot?"

"Yes."

"One of the ones who carries the Madonna?"

"I wish," he laughs. "It's not guys like me who get to carry the Madonna."

"Can you tell me something? Do you pray to the Madonna of Loreto before you fly?"

"To the Madonna and to Christ and all the saints. I don't take any chances."

He is offering me a friendly cigarette when two tall young women pass by on their way into the cathedral. Flavio stubs out the cigarette he has just lit, claps me on the shoulder, and wheels in pursuit.

In 1920, when the air force decided they needed a patron saint, they chose the Lady of the flying house. It was an inspired selection, though in 1936 it put Our Lady in the compromised position of watching out for Italian pilots as they bombed Abyssinian tribesmen with mustard gas. Today, happily, her job consists mostly of overseeing the daredevil maneuvers of the Italian synchronized flying squadron, the *Frecce Azzurri* or "Blue Arrows," who will make a daring pass over the piazza tomorrow, trailing the national colors in smoke behind them.

It is not only air force pilots, but civilian pilots and airline passengers, as well as pilgrims, emigrants and exiles who are invited to direct their prayers to Our Lady of Loreto. Her image accompanied the astronauts aboard Apollo 9, and Pope John Paul II, who has logged his fair share of air time, has composed a prayer to her. It concludes, "With your blessing, may pilots, technicians and auxiliaries work prudently, so that all who travel by air overcome every peril and reach safely the goal that awaits them." Amen.

In the old days, on the night of the venuta, the hills and fields for miles around roared with bonfires lit to guide the angelic pilots of the Holy House. Some were enormous, the collective efforts of communities who spent the days prior to the festival amassing firewood. Newly betrothed couples leapt nine times through the flames for luck, and the eating and drinking went on till three, the hour when the angels set the house down on the shore. Then, amidst bursts of fireworks, the renowned litany of Our Lady of Loreto, a recitation of the innumerable names of Mary, was sung. One local woman has written of "the thousands of lights that sparkled in the countryside, as if by magic. I had so many questions, and my mother explained to me, 'Tonight, the Madonna and the baby Jesus are flying with their house, but it's cold, so they've lit the bonfire to warm the air. That way, the baby won't get cold.'"

I step out on the terrace behind the piazza to scan for bonfires. There is one, directly below me. One glorious monster blazing among the pinpricks of electric light that dot the plain. Fire never grows old. This lonely anachronism is all that gives movement and vigor to the scene. The electric beacons are dead and cold.

THE HOLY HOUSE, OF COURSE, was the sort of thing that made Protestants and Freemasons pull out their hair. The house of the Virgin Mary? Flown over the sea by angels? For God's sake! Was there nothing the Pope would not stoop to in his pandering to popular credulity? No superstition he would not endorse if doing so filled his coffers? Rome didn't help appearances by muzzling the Bollandists, the Church's in-house fraud detectors, on the topic of Loreto.

In response to the sneers of the skeptics, the pious have always pointed to certain odd features of the Holy House: that unlike typical regional houses, it has no foundations; that three of its walls, to chest height, are built of stone, when no stone quarries exist near Loreto; that mysterious symbols have been scratched into some of these stones. The evidence suggests that the house is of foreign provenance. Is it such a leap, then, to suppose that this could be the House of Mary, transported from Nazareth to its present site by angels?

If your considered reply is "Yes," then you should know that in the thirteenth century, the ruling clan of Epyrus (across the Adriatic from Italy) went by the name of Angeli. A recently unearthed document, dated September 1294, three months before the legendary arrival date of the Holy House, records the marriage of Ithamar Angeli and Filippo of Taranto, a son of the King of Naples. Among the items of Ms. Angeli's bridal dowry are "the holy stones carried away from the House of Our Lady, the Virgin Mother of God."

So it was indeed the angels—or the Angeli at least—who conveyed the Holy House to Italy (though not, it would seem, by air).

Very well, then. The house was brought by "the angels." This still doesn't prove that the Virgin lived in it. The many fingers of Saint Thomas and heads of John the Baptist scattered across Europe offer proof enough of the naïveté of Christian relic-hunters in the Holy Land. One can almost hear the wheedling voice of the con artist: "Of course, of course, the House of the Virgin Mary, good sir. Yours for a very reasonable price." The Angeli were surely the victims of a scam.

Or were they? A venerable tradition relates that Mary's house in Nazareth was preserved after her death and used by Christ's disciples as a gathering place. In the third century, a synagogue-style church was erected above the humble dwelling. This church was succeeded by a Byzantine edifice, and a more ample basilica still was raised on the site by the French Crusaders. But a European pilgrim to the Holy Land, writing in 1288, reveals that the French basilica had fallen into a sorry state: "We came to Nazareth and found a great church there almost totally destroyed. Nothing remained of it but the chamber where the Madonna received the Annunciation; the Lord had spared it from destruction in memory of its humility and poverty." Yet recent digs on the site of the Crusader church have uncovered no trace of any "chamber of the Madonna." Could it not be that the Angeli, sometime between 1288 and 1294, disassembled the basilica's great treasure and transported it across the sea to safety?

One thing the archaeologists *have* discovered in the ruins of the church in Nazareth is a grotto hollowed into a soft rock face. It is of the sort used locally as the inner storage room of a dwelling. Of course, a house constructed in front of such a grotto would have only three walls, just like the Holy House of Loreto. To dispel any lingering doubt, experts have traced the stone of the Holy House back to Nazareth and identified the graffiti on its walls as typical of Nazarene churches. The rationalist, having sifted through all this detritus of facts and propositions—historical, linguistic, archaeological, architectural—ultimately discovers what the faithful have known all along: that this is the house of the Virgin Mary, brought to Loreto by the angels.

LITTLE BY LITTLE, IN THE two hours before midnight, the piazza fills up. The crowd seems a little subdued despite—or is it because of?—the bracing air. Most of the pilgrims are elderly or approaching that description. This is not their first time here. In twenty years, will their children still be coming in sufficient numbers to sustain the tradition? The doors of the cathedral are now closed, but the mass is being played on the jumbo screen, larger than life, for those who care to follow it. I prefer to savor the suspense and think about Mary's little house.

There are few relics of Mary. This is for the good reason that, according to tradition and dogma, her body was rapt up into heaven at her death. So though Chartres may claim to possess her tunic, another town her wedding ring, another her sash or her hair, no one possesses Mary. There was no body left to worship, no tomb to make pilgrimage to, no special place to pray or leave flowers or weep. This has helped render the Virgin ubiquitous; because she is nowhere, she can be everywhere. Perhaps, though, it has also made her more superhuman, more of a goddess.

Loreto brings Mary back to earth. Here is the house where the *woman* lived; not the airy Lady of Lourdes or of Fatima; not Chartres' stern Queen of Heaven; not the earth-born Virgins of the Camino; but the simple Jewish woman of 2,000 years ago named Mariám. Of all the 10,000 faces of Mary, this one is the most elusive. Loreto might be the place that brings the seeker closest to it.

Ah, but not tonight. A shiver runs through the crowd as the doors of the cathedral swing open. Out comes a long, double file of Red Cross nurses in uniform. After them, the regiments of the religious in their shimmering gowns. The children's choir, massed on the gallery over the piazza, breaks into the Magnificat. And there she is, draped in gold, pulsing with light, sailing above the crowd on the shoulders of her airmen. There is a roar of applause, cries, a flutter of white handkerchiefs—an outpouring of love for this Queen who has left her house tonight to be among her people. The woman beside me touches my shoulder: "Look," she says. "How beautiful!"

The voice on the loudspeakers is singing the litanies of Our Lady of Loreto: Mother of the Church, Mystic Rose, Mirror of Perfection, Morning Star, Fountain of our Joy, Merciful Virgin, Queen of Peace, Throne of Wisdom, Refuge of Sinners, Mother of the Creator. After each avocation, the crowd chimes in: *"Prega per noi,"* "Pray for us."

As the Madonna approaches, I reach for my camera. And only then do I realize that no one is taking pictures. Everyone is here, now.

IT SEEMS MY GUIDEBOOK is out of date. After midnight, the party breaks up fast. There is no feasting till three, no grappa, no bonfires, no wild boar sausages. All that's in the past now, it seems, or maybe confined to the outlying villages. Anyway, it's not here, not tonight. The world has been growing old of late. Old, listless and ready for bed.

The night has turned cold and the bars are closing down. I ask at one if they know somewhere I can put up for the night. They suggest the police station. Before I resort to that, I'll take one more look around town, just in case there's a bonfire somewhere that I've missed. My fingers find the medallion of Our Lady of Loreto jingling around with the change in my pocket. I give her a squeeze.

"Come on, Madonna of pilgrims. Help me out here."

I suspect this is not quite the tone to take with the Mother of God, but it's little enough I'm asking.

Near the south gates of the town, where the last pilgrim buses are pulling away for points all over Italy, I notice a "Youth Hostel" sign. It's nearly two o'clock, but who knows? Maybe there's a night watchman on duty. Maybe there's a floor I can sleep on or a life-sized presepio I can curl up in. Near the bottom of the hill, a sign points me to a quiet street of modern buildings. A light is on in the hostel. Someone is just now locking the door. I run and tap hard on the glass before he gets out of earshot.

"Do you have anywhere I can sleep tonight?"

"Tonight? No, I'm sorry. We're totally full. The pilots …"

"But a couch? The floor? Just somewhere inside. It's cold out here."

He sighs and blinks. "Well, come in. Let's see."

Behind the reception desk, glistening like a pearl of rare price on the wall of empty hooks, there dangles a single key.

There is a terrace outside my room. On the hilltop across the way, the dome of the cathedral still glows. But the lights have gone out on the plain. The one bonfire has consumed itself.

Here ends my trip, my pilgrimage. In a few days I will leave behind all these old things and fly in an airplane past the end of the world and over the sea of death. I will return to my rational life in the tidy, modern country of my birth. In a few days.

But for now the wind is blowing from the east and the clouds part to reveal a clear and starry sky. It's nearly three a.m. A good night for the crossing. I scan the firmament for angels, flying houses, signs of the Mother of God.

BIBLIOGRAPHY

Mary and Pilgrimage

Aradi, Zsolt. *Shrines to Our Lady Around the World.* New York: Farrar, Strauss & Young, 1954.

Turner, Victor. *Image and Pilgrimage in Christian Culture.* New York: Columbia. University Press, 1978.

Warner, Marina. *Alone of All Her Sex: The Myth and the Cult of the Virgin Mary.* New York: Knopf, 1976.

Zimdars-Swartz, Sandra L. *Encountering Mary: Visions of Mary from la Salette to Medjugorje.* Princeton, N.J.: Princeton University Press, 1991.

Paris, Chartres and Relics

Adams, Henry. *Mont-Saint-Michel and Chartres.* London: Constable, 1950.

Delaporte, Yvon. *Les trois Notre-Dame de la Cathédrale de Chartres.* Chartres: É. Houvet, 1955.

Dirvin, Joseph I. *Saint Catherine Labouré.* New York: Farrar, Strauss & Cudahy, 1958.

Durand-Lefebvre, Marie. *Étude sur l'origine des Vierges noires.* Paris: G. Durassié, 1937.

Geary, Patrick. *Furta Sacra: Thefts of Relics in the Central Middle Ages.* Princeton. N.J.: Princeton University Press, 1978.

Houvet, Étienne (revised by Malcolm B. Miller). *Chartres: The Cathedral.* Chartres: Éditions Houvet-La Crypte, 2000.

James, John. *Chartres: The Masons Who Built a Legend.* London: Routledge & Kegan Paul, 1982.

Saul, John Ralston. *Voltaire's Bastards: The Dictatorship of Reason in the West.* Toronto: Viking, 1992.

Sox, H. David. *Relics and Shrines* London: George Allen & Unwin, 1985.

Temko, Allan. *Notre-Dame of Paris.* New York: Viking, 1955.

Une lumière sur la terre. Strasbourg: Éditions du Signe, 1996.

Villette, Jean. *The Enigma of the Labyrinth.* Chartres.

Lourdes

Hales, E.E.Y. *Pio Nono.* London: Eyre & Spottiswoode, 1954.

Harris, Ruth. *Lourdes: Body and Spirit in the Secular Age.* London: Allen Lane, The Penguin Press, 1999.

Laurentin, René. *Bernadette of Lourdes.* London: Darton, Longman & Todd, 1998.

Marnham, Patrick. *Lourdes: A Modern Pilgrimage.* New York: Coward, McCann & Geoghegan, 1981.

Camino de Santiago

Atienza, Juan. G. *Leyendas del Camino de Santiago.* Madrid: Editorial EDAF, 1998.

Bravo Lozano, Millán. *Guía práctica del peregrino.* León: Editorial Everest, 1999.

Bouzas, Pemón and Domelo, Xosé A. *Mitos, ritos y leyendas de Galicia.* Barcelona: Ediciones Martínez Roca, 2000.

Davies, Horton and Marie-Hélène. *Holy Days and Holidays: The Medieval Pilgrimage to Compostela.* Lewisburg, Pa.: Bucknell University Press, 1982.

Frey, Nancy Louise. *Pilgrim Stories: On and Off the Road to Santiago.* Berkeley: University of California Press, 1998.

Laffi, Domenico. *Viaggio in ponente à San Giacomo di Galitia e Finisterrae.* Leiden: Primavera, 1997.

Letts, Malcolm. *The Travels of Leo of Rozmital.* Cambridge: Cambridge University Press, 1957.

Melczer, William. *The Pilgrim's Guide to Santiago de Compostela.* New York: Italica Press, 1993.

Franco, Zaragoza, Barcelona and the Spanish Civil War

Bolin, Luis. *Spain: The Vital Years*. London: Cassell, 1967.

Chadwick, Owen. *The Secularization of the European Mind in the Nineteenth Century*. Cambridge: Cambridge University Press, 1975.

El Pilar es la columna: historia de una devoción. Zaragoza: Ayuntamiento de Zaragoza, 1995.

Fraser, Ronald. *Blood of Spain*. New York: Pantheon, 1979.

Perry, Nicholas, and Echeverría, Loreto. *Under the Heel of Mary*. London: Routledge, 1988.

Preston, Paul. *Franco: A Biography*. London: HarperCollins, 1993.

Sanchez, Jose. *Anticlericalism: A Brief History*. Notre Dame: University of Notre Dame Press, 1972.

Wilford, John Noble. *The Mysterious History of Columbus*. New York: Knopf, 1991.

Fatima

Congregazione per la Dottrina della Fede. *Il Messaggio di Fatima*. Milano: Paoline, 2000.

Cornwell, John. *Hitler's Pope: The Secret History of Pius XII*. New York: Viking Penguin, 1999.

de Oliveira, Padre Mário. *Fátima nunca mais*. Porto: Campo das Letras, 1999.

Hebblethwaite, Peter. *In the Vatican*. Oxford: Oxford University Press, 1987.

Hebblethwaite, Peter. *The Runaway Church*. London: Collins, 1975.

Martin, Malachi. *The Keys of This Blood*. New York: Simon & Schuster, 1990.

Redzioch, Wlodzimierz. *Nuestra Señora de Fátima* Narni. (Italy): Plurigraf, 1996

Sister Maria Lucía of the Immaculate Heart. *Fatima in Lucia's Own Words*. Fátima: Secretariado dos Pastorinhos, 1998.

Thomas, Gordon, and Morgan-Witts, Max. *The Year of Armageddon*. London: Granada, 1984.

Rome and Loreto

Dejonghe, Maurice. *Roma santuario Mariano*. Bologna: Cappelli, 1969.

Fiori, Nica. *Le Madonnelle di Roma*. Rome: Tascabili Economici Newton, 1995.

Hibbert, Christopher. *Rome: The Biography of a City*. Harmondsworth: Viking, 1985.

Krautheimer, Richard. *Rome: Profile of a City, 312-1308.* Princeton: Princeton University Press, 1980.

Passa, Matilde. *Lacrime e sangue: viaggio nella religiosità popolare.* Baldini & Castoldi: Milano, 2000.

Peluso, Carmen. *Il sacro a Roma e in Vaticano.* Rome: Rendina Editori, 1999.

Santarelli, Giuseppe. *Tradizioni e leggende Lauretane.* Loreto: Congregazione Universale della Santa Casa, 1990.

Santarelli, Guiseppe. *Loreto: guida storica e artistica.* Ancona: Edizioni Aniballi, 1996.